When Pets Come
Between Partners

When Pets Come Between Partners

How to Keep Love—and Romance—in the
Human/Animal Kingdom of Your Home

Joel Gavriele-Gold, Ph.D.

HOWELL
BOOK
HOUSE

A Division of
IDG Books Worldwide, Inc.
An International Data Group Company
Foster City, CA • Chicago, IL • Indianapolis, IN • New York, NY

Howell Book House
An Imprint of IDG Books Worldwide, Inc.
An International Data Group Company
919 E. Hillsdale Boulevard
Foster City, CA 94404

Howell Book House is a registered trademark of Macmillan General Reference USA, Inc., a wholly owned subsidiary of IDG Books Worldwide, Inc.

For general information on IDG Books Worldwide's books in the U.S., please call our Consumer Customer Service department at 800-762-2974. For reseller information, including discounts and premium sales, please call our Reseller Customer Service department at 800-434-3422.

Library of Congress Cataloging-in-Publication Data available upon request.

ISBN: 0-87605-626-5

Manufactured in the United States of America

10 9 8 7 6 5 4 3 2 1

Contents

Contents

Dedication

For Christopher Joel

Aunts Janet and Gita

My father who loved dogs and horses

Art Robbins and Jean Getoff

Thank You

Acknowledgements

The Beyond Thank You Category:

Dominique DeVito, Publisher at Howell and chief inspiration who presented the seeds for this book, gave me the encouragement, and offered the field and sunshine of who she is to let things grow and become.

Alan Serchuk who took what was rolling around in my head and turned it into prose, who encouraged supported and transformed while teaching me the craft with great patience and understanding.

Carole Campana who held my hand by the lake, read, took me from the dreaded zucchini to the great French restaurant, suggested, questioned, encouraged, sent articles and kept me "on the path of my journey" while all the while saying, "This book will make you famous, Doc."

Thanks to the best of friends who stood by me: Carole, Juan, Bob and Debbie, Don and Barbara, Judy and Fred, Marianne, Joe Ford, Alan and Connie, Lisa and Steve, Annabella, Doug and Karen, Harry and Susie, Mary, Cousin Ron, Lee, Eddie and Jo, Pamela, and Barbara and Herb.

Thanks to the friends who thought I died, Risto and Analei, Bob and Andrée, Cousin Dova, Konstantin, and to the friends who did die, Beth Dugan, Job Michael Evans, Dr. Louis Gerstman, Jean Getoff and Dr. Lawrence Denson.

Thanks to the group, Art, Lois, Judy, Mary, Rick, Kathy, Lorraine, Nancy, and Jane for being there.

Thanks to my patients and students who taught me so much and "understood" after a night of writing beyond bedtime.

Thanks to all the people who agreed to be interviewed—at this point—too numerous to name.

Thanks to everyone who read, commented and suggested: Lisa and Steve Alfieri, Elaine Brandt, Rick C. Brandt, Dr. Carole Campana, Deborah Launer, Lorraine Lynne, Brian Maloney, Mme Pheff Modelski, Catherine Newsom, Doug, Karen, Blythe and John Ross by the sea, Paul Sagona, Mary Soyer, and Marianne Wickle-Schloss.

Thanks to Norma M.T. Braun, M.D. for the breath of fresh air and William Schiff, M.D. for the vision.

Thanks too to my editor, Nikki Moustaki at Howell for being cool and creative, Mike Singer, take a bow as well. Beth Adelman too deserves a bow for not nudging when she had a right to.

Thanks Dr. Stephan Cole, D.V.M. for being Dr. Stephan Cole.

Thanks to all the dog people on the block who kept asking how it was going and remembered to ask if I heard the one about . . .? Thanks—Pheff, Rick, Linda, Claudia, Norm and Annette, Shelly, Micki, the guys with the French bull dogs, and "Ricki" at B&N.

Thanks to all the doormen: Carlos at 205, Raymon, Robert, Shorty, Carlos at 210, the nice twin at 215, Antonio, and the rest of you who kept an eye on me when I was walking the dogs at all hours of the day and the night.

Thanks to Blackie, Rush, Gypsie, Sigi, Humphrey, Amos, Trøll, Tess, Élodie, Fergus, Charlotte and Broodje for supplying the unconditional stuff and teaching me to respect something much older and finer than the folly of man. I know Thor, Nina, Margriet, Athena, Maxine, Pepper, Chloé and Zoey will do the same for a new generation.

Introduction

This book discusses how the pets in our lives affect our personal and family relationships—how we integrate them into our families, and the way they mirror our own personalities. You will meet many characters here: pet owners and the people in their lives, plus a number of dogs, cats, and birds of one sort or another. A variety of other creatures also show up, including two ferrets, assorted fish, horses, and a snake. The common element among the pets is that each became an active member of the human household they lived in and helped the other people in the family see into themselves.

The stories this book tells are very personal ones in which a pet was the catalyst that helped those in its family recognize and learn to overcome those troubling problems we all experience but that sometimes take unacceptable control. These are also stories about how pets affected many family decisions made by their human owners.

In most of these stories, the people involved ended up in therapy to resolve their problems. However, that doesn't mean that only therapy can solve the problems you and your partner may be having with your pets. Rather, I have used these stories as a way to illustrate the concepts. You can then take these concepts and apply them to your own pet peeves.

The people in this book are among those I have met in my practice (of course, some details have been changed to protect their privacy), the pets they share, and the place those animals took in their relationships. Even if you do not have a pet, I think you'll find this book of interest because it will help you understand some basic ideas about how we humans function.

This is not a book about psychology, although it leans heavily on that art to explain the people-pet relationships you'll read about. This is really a book about relationships and what makes them tick—how each person contributes something to a relationship's success or failure. It came about as a result of the many therapy patients in my practice who reported that pets had become entangled in their human relationships; the animals had, in fact, become members of the family. As such, they were loved, abused, feared, ignored, pampered—in short, they received the whole panoply of human emotions and feelings.

THE PEOPLE/PET BOND

What became clear to me is that while a great number of people/pet relationships may seem straightforward, they can be just as complex as human relationships. Let's face it: When someone lavishes the degree of care and devotion that most of us devote to our pets, the animals become as much a part of the family as any other member.

Like everything else in our lives, pets can mean many things to us on many levels. They certainly give us joy and pleasure. As a psychologist, I can tell you from personal and clinical experience that pets can be a wonderful comfort when people cannot help. They definitely add to the fun and excitement in our lives.

And whatever else they bring to our lives, many kinds of pets offer us an opportunity to give and receive unconditional love. It is comfortingly obvious that the dogs, cats, and horses in our lives forgive us our mistakes and blunders.

Being a dog person, I am not sure how you define that quality when it involves, say, a boa constrictor and a human, or some of the other living creatures people keep as pets. My friend Alice, who has a boa, assures me that she experiences unconditional love from Crunch whenever he joins her in the bathtub or wraps himself around her ankle at the dinner table. Alice's former boyfriend, however, did not share her perspective. He bolted after their relationship had come to that moment of intimacy when Alice and he took a bath together and were joined by Crunch.

If anyone doubts a snake's ability to make its feelings known, consider a report written in *Modern Maturity* magazine from an owner of a boa constrictor in Georgia. "Once when we were away," the author wrote, "Dumpling, our 8-foot-long, 30-pound boa constrictor, went through our library pulling out books and throwing them on the floor as some petulant child might. As I picked them up, I noticed that every one of them was by my wife's favorite author, Danielle Steel. I guess Dumpling detected my wife's scent on the books."

Probably, few people who are not pet owners appreciate the bond that grows between animal and owner. I find that the most enjoyable moments of my day are when I am playing with my dogs (besides Fergus, I have two Bouviers des Flandres: Charlotte and Broodje). This is my opportunity to clear my head of all the day's demands. I take pleasure in watching the dogs enjoying my company and each other. I believe animals experience some, if not all of the same basic emotions as humans do: happiness, sadness, fear, jealousy, curiosity, disgust, and anger. In this book we'll look at each of these and how they affect us.

There are many wonderful reasons for people to have pets. Besides offering seemingly unconditional loyalty, pets also give us a sense that we're coming closer to nature and leading a less complicated way of life. People learn caring and affection from having pets as well. Children with pets learn about responsibility, care, and respect for themselves and others. Why would anyone take a totally dependent being into the home if that person did not care? Having a dog is somewhat like having a kid who is forever 2 years old.

Playing with and enjoying pets is a prelude to adult human relationships. It helps a child make the transition from caring for a pet and loving it to a human relationship. Puppy love is an introduction to adult love.

Couples, too, find that caring for a pet gives them some sense of what it is like to be responsible for the care and welfare of another living being, to be a parent.

Pets make you feel good, and the feelings seem mutual: You bring them into your family, and they accept you as part of their group. You are their provider, and in turn, they reconnect you with nature.

THE TANGLED WEBS WE WEAVE

According to the couples you will meet in these pages, at first glance it seemed as if their pet was causing a problem in the relationship. Certainly, most of the animals and other creatures we adopt as pets march to a decidedly different and not-too-human drummer. As each of these situations were explored, however, it became clear that the problem may have begun with chewed-up shoes, destroyed rugs and carpets, or inappropriate toilet habits—in short, a general disregard for human property and sensibilities—but the real trouble ran much deeper and began long before this particular animal entered the couple's lives.

In some instances, the pet's "misbehavior" seemed a relatively minor event, such when a dog in one of our stories was quite content to just lie about. At times the offense was more dramatic, perhaps when favorite furniture was used as a cat's scratching post. All too often, though, the person's reaction to the animal's actions harkened to an earlier time when his or her personality and life experiences were being formed. In one of the stories told here, you will see how the pet's owner unconsciously trained the animal—in this case, a dog—to be offensive with his toilet habits. Why would someone do such a thing? We'll explore the reasons.

This book also discusses some of the basic human responses to our family and our emotional environment and explores how they affect and are affected by the animals in the family. We'll look at jealousy, grief, rage, and the full range of human emotions and reactions.

How serious can these problems be? Veterinarians and people working in animal shelters have told me that they've met large numbers of people who, at their wits' end about an important relationship, have brought their animals in to either find a new home for the pet or to euthanize it. The animals became casualties of relationships in which one party found them to be an intrusion or even an offense rather than a newfound friend. It was astonishing to learn from veterinarians all over the country how many people thought the only solution to their relationship problem was euthanasia (mostly of the pet, not of the other person).

Before we go too far afield, let's recognize that animals are not all sweetness and light, no matter how much we love and adore them (of course, you might say the same of other members of your family). They are not always blameless when problems occur. They have their own personalities, they develop their own habits, and they come fully equipped with the traits and characteristics of their own species and breed (which are not always in keeping with the needs and habits of human society). And, as any animal owner knows, they are quite capable of challenging our authority when the mood strikes them.

What to Do?

This book is not about pet behavioral problems. Nor is it about animal psychology, toilet-training difficulties, dominant or submissive animal behaviors, nuisance and destructive behaviors, or health- and diet-related behavioral problems. This book is mostly about what happens when one or each of the parties in a human relationship regards the pet as a problem instead of finding where the problem really lies. This book is also about relationships in which the pet helps to keep the parties together and makes their relationship work.

In addition to those psychological issues that the animals in our relationships may force us to face, more pragmatic issues may be at work. What happens when you are in a relationship with someone you really like and you suspect that this person is quickly becoming the love of your life—except for one small problem: the pet? What do you do when you are either allergic to or just plain hate his or her cat(s), dog(s), hamster(s), horse(s), bird(s), boa(s), ferret(s), snake(s), or fish? What do you do if both of you have pets and the pets do not get along? You cannot envision giving up your pet, and the love of your life sees no way of ever giving up her or his pet(s). What to do?

In the course of this book, you will also meet people whose pet relationships are with other people's animals. This is somewhat like being an aunt or an uncle to a child—you get to enjoy the child without all the turmoil of raising your own. If you are dating and just beginning a relationship, for example, you can always announce when the going gets rough that it's time to leave so you can beat the traffic back home. Everyone understands. If you are in a live-in relationship, you can always point out that this is not really your pet and leave the other person with the problem.

But what happens when you are in a relationship in which neither of you agrees on how you are going to deal with the pet or pets? This can be as simple as formulating the proper diet for the animal, determining which veterinarian to use, deciding to neuter the pet, or boarding the animal if there is a vacation coming up. It can be as complicated as feeling second in importance to the pet or not being involved in decisions about the pet. And what if you are one of the many who are just not comfortable with keeping another being in captivity? These are all very real questions that must be addressed.

I may not have the answers for all these concerns. Nevertheless, you will have to face them for as long as the animal is part of your household—and that could be a very long time. Consider that a cat can live 15–20 years; dogs from 8–20 years (one friend had a dog who lived for 29 years); a parrot 80 years; boas longer than a mother-in-law; and who knows for sure about ferrets and fish. So here you are in this terrible situation, having finally found the love of your life but with an unwanted appendage. These are the same types of questions that must be dealt with when couples have children from previous relationships.

Lest you think these concerns are trivial, let me refer to a "Dear Abby" letter of many years ago in which a distraught young woman wrote to say that she was in love with a man who had two hunting dogs that she could not stand. "Abby, please tell me what to do," she begged. To this, Abby replied: "Never get between a man and his dogs—you will lose." Abby may have been right, whether it's dogs, cats, hamsters, birds, boas, ferrets, fish, or anything else on the face of the earth that might be claimed as a pet. On the other hand, many people have given up pets for love, sometimes with a happy ending and sometimes with a fall-flat-on-your-face unhappy ending.

Someone who's not an animal lover might raise the question, "Why not get your pleasure from other people—friends, family, lovers?" In other words, "Why animals?" They seem to be saying, "If you were really an adult and a well-adjusted person, you would not have to depend on animals for love." This is a little like telling a spaghetti lover that there is no difference between store-bought sauce (just add some garlic and fresh herbs) and sauce made from scratch. Yes, there are some really good prepared spaghetti sauces out there, but they just don't taste the same.

Put another way, *people* don't fill the animal lovers' need for *animals,* and animals may or may not fill peoples' need for people. Remember Dear Abby!

Part I

The Displacement Story

How Did Fido Get to Be Dear Old Dad?

Chapter 1

The Mechanisms That Drive Our Relationships

One of the most basic premises about relationships is the idea that *true love* means accepting the things that are most important to the other person. In the dispassionate language of the sociologist, this is regarded as part of being compatible. If knitting is her passion and baseball is his, the theory goes, shouldn't they be willing to accept each other's passions? Does not the same hold true for pets? Do you give up your pet for the love of your life who can't accept this creature that has become your loving companion? The answer to this question may depend on why you have the pet in the first place and what the animal means to you.

This is a tough topic to deal with. If you are in love with someone who has a pet that you cannot stand, or if the pet always seems to come before you, how do you manage to hang in there? For a person who has never had pets, the experience could be downright humiliating.

A key question to resolve in these issues is whether it is a simple like or dislike of the animal (there's nothing wrong with that), or whether something else is driving the problem. How much of what is going on, for instance, is really due to one of the parties in the relationship trying to dominate the other one? Maybe everyone is vying for control. Dogs, for example, are noted for their loyalty to their master; this may be part of their sense of pack hierarchy, and it certainly seems to be instinctive. That may not sit well with the newcomer who feels uneasy about sharing the would-be partner's attentions with an animal—or, worse still, a newcomer who is treated by the dog as an interloper. Then again, how much of what is happening reflects the newcomer's unconscious concerns and has nothing to do with the pet? In short, how much of the difficulty with the pet is really a *pet problem*, and how much is a *people problem?*

The answers to these questions are as varied as the people and animals involved. No one pat answer exists for any question in this book, and none will be offered because every relationship is unique. Instead, this book will try to explain some of the mechanics involved in the way human relationships develop. Most often, these mechanics are quite normal and even necessary to human development. We all develop feelings of jealousy and anger. We all suffer loss. We all learn fear. These things are part of growing up. They don't become problems unless they begin to unduly influence our lives. For example, fear is healthy; it helps us avoid dangerous situations. But if you are afraid to leave the house because you might be attacked, fear may have a negative influence on your life.

As for the animals in the picture, we are generally not concerned with psychological baggage they may have (most often the animal is an innocent bystander). We have animal psychologists and animal trainers to deal with the animal's problem.

A LITTLE SECRET ABOUT PETS THAT NO ONE EVER TOLD YOU

With pets being accepted as members of the family, it is natural that they also become players in the dynamics of the family. They may be seen by human family members as symbols of people, or they may represent incidents from the person's own past. In this chapter, we'll talk about how this happens.

Sometimes we are not aware that we have unconsciously placed unwanted aspects of ourselves onto the pet. That is, we use the pet as a metaphor for our own feelings. For example: "The dog has hated my wife ever since we moved here from Baltimore. I think he is missing his old girlfriend, Foxy." Possible translation: "I have been missing my girlfriend ever since we moved here, and I am beginning to really hate my wife."

Other typical examples: You may laugh when the bird defecates all over the silk embroidered pillows that your mother-in-law (whom you hate) just gave you, and you tell everyone what a great sense of humor Polly has. Or, you shiver with some twinge of something that you cannot name while watching your neighbor's boa constrictor devour a live rat.

Then there are all the situations in which our pets provide a focus around which we can re-create what I call "old soap operas." These are scenarios in which we re-enact past unhappy events in our lives in an attempt to tack on a new and happier ending to replace the familiar and disappointing results.

WHY WE BEHAVE THE WAY WE DO

Before going any further, let's examine some of the psychological principles that affect our lives as we mature. This won't turn you into psychologists, but it will help you understand how the characters in this book—and the people in your lives—behave the way they do. No, it does not all start with abusive parents or a deprived childhood; it is more a question of what our early experiences were and how well we were prepared to deal with them.

Three main mechanisms drive our relationships with ourselves and others in our lives. Psychologists call them **displacement**, **projection**, and the **repetition compulsion**. It is through this machinery that our pets get caught up in our internal dramas.

Displacement is the unconscious act of putting past thoughts, moods, feelings, images, impulses, and even actions onto present-day individuals and situations. For example, someone might fear a very large dog because of an association with an overbearing parent.

In *projection*, we unconsciously ascribe to others thoughts, feelings, and deeds we do not like or do not wish to acknowledge in ourselves. Who wants to admit hating a parent who years earlier accidentally killed a beloved pet?

As if the rational, logical world of intellect and comprehension is not interrupted enough by displacement and projection, we add still another component: the *repetition compulsion*. This is an unconscious and repeated acting out of an issue instead of moving it from unconscious memory into the conscious world, where we can deal with it and put it to rest. Through repetition compulsion, we attempt to change the past by unconsciously reliving, so to speak, unfinished business from an earlier period in the hope of finally tacking on a happy ending. With this going on most, if not all of the time, it's a wonder that we get any work done!

Very little is simple or straightforward in psychology, though. For example, although we can describe these three mechanisms individually, they are most often encountered in overlapping and interacting combinations. Displacement may lead to projection, which in turn could appear as a repetition compulsion. And, just to make things more confusing, these mechanisms often appear together, complicated by qualities such as anger, jealousy, and a need for control.

From People/Pet to People/People

The key to reversing the undue effects of these mechanisms lies in helping a person move his or her people/pet relationships into the realm of people/people relationships, where they belong. And that is a large part of what this book is about: relieving our pets of the burden of being what we cannot be or what we are afraid to be. We will also see how people build their household or family activity around the fact that there is an animal to be considered.

In exploring those three psychological dynamics, we will look at how intimacy, rage, envy, jealousy, grief, abandonment, loss, and other issues complicate them. Some of these problems may also stem from physical and sexual abuse, as well as dependency and separation issues. One thing that even psychologists must always be aware of is that analyzing or interrupting a person's psychological motivations is rarely a simple matter. In almost every case, a number of elements influence a person's behavior.

Furthermore, it's safe to say that in any relationship, everyone involved (pets included) contributes something—no party is totally right, and no party is totally wrong. Having said that, it's important to add that in many of the stories that follow, the analysis has been greatly simplified and often ignores the possible contribution of other parties in the relationship. This is simply to make a point more clearly. The objective is to illuminate the human dynamic involved, not to present a primer on the principles or practice of psychology.

THE UNCONSCIOUS

It is well accepted among psychologists that we all have thoughts and feelings that live below the surface of our awareness, a place we call the *unconscious*. Although these thoughts and feelings may live below the surface, they are nevertheless quite active; they play themselves out without our knowing it.

Those thoughts and feelings are a natural consequence of living and maturing. As we've already discovered (and as this book will emphasize many more times during the course of our journey), these feelings and thoughts are not in themselves an indication of some emotional disturbance or problem. We all harbor feelings of jealousy, anger, love, hate, fear—the whole panoply of emotions. Psychoanalysts and psychologists refer to these thoughts and feelings that live below our conscious awareness as unconscious thoughts, unconscious feelings, and sometimes as unconscious symbols.

As long as those feelings are a natural result of experience and do not exercise undue control over our actions, we are said to be "healthy." The problem arises when those feelings take on an importance greater than their circumstance warrants.

We will explore some of the ways in which we unconsciously appoint our pets as people, and how they can become either unwanted parts of ourselves or overly valued parts of ourselves. (If that sounds confusing, be patient; it will make sense shortly.) We will also look at a number of the ways in which pets are used to relive our former life experiences, in what can be called old soap operas and war stories.

In some of the case histories, you'll learn how the people involved let their pets get entangled in relationships that are deeply embroiled in other emotions and issues. Many times the people involved were not even aware of these feelings on a conscious level; the feelings stayed below the surface and played a powerful role in their interactions. It's fascinating to realize how many people have pets solely for the *unconscious* purpose of regarding the pet as themselves. It is as if the individual is showing the world how he or she should have been treated growing up.

Those three main mechanisms mentioned earlier—displacement, projection, and the repetition compulsion—seem to defy logic; there is nothing specific that you can put a finger on. It's not like, say, an allergy attack, where there are specific symptoms such as watery and irritated eyes, sniffling and sneezing, and clogged sinuses. When you have these symptoms, there is no question in anyone's mind that you have a problem. Even beyond allergy season, you know that you have a sensitivity to certain allergens, and you do your best to treat your condition.

That's not so in the world of feelings and emotions, however. These ongoing unconscious dynamics confound the rational, logical aspects of our relationships without ever being acknowledged, much less discussed.

PAIN REVISITED

One of the surprising experiences I had in researching the material for this book was the number of people who volunteered to be interviewed but who ultimately postponed, declined, or withdrew from the venture. Among the reasons given, some feared that they would be regarded as the bad guy in the relationship. A surprising number were concerned that I would not like them after I heard their story.

Also interesting was the great number of people I met who have given up their pets, voluntarily or otherwise, because of a relationship.

Some of these people reported incidents that occurred some 20, 30, and, in one case, 50 years ago. As they began to retell their stories, many were overcome with emotions and memories that left them in a flood of tears. Their loss connected to all the other losses in their lives.

Often the issue that arises is what the pet represents to one or both of the people in the relationship, and how those people interact. Sometimes resolving the issue is as simple as getting the person to verbalize what the pet stands for. Perhaps the death of a loved pet brings back memories of a lost family member, for example. In other instances, it becomes more complicated: It is necessary to follow the paths of symbolic meanings attached to the pet.

So, let's begin to explore the ways in which people relate to the pets in their lives, and let's delve into the psychological problems that may be operating beneath the surface.

Chapter 2

Let Sleeping Dogs (and Cats) Lie

How often have you heard someone say that so-and-so's St. Bernard reminds them of Great Uncle Ferdinand, who was so big and gruff? That happens to most of us pretty frequently, and we certainly don't think it's any big deal. Still, psychologists have a word for this (all professions have their private jargon!). They call it *displacement*, which simply means attaching some characteristic that you saw in someone from your past to some other being in the present.

Normally, this is not a problem. But if the person who thinks your St. Bernard looks familiar is afraid of the dog just because it reminds him of Uncle Ferdinand, that *is* a problem.

In fact, displacement is thought to be one of the most basic psychological mechanisms controlling many of our human relationships. A couple cases in point will help you understand how it works. First, meet Donna, Charley, and Angus, Charley's Irish Setter.

THE ANGUS CHRONICLES

When Donna asked one day if we could meet for lunch, I was delighted. I got to the restaurant—one of those Upper West Side eateries with a couple tables on the sidewalk that are popular in New York—a bit early and had some time to think about why Donna wanted to meet.

I did not wait long. Donna soon arrived, and we ordered lunch and talked a bit. She told me that her recent marriage agreed with her. She and Charley were having a great time getting to know each other and were doing a number of projects together around their new house. Then Donna confided that the only thing wrong with this otherwise perfect picture was Charley's dog, Angus. Angus looked like a normal enough Irish Setter—friendly by nature, long red hair, lean physique—but Donna had a complaint: "He does not behave like a dog," she said.

As a long-time dog owner, that piqued my curiosity. I asked what she meant by her comment. "He just sits around and waits to be taken care of," Donna explained. "He has no initiative or desire to do anything. He has to be practically pushed out of the house to go for a walk. He is not interested in other dogs and is not into any play activities. He accepts special treats, but only if a big deal is made out of them; he would just as soon roll over and go to sleep."

As a breed, Irish Setters are a little like Robert Redford and Uma Thurman: They turn heads, and everyone thinks they are fabulous. They are indeed beautiful to look at and fun to play with, but they do not do anything they do not want to do. Beauty aside, they are great bird dogs and love romping through meadows as well as along city streets. Of course, some of them would rather just hang around. Sometimes dogs are like that.

Donna looked more upset than her problem seemed to warrant. As a psychologist, I am always intrigued by such contradictions. I wondered if the dog was ill, but Donna said that Angus had recently had a complete set of blood tests and a physical examination and was fine. According to Charley, he had always been this way.

Donna said she often would just look at Angus lying around not doing much of anything and feel annoyed with him. In no time flat, her feelings of irritation would change to exasperation, and she would find herself grabbing his leash and fuming as she pulled him up from his reveries to take a walk. She found herself taking the dog out for walks even when she did not want to and when she had other pressing things to do. She resented having to feed Angus, and she found herself near tears when she had to pick up after him to comply with New York's "pooper scooper" law.

"Does Angus remind you of anyone you know?" I asked. Donna looked at me as if I should not have ordered the Bloody Mary I was sipping. After what seemed like a few minutes, tears began to flow and she replied, "My father."

"Okay, Donna, what about your father?" She explained that a couple years ago, he had been forced into early retirement, and that precipitated a radical change in his personality. "He became apathetic about everything," she said. Donna told me that her father had been a no-nonsense chief executive of his own corporation. Far from apathetic in those days, he expected obedience from all around him. He insisted that people do what they were told—now! And that extended to his home and family.

After a little more probing, the rest of the story came out. "Shortly before he stepped down from his job, my parents got divorced, and I guess that's when he started changing," she said. "Now he just seems to sit around his house and do nothing. When he was CEO of his corporation, he expected all of us to do everything for him. He has never done a thing for himself—he never had to. Now the spark, the demand, is gone. He is just vegetating alone at home."

As Donna thought about growing up in her father's household, her attitude turned from worry and concern for him and his obvious emotional upset to anger buried deep within herself. He was a man who always demanded that his family take care of him. He insisted that his wife direct all her attentions to him, but he never seemed to appreciate what was done for him. According to Donna, her father acted as though his only responsibility to his family was their financial support. Beyond that, the family was on its own.

This self-centeredness affected everyone. In Donna's family, everyone learned to fend for themselves with little thought for or concern from other family members. While the divorce may have been the beginning of her father's emotional reversal, it changed little in his attitude toward his family. When the divorce was finalized, both of Donna's older sisters were away at school. Her mother was left with Donna and her younger brother, plus an assortment of dogs, cats, birds, ducks, geese, and a horse to care for—and no help from anyone. Having grown up in such a household, it was small wonder that Donna had so much anger toward her father building up inside her!

Until our discussion, Donna thought she had gotten past those early memories. She certainly had no idea that they were coloring her attitude toward Angus. Donna was quite unaware of her unconscious connection to Angus.

All this may sound far-fetched, but when Donna got home and told Charley about our lunch and her reactions to our conversation about Angus and her father, he found the idea fascinating. As he thought about what she was telling him, he pointed out that she used the same language when she was complaining about her father and about Angus: "He's so selfish, he always wants his own way," and "He doesn't care about anyone else." Charley reminded her that she had often said, "Angus does not care if we live or die." He also told Donna that once she even said, "He just lies around here like he's a CEO or something." She laughed when she remembered saying these things.

Poor Angus! All he wanted to do was lie around and take life as it came. He was happy. He was fed. He was comfortable. It wasn't his fault that he reminded Donna of her father.

Angus and Donna are good examples of the idea of displacement. Donna transferred her feelings about her father to her relationship with Angus. In fact, the object of displacement can be anyone or anything, even an inanimate object. All that's needed is some characteristic to trigger the memories. The unconscious will take care of the rest.

A CAT NAMED BEAUREGARD

Here's another story involving Rachel, Bert, and Beauregard. Once again, an animal was just being itself and by doing so brought one of the humans in its family face to face with an old demon—and in the process the animal helped change that person's future. This time, it will be easier to understand what happened if we first look at the backgrounds of those involved.

Rachel's mother was severely depressed. From infancy and through early childhood, her mother had little energy to relate to Rachel in an animated way. For the most part, she seemed to just manage the bare essentials of child rearing.

Rachel remembered having a cat named Whiskey that was very playful and would chase around the house, taking fantastic leaps from what seemed like floor to ceiling. She recalled that sometimes the only action in the house would be Whiskey's frolicking. She also remembered wishing that she could be more like the cat. But one day Whiskey found his way out of the house, was hit by a truck, and died. Rachel recalled the moment she learned of his death as the saddest moment of her childhood.

Rachel's father fought in the Korean War and was away from the time she was born until she was 4 years old. By the time he returned, he found a sad and depressed little girl—and an even more depressed wife and mother. The return of Rachel's father helped a bit with her mother's depression. However, by this time Rachel had developed a pattern of acting the sad, depressed little girl around other people to stay emotionally connected with her mother. Even at that early age, she found that if she expressed other feelings around her mother, she would lose whatever connection her mother was capable of and then Rachel would be alone.

In contrast, her father was an animated, productive man with a lot of energy for work and for his family. After his return, Rachel, too, learned how to be animated. During our therapy sessions, she recalled how having her father home again helped her fend off her mother's depression and also showed her another way of behaving that she found emotionally more compatible. However, as she learned during therapy, the animated self that developed with her father's return only masked the sadness and depression carried by the little girl still within her.

Then Rachel met Bert at work. She was attracted to his quiet, gentle manner. And there was Beauregard: Bert had often spoken of his frolicsome cat getting into his things. The way he treated these incidents with humor rather than anger reminded her of the pleasure she experienced from her cat Whiskey. They began dating, and Rachel finally got to meet Beauregard.

Rather than the kittenish animal she had anticipated, Rachel discovered that Beauregard was an adult cat who loved to sit quietly in the sun on the windowsill, watching the activity outside. But Rachel saw sadness and depression in the cat. She had a sinking feeling as she sought ways to draw the cat out of what she described as his listlessness. "I don't know what it is, but the cat looks at me with sad eyes and just sits there looking out the window." (This was Rachel's displacement. As any cat owner knows, cats seem to love just sitting on a windowsill enjoying the sun and watching the passing parade). Rachel told Bert that she had never known a cat like Beauregard.

Away from the cat, Rachel was lively and funny. She gave a lot of energy to her relationship with Bert. For his part, Bert felt that she drew him out of himself, and he looked forward to doing things together. On one level of the relationship, Rachel was helping Bert come out of his shell in much the same way that her father's return had released her from the oppression of her mother's depression.

Bert saw Beauregard as a normal cat, but he also realized that Rachel's mood really changed around Beauregard. He said there seemed to be some kind of bad chemistry between the cat and Rachel—the cat even avoided her. At first, Bert thought it was because Beauregard wanted him all to himself.

Rachel said that when the cat just stared out the window, she sometimes "knew" that she was connected to her depressed mother. Before her father's return, her mother also spent a great deal of her free time sitting in front of the window just looking out. As a child, Rachel thought her mother sat at the window waiting for her father's return.

When Rachel was around Bert's cat, she said, "I would feel myself slipping into my old childhood feelings and could not stop myself, even when I told Bert what was happening and when he would do his best to help me talk about what it was like for me." Rachel not only felt depressed around the cat, but she also felt guilty about her reactions.

What came out of our work together was Rachel's realization that although she was aware of something about the cat that reminded her of her mother, she was not aware of the guilt she felt because of her father's return. Through him, she learned that it was okay to be funny and animated, but she had pushed away the memory of how guilty she felt when she was no longer feeling or acting depressed around her mother. Somehow Rachel saw that change as abandoning her mother; she saw herself as an uncaring, ungrateful daughter.

In this state, Rachel found herself sinking into feelings of self-loathing. In her mind, she knew her mother had done her best to raise Rachel by herself. But as soon as her father appeared, Rachel had dropped the sad and depressed character that she had developed to support her mother, so she felt that she had abandoned her mother. That guilt had been an awful burden for Rachel as a little girl. It was a guilt that she did not have words for. Only by exploring the dis-placed feelings generated by her relationship with Bert and with Beauregard—the cat with the sad eyes that liked to look out the window—was she able to recover those lost memories of guilt and self-loathing.

In exploring the guilt, Rachel came to acknowledge that she could never be angry with her mother. It is also interesting to note that Rachel's sense of guilt was of her own making. Her mother had never suggested that she felt Rachel had abandoned her after her father returned.

Sometimes we experience guilt instead of the anger we really feel. Rachel's guilt was a defense against her angry feelings. As a child, she had found it impossible to be angry with such a sad and depressed mother who was doing her best to make life as nice as possible for her daughter. After her father's return, she had felt guilty enjoying herself when her mother was around. To the young Rachel, having fun and enjoying herself—especially with her father—was like abandoning her mother. As an adult, Rachel could start to understand the price she had to pay as a kid to stay emotionally connected to her mother.

As so often happens, serendipity stepped in to help out. While Rachel was busy in therapy working through her feelings of anger and guilt, a family friend suggested that Rachel's mother try anti-depressants to help her come out of herself and start to enjoy life. It worked. Seeing her mother's renewed joy and emotional health also helped Rachel move away from her lifetime of guilt.

It also helped her understand why she had never connected with Beauregard. The cat who stared passively out the window, as her mother had so long ago, became the displaced target of Rachel's anger. As she worked through her feelings, she began to understand that Beauregard was just following his own cat nature. And as for Beauregard, I see him still on his windowsill, smiling like a Cheshire cat and marveling at the antics of his human family.

Chapter 3

The Siamese Code

··

Here's another example of a people-pet relationship and how displacement colored the lives of two people. In this case, though, the animals were not-so-innocent bystanders: a pair of Siamese cats and one stray puss. The human side of this relationship was well on its way to serious problems when I became involved.

When I first met Pete and Jackie, their relationship was all but over. At first look, the culprits were a pair of cats. Pete could not tolerate Jackie's Siamese cats. He tried to hide his dislike from Jackie and tended not to comment when she talked about her Siamese, but his feelings about the two animals were obvious.

It was not that Pete did not like cats in general; Jackie had a rescued stray cat that Pete did like. But the two Siamese were something else. They would jump on the bed the minute Pete walked into the bedroom. They would stare at him with looks that a guard dog might reserve for a burglar. If Pete walked into the kitchen while the cats were eating, they would stop eating and leave, not returning until Pete walked out of the kitchen.

The nonverbal agreement between the couple seemed to be that Jackie knew Pete would never do anything to hurt the cats, but he made no pretense about loving them. For a while, this helped keep peace, albeit a belligerent one. But now Pete's dislike for the Siamese cats had grown to outright hostility.

MINE IS MINE, AND YOURS IS MINE

Pete claimed that the Siamese had taken over the living space he shared with Jackie. People who know this breed of cat know that Siamese have no problems taking over a household and dominating the humans in their domain. Being quite intelligent, they make no bones about demanding human attention, and they can show their displeasure if they are not attended to. When they feel ignored, they are likely to retaliate by doing considerable damage to personal possessions and furniture. At the same time, they are capable of returning great amounts of affection.

The cats used the whole house as their personal domain. Pete felt intimidated moving around *their* house. He acknowledged that part of the problem was that he had moved into Jackie's house and had stopped insisting that they find a larger, more comfortable living space. For her part, Jackie said it was her own laziness that kept her from taking time to look for a new house with him.

I asked Pete what specifically he did not like about these Siamese cats. He said he found them repulsive, although he seemed to be perfectly comfortable with the stray. He called them arrogant and self-centered, and he complained that they pushed themselves into his space whether it was appropriate or not. Although many cat owners say their pets can be very loving and affectionate, Pete said these cats were not capable of a reciprocal relationship. (As anyone with cats knows, the animals can tell when they are not liked, and it is doubtful they would have extended any affection in Pete's direction.)

In contrast to Donna (whose story was told in Chapter 2, "Let Sleeping Dogs [and Cats] Lie"), who had buried her feelings of anger toward her father, Pete had no trouble connecting his feelings about the Siamese cats with his feelings about his mother:

> My mother was exactly the same way as the cats: arrogant
> and self-centered. She didn't seem to care where her kids

were in their lives [Pete had a younger sister and a brother]. She always came first; only her feelings and her needs were important. She would say we were always doing something *to* her. She could never see my point of view or what I needed, unless it coincided with her view of the world. There was no room to breathe in her house. She filled the house up with herself.

WHY KNOWING IS NOT ENOUGH

Later we'll revisit the need to bring such early memories to the conscious level so that we can appropriately deal with them. For now, you should know that being consciously aware of feelings and defenses is only part of the job. There is still the major task of learning to understand and deal with those feelings. Pete recognized the role his mother played in his psychological evolution, but as we shall see, he had yet to come to terms with it.

"When I see those Siamese cats, all I can think about is their self-centeredness and how familiar that feels," he told me. "They walk right across my face—literally. Never mind that this may be typical Siamese behavior to establish sway over their territory. I have no wish to get to know them better or spend any time with them. As for my mother, I see her only on holidays, and then I buffer myself from her with Jackie and with my brother and sister. She still fills up the house just the way those cats fill up our house."

Pete's father was not much help. Like Donna's father, he was a passive man who just wanted peace and quiet in his house after returning home from his job. He believed his responsibilities involved supporting the family and that his wife should be responsible for child-rearing problems.

I asked Pete what would help to make the cats less hateful to him. He thought for quite a while before he replied. Finally, he said it would be helpful if the Siamese had some limitations and were not free to roam everywhere all the time. Pete said he needed to know that he could have some privacy, an almost unheard of notion in his parents' house. Pete's mother's presence permeated his childhood home, and her impact and influence were everywhere. The kids were not allowed to decorate their rooms the way they wanted. Nothing could be hung on their walls without her approval. Every room could have been photographed for *House Beautiful* with just a few moments' notice.

Again, we have a situation in which someone is trying to change an animal's natural behavior because of a personal problem that has nothing to do with the pets. Old Angus just wanted to lie around enjoying the good life. Likewise, Siamese cats are territorial and make a point of letting everyone know it. One of the things new pet owners learn very quickly is that their cuddly new friends have instincts peculiar to the species—instincts that are not always consistent with life among humans.

SETTING SOME LIMITS

For Pete and Jackie, the talk came down to limiting the cats' natural territorial tendencies. They decided to make their bedroom off-limits to their pets. Pete and Jackie understood and agreed that not permitting the cats in the bedroom would be a major relief to Pete. Having a cat-free—and particularly a Siamese-free—area sounded wonderful to him. He noted that he might have been a different person if there had been a mother-free area in the emotionally overcrowded house in which he grew up!

From a people point of view, this seemed like a remarkably easy solution to the problem. It cost the cats a little bit of space and freedom, but it brought peace to the household. Was it a fair trade-off? Pete and Jackie certainly think so. I guess you'll have to ask the cats.

FEELINGS THAT WON'T GO AWAY

While the solution may have resolved the immediate situation, it did nothing to resolve Pete's lasting animosity toward his mother, or the way she still affected his life. A few weeks later, Pete and Jackie reported that life was much better without the Siamese cats in the bedroom, but Pete understood that his reaction to the cats was extreme and that he still had a problem. What particularly bothered him was that he felt he had always known there was a connection between his dislike of the Siamese cats and his anger toward his mother. And he was right.

The trouble in this family ran deeper—much deeper. Shopping with his mother, for example, was an embarrassment for Pete. All too often some salesperson would say something or do something that left his mother feeling slighted. So, she would take the matter to the manager, demanding satisfaction for the poor treatment she felt she had received. And, of course, it went without saying that Pete had to support her 120 percent, although even at an early age Pete recognized that some of these slights were quite insignificant and were even imaginary. (Think about some of the ways a pair of cats might demonstrate control of their territory, and it is easy to see how pervasive displacement can be.) To offer his mother anything less than total support would risk her withdrawing her affection and leaving him isolated.

It's not that Pete's mother was unable to give affection. When she felt loving, she could be very attentive; when she felt needy, though, Pete felt as though he didn't exist. The problem was that Pete's behavior had little to do with his mother's moods; his responsiveness to her needs had little effect on them. This unpredictability left him unsure of where he stood.

WAITING FOR THE PRIZE

Another aspect of displacement can be something psychologists call *intermittent conditioning*. As I explained it to Pete, this comes about when consistent behavior gets an inconsistent response: You never know if you will get a piece of chocolate or a smack on the head.

Pete could come home and report a B+ on an English test, and his mother might be thrilled and say, "How wonderful! I am so proud of my little man. I must call your Aunt Ellen and tell her right away." The same B+ on another English test three weeks later might be met with, "What is the matter with you? Didn't you study? You knew you had a test. Don't you care whether you go to college or not?"

The other mind-bending part of his mother's behavior was that everything was viewed in the extreme. Pete's mother spoke of him as either the most brilliant student of English or the all-time reject from English class. There was no middle ground for his mother; everything was all black or all white, the best or the worst. People were either all good or all bad, all right or all wrong. She had no interest in changing or developing any awareness of how there were shades of nuance in the real world.

With such a background, it is not difficult to see how a person like Pete can become trapped by intermittent conditioning. Not knowing what the response will be keeps many people locked into relationships forever. On the one hand, they are afraid to trust the approval they have received; on the other hand, they hope they have finally gained the acceptance so long sought. The same principle keeps gamblers hooked: They are always hoping for that big hit. And the occasional win just whets the appetite for "the big one," which, of course, is "just around the corner."

The reverse is also true. Ultimately, tremendous anger and hostility can build up because nothing you do seems to lead to that ultimate approval. The Siamese cats, in this situation, still treat you, at best, as incidental.

Pete began to have what I like to call *ah-hah* experiences as he came to understand the dynamics of his relationship with his mother. This happens when a present-day experience suddenly jogs a person's memory. For Pete, his growing awareness of how those early, growing-up experiences carried through into his adult life and colored his adult relationships only added to the anger he was beginning to acknowledge toward his mother.

WORKING THROUGH THE PROBLEM

But then, Pete's feelings began to change. After some months of working through some of the anger, he felt those angry feelings turning into sadness, which is not surprising. There is a real sadness underneath the anger of having never been heard or seen as a child. For many of us, being ignored can be more painful than physical abuse. At my suggestion, instead of trying to push it away because it was uncomfortable, Pete held onto that sadness. Once he was aware of those long-suppressed feelings, he was able to recognize them as ghosts from the past that were no longer factors in his life. Pete ultimately felt increased emotional strength and greater confidence in himself.

Psychologists call this process *working through*, a concept that is referred to throughout this book. This refers to the hard work of emotionally visiting and revisiting all the situations and circumstances that originally produced the discomfort, until it's possible to recall not only all the factual components of an important event, but also all the emotions that accompanied them. Once we are able to remember the events *and* recreate the emotions felt at the time, we can then examine the circumstances and begin to understand why they are able to so profoundly shape and affect our current lives.

As Pete started to connect to the sadness that surrounded his relationship with his mother, he began to see how fragile she really was emotionally—not at all the strong, domineering person she seemed to be. He began to understand that because of her frailty, the woman had to create a perfect family and a perfect household to cover her own feelings of emptiness and inadequacy. Understanding her life in this way helped Pete change his anger at her into sadness and a feeling of compassion. It allowed him to consider contacting his mother and perhaps resurrecting their relationship.

After this *ah-hah* experience, Pete got into the real work of therapy—an *ah-hah* experience is not the culmination of therapy, but when the real work of therapy begins. As Pete allowed himself to feel the sadness, he thought about all the energy he had expended over the years by carrying around an anger that would appear out of nowhere—anger that could turn a happy, joyful celebration into a gloomy event. He came to realize how much of his personal pain he had covered up with resentment and sarcasm.

But more importantly, this new realization allowed him to open up to new feelings. He started to really experience Jackie's love and caring for him: how much she truly listened to him, heard what he had to say, and understood who he was. He was able to see how Jackie understood his struggle with the sadness and pain beneath his smart-aleck veneer. Even the couple's friends commented on how Pete seemed mellower and less likely to become ruffled by unpleasant circumstances. He and Jackie grew closer together—and all because a couple of Siamese cats were doing what came naturally to them!

One important aspect of this story is that Jackie acknowledged Pete's feelings and was willing to make some adjustments to help him feel better. As for the cats, they continue to hold sway over most of the household, but they stay out of the bedroom!

Chapter 4

When You Know the Stand-In

· ·

Let's look at a somewhat different displacement issue brought to light by a people-pet relationship. Here, the main character, Dan, recognized the displacement and understood how he was allowing it to shape his relationship with Louise. But he did it anyway.

POLLY WANT A CRACKER— AND EVERYTHING ELSE

When Dan met Louise, he had already owned Murray, his African Grey Parrot, for 18 years. Murray was a lot of fun and had a working vocabulary of hundreds of words. Everyone loved Murray, including Louise.

But even on Mt. Olympus, nothing is perfect. Here, in Dan and Louise's world, the problem was that Murray had the run of Dan's apartment—and, birds being birds, Murray left calling cards everywhere. Before they were married, this did not seem to bother Louise very much, even when she stayed at Dan's place during their courtship days. Dan simply scraped the droppings up when they dried out, and they never really smelled that much (so he said).

But there was more: In spite of the name, Murray was a female and showed what is considered to be typical female parrot behavior. This added to the problem—we'll get to that in just a bit.

After they were married, Louise felt differently about the bird. Evidence of Murray's presence was everywhere, and there was no respite. Louise began to complain, first about the fact that Murray was free to move about the apartment at will—and, birds being birds, her droppings were everywhere. In addition, whenever Murray's nesting instinct kicked in, she regurgitated most of her meals as a sign, in true female parrot fashion, of affection for Dan. The regurgitations were not attractive, but they did not bother Louise as much as the guano. Besides ruining drapes, rare carpets, and the expensive upholstered furniture Louise brought with her, Murray was ruining Louise's valuable paintings.

There was more. Murray was becoming what we will call jealous of Louise. Dan was spending more of his time with Louise, at Murray's expense. African Greys typically start screaming when they feel they are not getting enough attention, and Murray was no different. Unfortunately, Dan and Louise reinforced the screaming behavior by trying to quiet the bird before the neighbors complained—in essence, giving her the attention she wanted as a "reward" for screaming.

If the competition for Dan's attention wasn't enough to upset the bird, Louise rearranged the furniture when she moved in to accommodate her possessions. No one discussed the matter with Murray, who began having stress reactions, the worst being feather-picking. Now, don't laugh. Almost anything an African Grey finds stressful may lead to feather-picking. This activity can become a serious health issue if it continues because it can damage the feather follicles.

Louise began petting Murray in an attempt to reduce the bird's stress. Although African Greys do not always enjoy human touch, Murray responded well to Louise's holding and petting. Louise concentrated on quietly talking to Murray while rubbing her stomach and beak.

Note: A number of parrot owners say it is vital to discuss life changes and physical changes with your parrot before actually making a change. Dan had never discussed Louise's moving into the apartment with Murray. (If you are not a parrot person, the idea of discussing changes with your parrot could sound pretty silly, but it is recommended by those in the know.)

With all this going on, it is easy to see why Murray had grown into a major bone of contention for Dan and Louise—serious enough for them to come to me for help. Louise and Dan appeared to agree about everything in their relationship except Murray. When we met, I asked Dan who Murray reminded him of. He replied without hesitation that Murray was himself and that Louise was his mother. It wasn't until later that Dan realized just how all-consuming that relationship had become. As Dan explained it, he had grown up in a house with a very controlling mother. There was only one way to do things, and that was her way. In particular, everything had to look pristine for visitors and company.

Coming to know Dan's mother and her background, it was not hard to understand what was driving her—not that it made Dan's life any more bearable. Dan's mother had come from very humble beginnings and was never regarded as good enough by his father's family. Rather than showing the anger she must have felt, she taught herself everything there was to know about homemaking and interior decorating. One result of this was a living room decorated with white furniture and powder blue wall-to-wall carpeting. No one was ever allowed in the living room—except, of course, his father's family.

Dan always felt he was second-class in his mother's eyes. He believed she saw him as someone who could not be trusted to respect her things and keep them clean. Somehow, he had interpreted her off-limits house rules as a suggestion that he was dirty and not dependable. That set the scene for the way Dan and Louise's relationship developed with Murray around. In some psychological feat of displacement, Dan had cast Louise into his mother's role, but in a way that reversed things and put him in control. (Who said the idea of displacement was a simple one?)

By letting Murray continue to have free reign of the house after Louise had moved in her valuable possessions, Dan was unconsciously setting Louise up to feel as disregarded as he had felt growing up. He was, in fact, making a very dramatic statement to his mother, one that he could never make to her directly.

I helped Dan to understand that unconsciously he was torturing Louise with Murray the same way he had felt controlled and tortured by his mother. Louise was getting the brunt of Dan's anger and anguish simply because she had come into his life. Louise understood also and acknowledged feeling disrespected and tortured since moving in with Dan. I pointed out that in this form of displacement, the wrong person was getting punished, although for the right reasons. I also noted, with a touch of sarcasm, that Dan should have sent Murray to his mother's house to live!

To show how devious displacement can become, Dan had transferred his childhood identity to Murray before he had met Louise, while he became the free-spirited, free-wheeling, noncontrolling and carefree mother he always wished for. In that household, Murray had the freedom that Dan never had.

Of course, important as these understandings were to Dan and Louise and their relationship, the problem with Murray and her screaming and toilet habits was very real and not a bit psychological. Though a jungle-tree-dwelling bird by instinct, she lived among people in a home. Together Dan and Louise worked out a schedule for Murray that gave the parrot plenty of exercise without destroying the house. They decided that Murray could be released to roam her "jungle," but not until she had expelled most of what she had ingested. Once again, the problem was resolved by a combination of understanding what was really going on and making some adjustments that enabled everyone to get what they needed.

LEARNING TO BEAR IT

The story of Nancy, Albert, and Bear, a St. Bernard, came out during therapy sessions. This gives us yet another example of the workings of displacement and shows how complex such relationships can be. At first glance, it seemed as though Nancy was bearing the brunt of

Albert's recent divorce. That was one factor in their problem, but the main story was much deeper, as you will see.

When Albert met Nancy, he had been divorced about two years. As Albert told it, the process cost him dearly. His ex-wife, Fran, "took him to the cleaners." About the only thing she did not want was Bear, the St. Bernard Albert had bought her as a first anniversary gift. According to Albert, Fran told him that the only thing she wanted to remember him by was his money. To say the least, there seemed to be nothing but bad feelings between Albert and his ex.

Everyone who had known Fran agreed that she was the least nurturing, most cold-blooded human being they had ever known. Albert was a fairly quiet, reserved guy who seemed good-natured and sensitive. No one had been able to figure out this match, nor was anyone surprised when Fran left Albert for a prosperous land developer in Florida. What made the marriage possible was the fact that Albert did not expect the love and tenderness one would expect from a marriage—but we're getting a bit ahead of the story.

Shifting the Responsibility

After the divorce, Albert said that Bear began acting strangely, often lying about listlessly whenever Albert prepared for one of his overnight business trips. Although Albert returned early in the morning, the dog definitely showed his displeasure at being left alone. I dare say that a good many dog owners are treated the same way by their pets; just go away for a day, and you return to find that your dog has chewed up one or more shoes or has done some other damage that lets you know how bored he was while you were away. And when something as large as a St. Bernard misbehaves, you have to take notice. By the time Nancy came into the picture, Bear had become a really aggressive dog who thought he was the master of the house. While St. Bernards are not known to be aggressive, Bear would sometimes fight with other dogs.

Bear was Albert's dog, but when Nancy moved in with him, it seemed everything became reversed. Nancy took Bear to obedience school, and she became his primary caregiver. Albert seemed to abdicate most of the responsibility for the animal.

This shifting of responsibility adds yet another wrinkle to our story of displacement. As you'll see, Bear was indeed being used by Albert to satisfy an emotional objective, but the big dog had developed some of his own characteristics that exacerbated the human relationship.

Nancy thought it was strange that she was now taking care of the dog Albert had bought as a gift for his first wife. "The dog had become the focus of our relationship," she said at one of our therapy sessions. "We were just beginning our life together, and suddenly I was responsible for another woman's gift. Besides the emotional aspects—trying to build a loving and intimate life with each other while a very large and demanding animal interfered—there were physical problems, too. It was a very small apartment, and there were certain areas where I did not want the dog. It became like a territorial thing."

Albert interrupted Nancy during one of our therapy sessions to say that he knew he had a lesson to learn about boundaries and limits, but he did not want to hear about it just then. That was more than Nancy was willing to take. "You care about the dog more than you care about me, even though the situation is making me unhappy," she told Albert. "You actually said the damn dog was more important to you than our relationship. I still cannot believe you told me that if the relationship was going to work, it was my responsibility. You wanted the relationship, and you wanted the dog without doing any of the work."

She continued, "It made me angry that he kept saying it was his ex-wife's dog. It made me feel very insecure with our relationship. I wondered where he was in his head with his ex-wife. I thought if I could solve the dog problem, I would have a clearer idea of what my real feelings were for Al. Bear used to run away, and I would always hope he would not come back."

As the therapist, I wondered if keeping this dog was Albert's way of holding onto his first marriage. He acknowledged that might have been the case just after the divorce, but he did not believe it was the case after he met Nancy. I pointed out that listening to the both of them left me feeling that Fran, the ex-wife, was also in the room with us. Nancy agreed. "When we first met," she said, "I felt bonded to him. If we were going to be together, I felt that I had to agree to keeping the dog, otherwise we could not have a relationship. Bear is like a shadow to Al and does not let him out of his sight."

Ex-Wife? Mom? Dad?

She explained, "The dog was becoming the focus of everything. To me, it represented his former marriage, so it seemed like he was still committed to that marriage and not to me. We were not finding a way to work together."

Then a new element was introduced into the story that helped explain why Albert had entered such a cold marriage with Fran and why Bear played such an important role in his life.

Nancy said she thought another reason why Bear was so important to Albert related to his childhood. Albert explained that his mother had died suddenly when he was seven, and his father remarried a year later. The death of his mother was a great loss to Albert. However, Albert found some solace in his attachment to the dogs his parents had. The animals gave him companionship, friendship, and devotion and asked little in return. But even that was temporary. "Two of the dogs ran away and never came back," he said. "One of the dogs was given away because it was wrecking the house, and the other one got sick and they gave him away as well. I felt it was unfair, and I did not want to be like that."

Little wonder that Albert had very powerful emotions about not giving up Bear! He said it would be bad to get rid of this dog "even if the dog is a pain." As the therapist, instinct told me that we were on the right track. There was still another level to be worked through, but it was coming.

Nancy did not grow up with pets, although she had always wanted dogs. But, she indicated, Bear was something else. "Bear could not be left alone because he would be so destructive, so I would take him every place I could. Al took him to work with him sometimes as well." I noted that Albert apparently did take some part in their life with Bear. One of those times Albert took Bear with him to an apartment building where he was redoing the bathroom, with comic consequences. There was no floor where the work was being done, but there was a suspended ceiling three feet below. The dog, in his lumbering about, fell through the ceiling and landed on the people below. They never knew what hit them!

I asked Albert and Nancy if they felt his former marriage would have intruded if Bear had not been around. Nancy said she wasn't sure. She had come to realize that Albert was more comfortable with Bear than with people. Despite the fact that the care and training of Bear had fallen upon her, she believed that the dog really was his best friend. Nancy was the only person Albert ever trusted to care for Bear. She was also becoming aware that their problem together was not all about Albert holding onto his ex-wife.

Sole Source of Comfort

As our sessions continued, it became apparent that Albert had great difficulty accepting comfort and nurturing from Nancy (and probably wouldn't have accepted it from Fran, which could explain why he was able to be married to her). Bear became the only source of comfort that he could accept. Albert saw the dog as really loyal, someone who would not abandon him the way some people had. All he had to do was hold on to Bear and protect him. From there, we got to Albert's fears of abandonment and how awful it was for him to have lost his mother at such an early age.

As a psychologist, I am constantly reminded that emotions most often are anything but logical or rational. In Albert's case, he converted his mother's death from a deep loss into a case of abandonment. He consequently felt that he could not trust people to stick around and be there for him. To children, death is always seen as abandonment.

Of course, Albert's first marriage proved him right. In marrying what one of his friends called "the least-nurturing person in America," he created a self-fulfilling prophecy. As it turned out, Fran would have left anyone if the price was right. When Albert married Fran, he had never intended to rely on her, and he could not even conceive of the idea of getting any love or support from her. For Albert, she was a safe bet because he did not have to make an emotional investment in her and did not have to worry about grieving if she left. Then came Bear, whom Albert felt would not leave him. Bear offered the dependable companionship with unconditional love that Albert felt humans could not provide.

Nancy was a new experience for Albert. She was warm and caring, and she genuinely liked him. Still, Albert never intended to get serious with her. But Nancy was willing to work at building a relationship; she was determined to help Albert and the dog. The four of us (including Bear) worked together, and gradually Albert was able to understand that his abandonment fears had become so powerful that they overpowered the reality of his relationship with Nancy, who demonstrated in every way she could that she wanted to stay and be with him. Finally, Albert was able to acknowledge that anyone who was willing to go through what Nancy went through with Bear must really want to be with him.

The important displacement here was the result of the fact that Albert had never really dealt with the loss of his mother. When she died, he unconsciously decided not to make real emotional investments in people who might die or otherwise abandon him. Fran was a great choice because she offered nothing for Albert to lose—and her behavior at the divorce "proved" to him that people cannot be trusted. Nancy, however, was willing to stay with Albert and fight to prove that she would not dump him or Bear.

With more stability in his household, Bear, too, settled down to a peaceful life as a well-behaved member of his family.

Chapter 5

Animal Actors

In the world of displacement that we have seen so far, the recipients of those displaced experiences—the pets—have played a mostly passive role, just doing what came naturally to them. Animals in general probably see humans simply as other inhabitants of their world. As pack animals, dogs, in particular, just assume that we are members (although strange-looking ones) of their pack.

Frequently, however, the dog, cat, parrot, or whatever becomes an active player. That was the case with Judy. The story of Judy and Buster, the dog that ruled her life, provides a view of displacement in which the pet, an otherwise lovable dog, helped the person act out her displacement.

Judy's story illustrates another aspect of displacement and, in fact, therapy in general: Analysis does not come easy to patient or therapist; there are precious few *ah-hah* experiences. More often than not, the patient throws up obstacle after obstacle to avoid facing the emotional pain of past experiences (psychologists call them *defenses* or *resistance*).

Defenses are costly to the person who uses them because, even though they help avoid pain and other difficult emotions, the relief is only superficial and the process uses up untold amounts of emotional energy. In addition, sometimes holding onto childhood defenses keeps us from maturing emotionally. Our reactions to life situations and relationships get stuck at an immature level. Most of us know some-one who is an adult chronologically, yet often responds to adult situations in a childish way.

I'M IN CHARGE—YOU SAID SO

When I met Judy, her dog was 9 years old and still used her Persian rug as his toilet. (Murray, the parrot, whom you met in Chapter 4, "When You Know the Stand-In," had nothing in his genetic code to tell him it was wrong. Dogs, however, are trainable; given the choice, they generally will not soil their den.) Judy viewed the situation fatal-istically. She said there was no point in replacing the rug because Buster was sure to do the same on any other rug. She had worked with a trainer plenty of times, but as she said, "Buster just keeps doing what he has always done and never pays any attention to me except when he is hungry."

When she took Buster for a walk, Judy said he was too busy being social to eliminate outside; either he played with other dogs, or he was busy looking around to see if any of his friends were coming. Judy told me about all the trainers she had lessons with and related their good advice. One told her about the need to develop eye contact with Buster so that he would pay more attention to her, both at home and on the street. While Judy agreed that establishing eye contact with Buster would give her more control, she also admitted that she lacked the patience to consistently apply the methods the trainer suggested.

Another trainer suggested soaking newspaper in the urine spot on the carpet, then taking it outside and placing it where she would like Buster to go. But Judy said she could not organize herself to follow that advice. She thought perhaps it had something to do with her erratic work schedule as an airline flight attendant.

As any dog owner knows all too well, tending to a pet's needs can take a bit of time management. All Judy's assignments were one-day trips. The overnight trips started in the late afternoon, so she usually returned by mid-day the next day—certainly not an unusually long time for a mature dog. And sometimes other people would care for Buster.

If Buster were human, I might think he was suffering from separation anxiety—the symptoms were all there—but experience has taught me that first impressions are not always accurate. Buster did destructive things, as well as urinating on wall corners (as many animals do to mark their territory). If there was a newspaper around, he tore it to shreds. Anything lying loose on the kitchen counter might be destroyed or taken to some other part of the house. When Judy prepared for a trip, Buster became agitated. Perhaps seeing her with a suitcase triggered some knowledge that he would be alone for more time than he wanted to tolerate.

Buster was not always alone during Judy's trips, though. Judy had a more-than-casual relationship with Don, who seemed to like Buster and would often take the dog out for very long walks. As it turned out, though, there was more going on than a man and a dog out on a walk. It took Judy about two years to catch on to the fact that Don was meeting lots of available women attached to the far end of the leashes of Buster's friends.

Judy came to me when she finally found out about Don's fooling around. Not surprisingly, he refused to come to the session with her. Judy loved Don and was broken-hearted. She did not want to lose him, yet she could not bear his faithlessness. Judy said that in a lot of ways, Buster and Don were alike: They always seemed to do exactly what they wanted to.

Not only did Don use Buster as a way to meet other women, but he also used the dog as a way to rationalize his own behavior. When Don and Judy had a disagreement, he would point to Buster and say, "You let him get away with all kinds of stuff, but you are on my back for every little thing." (Nothing like a little guilt to try to take the heat off!)

Ultimately, Judy began to complain to Don that she was seeing too little of him and that they hardly ever seemed to really talk. Don's response was, "What you see is what you get. I am just fine the way I am, and I am not changing for anyone." As Judy related these events, I suggested that if Buster could talk, it seemed that he would be saying the same thing: "I'm just fine the way I am." Judy agreed and said she did not know what to do.

Who Do I Remind You Of?

I asked her if the way Buster and Don behaved reminded her of anyone in her family. She said no, but we began to examine her childhood anyway. "We lived on a farm," she said. "Dad could never make any decisions about anything. He would talk it over with Mom, and she would tell him when to harvest and what price he should take for the crops and what to plant for the following year."

"So Mom made all the decisions?"

"Yes."

"What else was she like?"

"Well, when Mom got mad, she got fighting mad. We used to say when she got her Irish up, watch out! If you really crossed her, she could get real mean and stop talking to you. Once she got angry with me and stopped talking to me for nearly three months. I think I was around eight years old then."

"What did you do or say to upset her so drastically?"

"Oh, I don't remember. It didn't take a hell of a lot, though, to set her off."

"Don't you think that is pretty crazy to stop talking to an eight-year-old for three months?"

"Well, I wouldn't do that to a kid of mine, but that was Mom."

I asked how the other kids in the family dealt with Judy's mother. "Pretty much the same way as I did," she replied. "You stayed out of her way and tried to tell her what she wanted to hear, and you tried to feel what she wanted you to feel. Otherwise, all hell broke loose."

I told Judy that it seemed to me she was treating all living creatures as if they were her mother. She imbued everything, including Buster, with more power than they had; she allowed everybody's needs to come before hers. Even her work as a flight attendant was basically serving people, being a helper, and wearing a smile, no matter what.

As this applied to Buster, Judy giving up on his training was much like her giving up on getting her mother to accept the idea that she had feelings of her own. It may seem strange, but Judy regarded the dog the same way she did her mother, as not caring about her feelings. Such is the way of displacement.

As this reality started to sink in, Judy began to cry. She had always had to give in to her mother's wishes. There was only one way to do things, and that was Mom's way. You did not cross Mom because she could give you a look and stop talking to you for three months. Now, years and miles later, Mom was as close as ever in Judy's life. Judy had never let go of her.

Separating from her mother was very hard for Judy to do. So often, it seems, it is most difficult to separate from the people who give us the least of what we need. Unconsciously, we hold on, always hoping finally to be seen and heard and to have our needs met. Just once in her life, Judy would have liked to have known that her mother was aware of what she needed and felt. (Remember the story in Chapter 3, "The Siamese Code," of Pete, Jackie, and the Siamese cats? Pete, too, was looking for recognition and acceptance from his mother.)

PAINFUL SEPARATION

Judy understood almost instinctively that she had to find a way to separate from her mother emotionally. The problem was that somehow she came to feel that the only way to make the break was to become enraged at the way her mother had treated her, and this made her uncomfortable. As a result, she avoided dealing with questions about family situations and incidents for fear that her responses might force that rage to the surface, making any further relationship with her mother impossible. She would then never get the acceptance she required! This may have been the same thing that kept her from demanding a level of obedience from Buster: Expressing her anger and frustration to her pet might somehow cause him to reject her.

To protect herself from exploring the events in her early life, Judy's responses to most questions were "I don't know" or "I don't remember." These responses are a typical defense against experiencing the feelings that go along with knowing and remembering. In a sense, these responses for Judy were a way of lying to herself to avoid facing the rage she really felt. While such defenses may give the person some time to recover from a difficult situation, in the long run they are largely unproductive, as they were for Judy.

As Judy began to acknowledge those unresolved issues in her life with her mother and saw that her problems with Buster were related, she became increasingly exasperated with the dog's behavior. She was ready to give him up for adoption, until I pointed out to her that she was becoming exasperated with the wrong character. Buster was doing nothing new or different. In fact, he had quieted down considerably since he was neutered and was becoming more easily trainable as he got older. But things actually got worse before they got better.

Judy's was not some minor transient problem—it was serious. The prospect of having to deal with her feelings about her mother became so frightening that she took a break from therapy. Little changed in the interim. The old fears were still in control. Buster's behavior had not changed. Judy had become more dependent on Don, who, in turn, resented her neediness, possibly because it interfered with his dalliances. The more she made requests of him—mostly about spending more time together—the more he withdrew and complained that she was demanding and unreasonable.

Finally, Don began muttering that he was thinking he wanted to date other women (more accurately, he let her know what he had been doing all along) and that perhaps he just needed a break from the relationship to think things over. At this point, Judy returned to therapy. "I'll do anything to keep him," she said about Don. "Just tell me what to do. I do not know what I will do if he leaves me. I can't go through a break-up."

When I told Judy that even if I told her what to do, I felt that she would not be able to follow my suggestions any more than she could follow those of all the dog trainers and behaviorists, she became extremely irritated. And that gave me the tool I needed to cut through her fear of acknowledging the rage within her. It took a couple of months of needling her irritability, but it worked. "You are really annoying me, and I don't know why I am coming here anymore," she stated at the end of one of her sessions. The woman who could never get angry with anyone for fear they would stop talking to her was having no trouble being furious with me! Judy had finally learned that it was possible to have her own opinions and feelings, and that expressing herself did not mean that a blow-up was inevitable.

The result? Judy let Don know that she had met a man in one of the cities she flew to with some regularity. She reported that she was also really disliking Buster and becoming impatient with him. She began scolding the dog for his misbehavior and actually found herself becoming more consistent in her corrections as she began to feel her anger. She let him know that he and the carpets were on their way out if he did not shape up.

After all these years, Buster knew that this time Judy meant business. The carpet did get thrown out. Buster and Don sensed something different and stronger in Judy, and they began responding to her as if they were hearing her for the first time. Don volunteered to take Buster to obedience classes. He even agreed to try a few sessions of couples therapy with Judy. The two are still together and are doing well.

Chapter 6

The Pet in the Middle

Here's another type of displacement: Rather than the passive embodiment of a person's unresolved childhood issues, a certain pet was, in a manner of speaking, victimized by it. Everything started with a case of kidnapping—or, should I say, dognapping. Meet Diana, Chad, and Heidi.

ABOVE AND BEYOND

When Diana took care of her friend Betty's Bernese Mountain Dog, she became obsessed with the dog and would not give him back when Betty returned from vacation. People thought Diana had lost her mind. She would not answer the telephone, and she drew the curtains on her windows. Finally, after a week of this strange behavior, she returned the dog and apologized profusely. Her husband, Chad, thought she should see a therapist; Diana refused, saying all she wanted was a Bernese of her own.

Diana got her wish, and she named her dog Heidi. Heidi went everywhere with her and received all her attention. Chad, who is very much a live-and-let-live kind of guy, thought Diana was going through a phase and would eventually be okay. But this wasn't just a phase.

If Heidi so much as coughed twice, Diana rushed her to the emergency room at the Animal Medical Center. (How many people have we met who treat their pets as though they were super-sensitive first children?) These events gradually became more frequent—sometimes two or three times a week—but the important point was that nothing was ever wrong with Heidi. Bernese Mountain Dogs are exceptionally hardy, sturdy dogs, and Heidi was as healthy as they come. Although Chad and Diana's friends pointed out that her over-protectiveness was destructive to everyone involved—including Heidi—Diana would hear none of it.

Vacations always included Heidi. Everyone said Chad was a saint, but Chad did not think there was any problem. He grew up in a house where his mother had 13 dogs, so one dog was never an issue for him. But that was Chad.

Diana's behavior with Heidi was obviously much more dramatic than could be explained by her being a first-time pet owner. As it turned out, her overprotectiveness was a mask that hid very deep pain. Close to the surface, Heidi had become the child Diana and Chad had lost in childbirth about a year before they got the dog; it would have been their first child. When Diana talked about the loss of the baby in our therapy sessions, she indeed said that the dog was the child she was not able to mourn. "I have to stop myself and say she is a dog," Diana told me.

Chad thought Diana's great bond with Heidi came about during a visit to the cemetery, when the dog seemed to go straight to the baby's grave. Chad believed there was a way that Heidi could almost read Diana's mind.

As we delved more deeply into Diana's past, I learned that her parents were divorced when she was eight years old. Her mother had been an extremely self-centered woman who had refused to let her husband have custody of Diana, despite the fact that she did not want the child to live with her. She had insisted on putting young Diana in private schools. "I've always believed my mother had a lot of anger toward me and blamed me for a lot of what was wrong in her life,"

Diana said. "I suppose if I had not been born, she would not have stayed with my father as long as she did. She is the type of person who would kill someone and blame the person she killed."

I noted that it must be terrible to be the child of a mother who did not want you. "Your exceptional overprotectiveness of Heidi is exactly the opposite of your mother's lack of caring," I observed. "It is as if you see yourself in Heidi and are giving to her everything that was not given to you. I wonder if, when you look at Heidi, you are thinking something like, 'She is me and I am her.' It is amazing how all these thoughts occur in silence with such a sadness underneath it all."

With flowing tears, Diana acknowledged the truth of my observation and said, "I don't have time for my mother now. She hates Heidi, but she says that if anything happens to me, she wants my dog. Isn't that crazy? There is no love for me or Heidi, only possessiveness and competition. I cannot bear to admit this to anyone, much less to myself."

Diana had always been in touch with her anger at her mother; that was nothing new for her. But she had never allowed herself to experience the pain of not having had a loving mother. It was not until Diana and Chad lost their first child that Diana's pain came to the surface. At first it was cloaked in her kidnapping of Betty's dog and then in her exceptionally overprotective relationship with Heidi, a relationship that was becoming all consuming.

Chad's tolerance for Diana's relationship with Heidi was phenomenal. It was also a product of his own childhood. During one of the early sessions we all had together, Chad described his mother as something of an airhead, but with a heart of gold. He asked if I ever heard anyone say, "I wish I could go down to the dog pound and just take all of them home." I said I thought I had heard myself say something like that from time to time. Chad said that is just what his mother did one day. She came home with about 20 dogs and found homes for six of them and kept the rest. With the dogs and eight kids, she had a grand old time. Chad's father had no problem at all with the situation.

It was probably because Chad's mother had enough love for her kids and the dogs that Chad had so few concerns about jealousy. Unlike people who cannot tolerate the feeling that they are not loved as much as the pet in a relationship (as we shall see in Chapter 20, "Jealousy, the Complex One"), Chad said, "I'm not second to the dog. People have different love relationships. Diana's love for Heidi is deeper than the average person's and is much more complete. Still, it is just different from her love for me."

Ultimately, Chad and Diana had another child, a little boy they named David. Diana's attention and love for Heidi did not diminish at all with the birth of David. What changed was her urgency in attending to Heidi. David's birth, combined with the lessons learned in our therapy sessions, helped put her concerns about Heidi's health in their proper perspective. They became a concern for the dog rather than a displacement of her anger at her mother. The neurotic part of excessively worrying about Heidi's health dissipated. Heidi became a constant companion to little David and lived through his childhood before peacefully dying in her sleep at the age of 14.

The strength of Diana's displacement to Heidi came from two sources: The trauma of losing her infant caused her to be overprotective of the dog. Adding to that, she was unconsciously displacing her feelings about the lack of care and love from her mother by being the kind of mother to Heidi that she herself wished for.

CONNIE, WHO WAS EVERYONE'S BUDDY

The need to care for another can be very strong. In this next story, the pet not only highlighted his owner's emotional problem, but, unlike Heidi, may also have benefited from it.

This story is about Connie, a woman who came to see me because she never seemed to be able to hold on to the men with whom she got involved. They always complained that Connie was more concerned about her dog than she was about them.

Connie's last relationship (of five years) ended abruptly when Vito announced he was marrying Theresa so that he could keep his job working for Theresa's father. (It sounds like an Italian opera, but it was real, serious, and very distressing to Connie.) If this were an isolated incident, it would have been just one sad story—such things do happen. But for Connie, it seemed like a way of life.

I asked Connie about Vito's specific complaints about her dog. She said that, like most of the other guys she had dated, Vito mostly complained about her having to take time out to walk the dog and feed him. I asked what she thought these guys expected from her, and Connie said they all wanted her undivided attention when they were around. But it seemed to be a one-way street: At the same time, they also wanted the freedom to come and go as they pleased. Typically, they told her that if they didn't call for a week or two, she shouldn't call them. She had to understand that they were busy, and that was just the way it was.

In therapy, it did not take Connie long to realize that she kept picking the same type of guys over and over again. Somehow, she allowed them all the power and control in those relationships, and she was expected to be grateful for their attention and whatever time they could spare her. Quite naturally, her dog came to be regarded by these men "friends" as an interruption. I noted that, for this kind of selfish guy, feeding the goldfish would be an interruption. Little wonder that Connie became so attached to her dog!

Besides choosing men who were more interested in being serviced than in having a relationship, Connie also kept picking men who were unavailable. Over the years, her unavailable choices had included three gay men, two Mafia-connected characters, and a boy toy 15 years younger who had left her for a girl toy. What was going on here?

I learned from Connie's family history that she grew up in a fairly happy home and was her father's favorite of five daughters. In her midteens, Connie's father suddenly died from a heart attack while attending a football game in another city. He died instantly and alone, without his family.

As we talked about this tragedy, Connie realized that she had never recognized the anger she had developed over her father's sudden death; she had never recognized how abandoned she felt from that moment on (again, death is seen as an abandonment). In explaining that this is not uncommon, I showed her how she had come to expect very little from relationships, feeling that they would end suddenly, without much notice—which they did.

This experience colored her choice of pets and her choice of men. All of Connie' pets were shelter animals rescued from destruction—at the eleventh hour, so to speak. The animals she rescued always needed to be cured of some illness or required expensive surgery. Somehow she would always be attracted to the pup who needed a hip replacement. She now became aware of the connection between rescuing animals and the fact that she had not been able to save her father. Our emotions often unconsciously connect to symbolic meanings. (I told you that emotions are not logical!)

By working through her anger at being abandoned by her father, emotionally speaking, and by seeing how that fit into her overall grief, Connie was able to see the men in her life more clearly. She was no longer duped into believing that she should be grateful just to have a man's attention. (Remember the example in Chapter 3, "The Siamese Code," of the gambler always looking to get that big payoff?) Instead of waiting to be chosen and discarded, she found herself taking the initiative to find men who were looking for a relationship based on cooperation instead of control.

Connie's pets are still shelter animals that need a home with loving care and attention. However, the emotional intensity of her need to save them the way she could not save her father has greatly diminished.

Chapter 7

So What Does It All Mean?

Now you've met some of the players in the first part of our story about people and the pets in their lives, and you've seen how those animals triggered emotions from their human family members' past—emotions that lay hidden but that nevertheless affected their current lives. All this, while the animals did little more than what comes naturally to them!

You've also been introduced to one of the basic mechanisms in a person's emotional growth: displacement. We'll talk shortly about the other two—projection and the repetition compulsion—but first, let's spend a little time examining why it is possible for past experiences to affect present behavior and why their effects diminish so slowly. The next few pages may be a little slow going, but they will improve your understanding of the interaction between our pets and their human families, and will help you understand why those creatures are able to affect us so deeply. This chapter will also lay the groundwork for the discussions to come. Along the way, remember, the seeds of displacement and those other defense mechanisms are planted almost at birth. They are the normal consequence of growing up and becoming an adult.

To start, let's look at the problem of separating from a less-than-adequate parent. For both Judy and Diana, this was extremely difficult. Just admitting that they did not receive the parental love and acceptance they needed was a huge accomplishment. In each of these instances, the catalyst for this breakthrough was a pet: Judy had Buster, and Diana had Heidi.

Separation is a normal lifetime process, with many stages of evolution. It is an integral part of growing up, starting in infancy. Traditional separation anxiety is evident in infants at around 8 months old. They begin to notice the physical separation between them and their mother, and that mother is not always immediately available to satisfy their needs. Later, the child is sent off to begin elementary school, and mother is no longer in sight. Then there is the first love that ends, the move to the college dorm, the job, the friends—it is easy to see how separation evolves and is a natural consequence of growing up.

Yes, these are physical separations, but they always have emotional consequences. At the very least, there is the challenge to the person's sense of security: "Will I be able to survive in this world without my parents?" That is natural. But when the normal process of separation and growth is interrupted or is somehow distorted, difficult emotional reactions can develop.

Consider that we start experiencing ourselves as a part of our mother—literally before birth. At some point we discover this is not so, that mother sometimes leaves us, and we become anxious about the comfort and security that we rely on her for. In the process, we find that while separation brings anxiety, it also brings a new freedom to explore and have new experiences. Our ability to grow and expand with that new freedom depends entirely on how well we come through those early separations from parents and family and whether we are able to discover that separation does not mean danger or loss.

The people who got the least of the love, affection, and acceptance they needed as kids seem to suffer the most as adults. There are lots of ways that we unconsciously yet stubbornly try to hold on to what we remember as our childhood, hoping that if we do so, maybe somehow we will finally get the love and attention from our parents that we missed.

At the same time, while still yearning for a better past, we do our best to convince ourselves that we have risen above that loss. We believe that by talking about our parents sarcastically and contemptuously—in short, with disrespect—we have separated ourselves from our past. Some of us believe that seeing parents infrequently proves that we have separated and grown beyond the need we felt for a loving family, when in fact there is no known correlation between low frequency of visits and separation from parents. Some of us act as though not talking to our parents proves that we do not need them and that we do not have to ever acknowledge what we did not get from them. But these are defenses. It would seem that by having less contact with them, we avoid conscious reminders of our loss.

Still others of us go the other way, bending over backward trying to accommodate our unfulfilling parents, hoping that now, when we are adults, we will finally receive their much-needed approval.

ENTER THE ANIMALS

The results of those early childhood experiences stay with us throughout our lives. They have an effect, good and bad, on all of our relationships. For many of us, our choice of our pets and how we regard them often reflects how we handled the issues of separation from our parents. Having a dog, or any other pet that offers unconditional love, certainly reflects a wish in all of us for some kind of compensation for the lack of unconditional love we may have experienced in childhood. Holding on to a pet at all costs, including at the expense of a human relationship (as Albert risked with Nancy), may connect to our own fears of being abandoned in childhood. A number of my clients who were sent to live with relatives or friends because of family problems, or who were sent off to boarding or military school, have never forgiven their parents for rejecting them and abandoning them to some other caretaker. For these people, giving up a pet can be too painful to bear.

Other people adopt an air of indifference to their own experience of rejection and abandonment, and they constantly give pets up for one reason or another, or even euthanize them. One woman whose mother had placed her in an orphanage so she could continue working as a prostitute reported that she had more than a dozen dogs and cats euthanized, getting rid of them whenever she felt they no longer loved her. She did not think she had an abandonment issue involving her mother, and she claimed, as did Marlene Dietrich in speaking of a father she had never known, "You cannot miss what you never had." Euthanizing animals is very extreme behavior, but you can recognize the same kind of avoidance that was discussed in the story of Judy, Don, and Buster, the dog who was not housetrained.

For many people who cannot acknowledge their dependency on their parents, a cat seems like the perfect pet. Independent, smart, and self-contained, a cat reflects an air of not needing anyone or anything. Of course, as most cat lovers will tell you, cats often become trapped in their own mythology. They can be as affectionate and needy as a dog—it all depends on how you treat them.

Lots of people with reptiles—particularly people with snakes as pets—report childhood households that were full of chaos, messy, and even unclean. Probably there is no cleaner animal than a snake; it is also an animal that demands little and does not really bond to humans, although some snakes do respond to voice and vibration and seem to come when they are called. One woman I know who has a boa reports that there is nothing more comforting to her than having her snake crawl over her. The snake feels tender and gentle and is capable of giving her "hugs."

Where there were environments full of noise and screaming, kids get a message that keeps them in a hyperactive state. Having the gentle song of a canary or another songbird as a pet is a source of comfort for many people who struggled through a childhood of chaos and confusion.

THE *AH-HAH* EXPERIENCE

Somewhere, perhaps in a left-over scene from one of those old 1940s movies, is the therapeutic version of the *ah-hah* experience. Imagine this: The patient lies on the analyst's couch for a number of years, talking about all kinds of things but never getting at the real problem. Suddenly, a present-day experience jars the person's memory, and a long-lost piece of the puzzle—a memory that has been missing for decades—is unearthed by the patient and is interpreted by the psychoanalyst. The patient has had an *ah-hah* experience and rides off into the sunset, cured—a new person.

Wouldn't it be nice if everything in life could be that easy? It isn't, of course—certainly not in psychotherapy. For us, the *ah-hah* experience is the beginning of the work, not the end.

The *ah-hah* brings a past thought, memory, or experience from a preconscious or deeper unconscious level into consciousness. The preconscious level is a kind of way station between the unconscious (where information on past experience is not accessible) and the conscious (where all the information is available). Much of the work of therapy is involved with helping the client get into that hidden personal material and bring it into his or her conscious world, what therapists call *working through*. As the therapist listens between the lines of what the client is saying—or may not be saying—information is gained that helps the client make that transition.

Exploring—and Avoiding—the Past

The hidden experience has always been a part of the person, but it is not accessible because it has been repressed, locked away in those unconscious areas where the person fears to tread. Whenever we have an impulse that is too dangerous to act upon, or a thought or a feeling that is too painful to feel, we hide it from ourselves by using the many psychological defenses available to us—defenses that keep us from having to face the unfaceable, yet that constantly remind us that there is something buried there. We'll get into other kinds of defenses later on in this book, but here's a typical example of how the defense mechanism works.

Rather than facing uncomfortable feelings such as sadness, hurt, pain, anger, and grief, we often rush to forgive the person who has hurt us, without giving ourselves a chance to fully experience the emotions connected to the offense. Most of us expend considerable energy in avoiding those uncomfortable feelings. If it will help short-circuit experiencing those emotions, we may go straight to exoneration. In other words, forgiveness itself can be a defense against having to deal with difficult feelings.

While such avoidance may relieve the emotional pressure in the short term, for long-lasting relief you must really work through the feelings. This means recalling and examining all the situations and circumstances that produced the discomfort. For example, Donna worked hard during her therapy to get past those defenses that protected her for so long, to recall and emotionally re-experience as many instances as possible in which her father had expressed his unreasonable expectations without giving anything emotional in return. In so doing, she relived those early feelings, but with her now-adult perspective. Donna was able to see her father's behavior for what it was: arrogant and self-centered. It had nothing to do with Donna personally; he showed equal disregard for everyone. As an adult, she was able to accept that the past is gone, that it is time to let go.

As part of her new understanding, Donna was able to let go of her irritation with Angus, which was a displacement reaction to her father. She recognized what had upset her about her father and began to understand how those feelings had interfered with her marriage. Donna realized something else, too: She feared that Charley, her new husband, might become like her father, and she was startled by that connection.

Lest I give you the wrong impression, all displacement states are not necessarily bad. Just because I mention some aspect of displacement in the context of a personal problem does not mean that all displacement mechanisms are symptoms of emotional trouble. The fact is, all human and animal relationships contain a mixture of reality and displacement reactions. To put it another way, displacement in its many guises is normal. We all engage in it at different times and in different situations.

Whether a particular displacement reaction should be considered a sign of trouble depends on what is happening in the real world as a result.

OUR RELATIONSHIP MODELS

The way we relate to the people who spent the most time with us during the first few years of life determines, to a great extent, the style and manner in which we relate to the rest of the world. What we learn from our early environment comes in a number of ways. Humans learn by identifying—that is, copying their parents. We take in their view of the world. We learn cultural, social, and religious values from our parents, or from those acting in that role. We also learn from them about how we are perceived by others.

Our first relationships (mother-child, father-child, nanny-child, sibling-child) become the models for all other relationships in our lives. While almost everyone we relate to in those early formative years has some effect on our development, the uniqueness of the mother-child relationship—good, bad, or otherwise—is like no other we will have. In some ways, what we seek in all our relationships is a reconnection to what was good and warm and nourishing in that first relationship.

Both parents play their part, of course. The father-child relationship seems more slanted toward supplying a child with a sense of the reality of the world, while the mother-child relationship supplies comfort and nurturance. The combination of what both parents give to their relationship with their newborn determines how well the child will be prepared emotionally and psychologically for the life before him or her.

Of course, all of that presupposes an ideal world. Some people did not have a father or a mother, or some other male and female parent figure, to supply what was needed from that particular parent. Perhaps there was an early loss of a parent through separation, divorce, adoption, foster care, or death. For some people, growing up with only one parent might have been a preferred alternative to growing up with both parents, depending on what kind of people they were, how they treated you, and how they treated each other. For others, having both parents may have felt more important than whatever conflicts were involved. It is important to note that a model family is not a necessary ingredient for success. Children from single-parent homes, adoptive families, and even foster care do grow into well-adjusted adults.

The fact is, we yearn for what we did not have, whether we consciously admit it to ourselves or not. The needing and wanting remains and can take many forms. As a case in point, consider Marlene Dietrich's comment about not missing what you never had. Perhaps nothing could be farther from the psychological truth, but that point of view certainly shaped Dietrich's personality and how she viewed men and the world. In the same interview, Dietrich said most of her films were not really great, and although she was viewed by the world as a great star, she regarded herself as artistically inadequate. One can only wonder if she was unconsciously reporting that she could not experience herself as a whole person or a world-famous star without the love and approval of a father.

What we take in from the real world is filtered by our growth experiences and adds to our psychological makeup. It also goes a long way toward determining how we perceive and react to new experiences.

As an experiment to see how this works, read a story to a group of people and ask them what the story was about. Researchers who have done this experiment scientifically have found that the variations in people's answers depend upon how each person was really hearing the story. Those whose physical, intellectual, and emotional energy is unhampered with emotional baggage from their past have no problem recalling the details of the story. Others may report distortions of the story, depending on what is going on within them and what they are experiencing in the world around them. Put to the same test a few years later, the results may be different. We all do it in many ways as we grow.

Am I saying that everything you experience is destined to become buried in your unconscious? Not at all. We humans do our best to get rid of what we don't want. How well you are able to sort things out depends largely on how well you weather your psychological growing-up.

We are always taking in the world, holding onto those experiences and memories that please us or that seem important, and discarding the rest. Whatever we take in affects what we already know about ourselves and the world. Sometimes, though, what we experience is not acceptable, so we try to reject parts or all of the experience.

FINDING A COMFORT ZONE

Discarding and **discharging** are our ways of creating a comfort zone to avoid emotional fear and pain, real or imagined, whether it comes from our thoughts or our feelings. Again, it is natural to do this; it is the way we protect ourselves from emotional hurt. It is only when we refuse to acknowledge those rejected elements and the effects they can have on us that we get into trouble.

From your first breath onward, you try to take in what is experienced as pleasurable and avoid anything that interferes with your comfort and well-being. By the time you get to school, you discover that the world can be a frustrating place. You have demands descending on you from many directions. Reality begins to interrupt pleasure. Responsibilities and rules regarding the needs of others replace pure pleasure and the concept of me-first. Paradise Lost replaces the Garden of Eden, and we realize that growing up is hard to do.

If you think about the concept of displacement for a moment, you will see that there are many ways in which our parental relationships appear in our thoughts and feelings. For example, let's look at the ways in which you regard power and authority. Name any authority figure— the President of the United States, your town's mayor, a police officer, your boss, anyone—and think first about how that person reminds you of how your own mother and father dealt with authority issues, and then about how you regarded their parental authority.

Were you a defiant kid attempting to rebel at every turn? Were you a "good," compliant child who appeared to have no problems obeying the rules? Did you go back and forth between being defiant and compliant, depending on who was representing the authority—mother or father? For most of us, authority issues from childhood are carried over into our adult lives and into our relationships with other adults, with kids and with our pets. Maybe we automatically defy every rule we encounter. Maybe we have trouble resolving conflicts over the rules we disagree with. Maybe we think the whole idea of rules is silly or too restrictive. Maybe we think the rules ought to be followed, no matter what. (In Chapter 21, "Control Issues: Who's In and Who's Out?" we will explore the idea that many people with unresolved authority issues fall into control situations in which they either become control freaks or are involved with them.)

One of the ideas I've been hinting at is that the mind, particularly at the unconscious level, is very creative and very selective in the way it chooses to protect itself. In trying to analyze why one person reacts to another person or a situation in a particular way, therapists often find that things may not be what they seem. When we engage in displacement, our actions may connect only to parts of a relationship and not to the whole relationship. So, we may have a reaction to only some components that trigger our old feelings and behaviors.

For instance, my friend Della was sent off to boarding school when she was four years old. She was not around her mother enough to have stored up memories of her. Her displacement reactions are to the good and bad teachers from this time in her life.

The most important part of deciphering our displaced reactions is to determine who we are reacting to. When you get mad at the dog or your spouse, are you having a reaction to your mother or to your father? Is this a reaction to other meaningful people, perhaps a sibling, a grandparent, or a teacher?

Chapter 8

How Can You Tell If It's Displacement?

So, after all this discussion, how do we know when something that is going on in the present is a displaced reaction? A good way is to imagine how others see it. If you were to film your involvement in a particular situation, how might a viewing audience see it? If a neutral observer might feel that certain responses (or, perhaps, lack of response) were inappropriate because of their duration, timing, or depth, this could be a displaced response.

When I was growing up, one of our neighbors continuously ranted about the local utility company. According to her, the company lied, cheated, and attempted to gain illegal access to her apartment. She was always embroiled in arguments with their representatives. This was not a crazy lady. However, her complaints about the utility company always sounded exactly like her complaints about her parents, who were long since dead and preserved in sacred memory. By displacing her unhappiness with her parents onto the utility company, she held onto her memory of her "saintly" parents. When she came to understand that, she had no further need for her fights with the utility people.

The more you know about yourself and the more you know about your emotional history, the less likely you are to displace your past onto the present.

THE UNCONSCIOUS DEMYSTIFIED

The unconscious can be regarded as the storehouse of all that has passed through our senses. If you compare the unconscious to where you live, it's like not realizing how much stuff you have stored in your attic until you have to move it.

Almost always, our need to displace old relationships and feelings onto the present operates in the unconscious part of the mind until it is made conscious, usually through therapy. Part of the way to resolve the problem is to put all the displacements into perspective—that is, to make them conscious enough so that you can see the true role they play. This is the only way to avoid rekindling the same problem over and over again.

People relate to each other in the world on many levels of awareness or consciousness. If you are trying to hear the words to a new song for the first time, your level of concentration and consciousness becomes obvious to you. You may move your head closer to your stereo and tilt your head so that your good ear is facing the speakers while you are listening to the song. Your brow may be furrowed to lend greater concentration in taking in the new words. You can recall instances when your awareness was at a peak and your consciousness was right there in the moment.

It is also possible to operate on two different levels of consciousness. Your attention, for example, may be focused on a fascinating television documentary, while at the same time you're knitting a sweater or putting your recently returned canceled checks from the bank in numerical order. When you are doing two things at the same time, you are operating at different levels of awareness or consciousness. At one moment your attention may be more focused on the TV screen, and the next on your checks. Some people may even refer to our ability to attend to different things at the same time as operating in altered states of awareness.

Altered states vary from complete and focused concentration and awareness to zero awareness, from operating completely at the conscious level to living at the unconscious level. When a person is at the conscious level, we say he or she is paying attention. If you have even the slightest awareness of something going on, you may say you are consciously aware of whatever it is. If you connect to something only after it has been pointed out to you by someone else, you may say you have a *preconscious* awareness.

The old Hollywood term for preconscious awareness is *subconscious*. Whatever is at the subconscious level can either become fully conscious or move in the other direction, closer to becoming unconscious. We have all experienced a sense that there is something— a thought, a feeling—just slightly out of our reach. You almost know what it is, but it eludes you and dances away from your knowing. This preconscious state of awareness is moving toward consciousness but is not quite there.

Did you ever have a dream that made you wake up wondering if the dream had any meaning? Whenever you remember your dreams, it is an invitation from yourself to explore your feelings and motivations on a deeper level of knowing than that of your waking hours.

The things we know are on a conscious level. You know who you met yesterday, what you had for breakfast, what you were thinking on the way to work, and what you were feeling when the phone rang for the first time this morning. At the same time, you do not always know why you do certain things. For example, why do you avoid walking under ladders when you tell yourself that you are not superstitious? You have feelings that do not necessarily make sense to you. That is, you don't know why you are feeling them at a particular time or with a particular person or in a certain situation.

Why do we have one thought that becomes more conscious than another thought that is occurring simultaneously just below the surface? The reason is still a mystery. We are just beginning to learn how our senses prioritize what we experience consciously and what we experience without being conscious of what is occurring. Does our brain make the choice of what we attend to, or does it depend on our mood or some chemical combination of what is happening in our brain and body? We are still learning the answers.

SO WHAT ABOUT DISPLACEMENT?

Displacement is the unfinished emotional business of childhood that is still floating around in the present day. Lingering separation problems are among the major contributors to present-day displacement problems. Here are several thoughts that may help you understand how displacement works:

1. Realistically speaking, displacement and displaced feelings make the world go around much more than love or power.

2. In any relationship, people always displace thoughts, feelings, attributes, and motivations from old relationships onto present-day relationships. The importance of that displacement lies in the degree. The more you are involved in displacement, the less you deal with the real people and the real today. Ultimately, you can displace yourself right out of reality.

3. People displace past relationships onto pets, other people, inanimate objects, and situations in their current life.

4. The earliest caretakers and the other significant people in a person's childhood are the original models for their human relationships. These are usually parents and siblings, but the list can extend to nannies, housekeepers, grandparents, aunts, uncles, cousins, neighbors, teachers, and anyone else who had an important influence, positive or negative, on our formative years. The way we saw these people and their relationships teaches us how to interact with others.

5. Sometimes we treat everyone in the world as though they were mother, father, sister, or brother—including our pets and other people's pets. When that happens, it means we are not living fully in our world of today.

6. Part of understanding how we use displacement of thoughts and feelings lies in understanding how we operate

simultaneously on the various levels of human consciousness, from unconscious through preconscious thoughts, feelings, impulses, wishes, fantasies, dreams, and motivations to conscious awareness.

7. The more conscious and comfortable you are with your self and what makes you tick, the less your unconscious needs to displace your past relationships onto those of today—human or pet. Knowing what is happening on the various levels of consciousness is vital to examining those relationships that are threatened by displacement problems.

8. We displace as a form of discharging what is uncomfortable to hold onto within ourselves, both in thoughts and in feelings.

9. What you bring into a present relationship may be a partial or complete displacement from your early years.

10. As you grow through infancy and give up the belief that you are the center of the world, reality enters your life and demands that you attend to today's duties, responsibilities, and obligations. The degree to which you experience these demands as uncomfortable influences, determines what gets displaced to people, pets, and objects outside of yourself.

11. Screening out what you do not wish to deal with is a pre-emptive step in avoiding the need to later expel it. Never allowing the uncomfortable stuff into your conscious mind in the first place is one way of dealing with the problem. The only trouble with that approach is that you often loose a lot of good experiences as well. It's a little like throwing the baby out with the bath water.

12. To see if displacement is occurring in a relationship, view the issue as if it were being played back on a video. If you believe an audience viewing the program thinks the players are over-reacting and under-reacting to the situation, that audience might be viewing displaced reactions.

13. If you still have old reactions that are not getting you what you want and need in your present life, then it is likely that you are displacing something from an early relationship.

14. Here's another clue about the influence of displacement: If you find that you are able to anticipate how a given situation will turn out long before it plays out, then it's likely that you are in the middle of your own displaced reaction.

Displacement is something moved from the past onto someone or something in the present. In the next section, we'll look at projection, in which we unconsciously ascribe to others those thoughts, feelings, and deeds that we do not like or that we don't wish to acknowledge in ourselves. You might say it is displacement involving yourself instead of another being.

Part II

The Role of Projection

I'm Just Fine: It's Your Problem

Chapter 9

Getting Rid of the Unwanted

....

We have seen how pets can *become* people and, usually through no fault of their own, are cast in a disruptive role in a human relationship. Animals, like people, come equipped with a host of natural behaviors—we call them instincts. Sometimes the pet adds to its basic equipment—again, just as we do—and learns other behaviors. Although some of the learned behaviors may be annoying and damaging to the humans in the household, remember that the animals learned those behaviors from their owners. Think back to the story in Chapter 5, "Animal Actors," of Judy and her dog, Buster, who ruled her life.

When one person in the relationship relates to the pet as if it were someone in his or her sphere, we call that a displacement. This is based on something unresolved from that person's life that interferes with a real relationship. In such circumstances, the person involved responds to the pet as if it were a person from the past. In the process, the person may also attribute unwanted parts of him- or herself to the pet. When this occurs, it is called *projection*.

We all have psychological parts of ourselves (emotions and thoughts) that we do not want to acknowledge. For example, feelings of greed, hate, envy, and sometimes even sexuality are not always easy to acknowledge within ourselves. It is much easier to ascribe them to someone else, whether real or imagined.

People may project their good traits onto their animals. The message they send is, "my soft, furry animal" is the lovable part of me. If in the constructed reality the person sees the animal as rejected by other people, he or she feels rejected. And, as we have seen, very few things are straightforward in psychology. The same kind of construction allows people to see their fears as "the worst parts of me" and to project them onto an animal: "Your dog is mean, vicious, spiteful, and dangerous. I am terrified to go near her."

Not all our projections are negative. Sometimes we lay things on our pets that are very complimentary. When the pet is regarded as having the positive characteristics of someone's parents, siblings, or significant others, there is really no problem. At worst, one or another of the people in the relationship is assigning human qualities to the pet and perhaps making the pet into something it isn't. As long as the result in not destructive, there's nothing to worry about.

For example, when my old Labrador Retriever, Troll, was waiting for me to throw the ball, his facial expression and furled forehead made him look, to me, exactly like my childhood friend Efron. I had fond memories of Efron, so I would always get a kick out of Troll's expression. Now, if Troll had looked like my cousin Ed, whom I cannot stand, perhaps there would not have been a lot of ball-retrieving in Troll's life.

Projection is related to displacement, but it operates somewhat differently. In the previous section, the people-pet problems arose because the animals reminded the people of someone with whom they had an unresolved issue. That was displacement: The person attached something from the past to the animal. Displacement can become a problem in a relationship when it involves an unconscious negative association with the person's past. If the pet stirs up feelings and memories of an abusive father, a non-nurturing mother, an older brother who got all the good stuff, or a younger sister you had to drag everywhere, the present relationship will suffer because of the displaced reactions.

Projection, however, occurs when we put a piece of *ourselves* into another person or a pet. That piece could be a feeling, or it could be an idea. We do this all the time in one way or another. It is built into our human wiring to take in what is good and spit out what is bad— and that is not limited to the psychological! Through our natural evolution and our environmental experiences, we have learned that when food smells putrid, nausea takes over and warns us by way of the gagging reflex that it is a good idea not to eat whatever is giving off the foul odor. If we eat something toxic that the body cannot handle, we will discharge it by vomiting or diarrhea, or both. Of course, sometimes we can be fooled, as with the beautiful but toxic mushroom that gives off no odor.

Psychologically, we operate the same way we do biologically. We hold onto what we find pleasant and forget those things that we feel are dangerous, that are humiliating, or that cause us anxiety. We hold onto what we see as our positive attributes and spit out the thoughts and feelings that are too painful to accept in ourselves. This is the way we defend ourselves against the stuff that makes us uncomfortable about who we are. We project onto others those aspects of ourselves that we either have not acknowledged or prefer not to own. To turn around and face those unpleasant parts of ourselves that we project onto others takes courage and persistence.

Because projections operate unconsciously, you only learn of them when someone points them out. The person who is the recipient of your projection is often too busy defending against the assault to figure it out. Frequently, the recipient feels strangely uncomfortable but does not know why.

Often we become aware of our projections only after the process of psychotherapy begins. It is extremely difficult, if not impossible, to become aware of projections on our own.

AND THEY CALL THEM "DUMB" ANIMALS

One of the most basic and best examples of projection I have encountered involved Barry, a young man who reported that the family dog, Fred, had become hostile to Barry's wife, Estelle. Barry told me that the dog had liked his wife very much until their recent move from

New Hampshire to New York. Since the move, Fred had been growling at Estelle and urinating on her side of their bed.

Barry thought it was because Fred was missing Misty, his Collie "girlfriend" back in New Hampshire. He seemed surprised when I asked him if he had a girlfriend back in New Hampshire as well. Turning red and looking down at the floor, he wanted to know what made me ask a question like that.

When we moved Barry's hostile feelings back into Barry and out of Fred, we talked about his unhappiness in his marriage and how much he was missing Yolanda, with whom he was having an affair. Barry did not want to acknowledge how much he was missing Yolanda or how much he had come to hate Estelle during the course of their marriage. Fred was picking up Barry's hostility toward Estelle. So was Estelle, and she was taking out her own anger on Fred, causing him to be aggressive toward her. She had been yelling at him often and had forgotten to feed him on a couple of occasions. No wonder Fred urinated on her side of the bed!

Once Barry acknowledged his hostility toward Estelle, we were able to discuss possible alternatives for him. Because Estelle did not want to work on the relationship, they ultimately divorced. Barry and Yolanda married, and Fred was just fine with the outcome.

The psychological mechanism here was simple projection. Barry was projecting his hostility toward Estelle onto Fred. Fred, in turn, was picking up that hostility. For her part, Estelle also sensed her husband's hostility and took it out on Fred, who was only reacting to her hostility (sounds positively Shakespearean, doesn't it?).

Projection is slippery stuff. It sometimes is influenced by and intermingles with displacement, which we have already talked about, and with the repetition compulsion, which we have yet to talk about. We know projection is there, but we frequently have trouble putting our finger on it. It's a little like trying to pick up a piece of mercury: You can see it, but when you try to touch it, it moves away. Even psychologists find it difficult to give a coherent definition of projection because it operates in conjunction with so many other psychological defenses.

While displacement and projection may appear together, it is important to remember that they are different. Displacements come from a person's past and appear in some present situation. A projection is a long-standing part of an individual's personality that he or she would prefer not to deal with. Projections may not be the most positive or complementary attributes, in that person's view.

The process of projection as a part of a person's character begins to develop at an early age. By the time we enter kindergarten, all the ingredients are in place within us to form our personalized projections. We have learned in one way or another what is acceptable behavior and what is not. We have discovered what we like and don't like. We have learned about unhappiness, shame, and embarrassment. We also have learned about joy and pleasure and the excitement of being accepted.

Projection is our way of unconsciously rejecting those memories and feelings that we associate with painful and unpleasant events. These are usually the parts of ourselves we would rather not think about, much less have to deal with and look at.

There is no way of avoiding projection entirely. Consciously or unconsciously, there is a reason for the way we act. The way we respond to people and events reflects an attempt to resolve or relieve some personal issue. The trick in dealing with it is to be aware of what projections are and how they may be distorting your current relationships with people and animals.

Projection also can be seen as an adaptive process by which you attempt to get rid of what is uncomfortable inside yourself. Unfortunately, it is not like throwing something into the garbage; in this instance, the garbage throws it back. If you project something onto someone else, that other person reacts in a way that affects your reasons for projecting in the first place. Whether we like it or not, we do not live in isolation. As long as we are in relationships, everyone around us will have an effect on our lives. Similarly, everything we do affects those around us.

With this in mind, it is easy to understand the importance of becoming aware of our projections and keeping them in the conscious realm. Once this awareness is achieved, real change can take place within the individual—change that allows for greater emotional and psychological growth.

Sometimes projection takes the form of expecting others to do what we do not want to do. When they don't meet our expectations, we resent them for not cooperating. For example, we may project a need for people to be more polite or more honest than they are, even though, under the same circumstances, we might be just as impolite or dishonest as those around us.

As a psychotherapist, I need to remember that a client's projection represents a tool or pathway that I can follow to the root of the problem. But first I must be sure of what is a projection and what is reality. Whatever else a projection may involve, there is always an element of reality. If a client tells me I am always late for therapy sessions, for example, I must determine if I really am before I label it a projection. Further, if I am indeed always late for the sessions, I must look closely to see if I am somehow projecting some problem of mine into the therapeutic situation. That said, let's look at a couple more projections in action.

Chapter 10

The Tales of Two Cats

....

The two cat stories in this chapter are excellent examples of projection at work. In both of them, the cats were just being cats. Through the mechanism of projection, though, they took on larger roles in their owners' lives.

DUMB AND DUMBER

By the time Margie was in college, she had been dating Keith for three years; she liked him very much and hoped they would marry. Wonderful though their relationship was, there was one fly in the ointment. Margie, a social worker, often wondered about Keith's intelligence. He was a saxophone player, and Margie worried that he seemed to lack intellectual curiosity. That was her projection, and it had to do with his cats.

Keith had two cats, and that bothered Margie very much. Although she claimed she did not agree with her mother, who maintained that only stupid people have cats, she was concerned about the amount of time Keith spent playing with them. She worried that perhaps he was not as bright as she would have liked.

Margie become critical of Keith and kept telling him that she thought he should be doing more educational things instead of spending so much time with his cats. Margie actually started testing Keith's intelligence by initiating conversations about current events. Ultimately, Keith caught on to what she was doing. Margie, however, denied it and said he was imagining things and that he was being too defensive.

In fact, there was nothing wrong with Keith's intellect. Both his parents were university professors. His sister was an endocrinologist and his older brother was a NASA rocket scientist. Keith, however, had natural musical talent and preferred to direct his intellectual capacities in that direction.

Things went from bad to worse for this couple. Keith was offended and objected to Margie's criticisms of him and his relation-ships with his cats. He told her that at least the cats appreciated him as he was and were not worried about how smart he was. Finally he told Margie that if they could spend more time having fun together, she might appreciate him more instead of trying to make him into an Einstein.

Margie was a social worker because it satisfied her strong sense of compassion and desire to help people, but she did not find her work intellectually challenging. She also had an unconscious need to be appreciated for her intellectual capabilities. In her mind, a strong intel-lect commanded attention and respect. Now Keith was trying to get Margie to accept him as a person and not as a walking encyclopedia.

As you can imagine, by the time the three of us met, Keith was ready to give up on his relationship with Margie. As he put it, he loved his music, he loved Margie, and he loved the cats. And he felt that the only problem with the cats was in Margie's head. Keith believed that Margie had fixated on her mother's opinion about cat owners, in spite of the fact that she knew her mother was wrong. This hold that her mother's opinion had over her was ruining their life together.

Margie understood Keith's feelings but said she could not help herself. Something inside her kept insisting that Keith must not be intelligent if he spent so much time with the cats. They both agreed that jealousy was definitely not the problem.

I asked Margie straight out about how she regarded her own intelligence. She let out a great sigh and began crying as she described her fear that she was too dumb to get anything right. Her mother always left Margie feeling as though she could never be as smart as Mom was. By creating such feelings of inadequacy in her daughter, Margie's mother was able to avoid her own feelings about being deprived of the opportunity of pursuing her dream career: nursing. She projected her own fears and anger onto her relationship with her daughter by stressing Margie's failures.

Margie's mother carried her own emotional baggage. She was a poorly educated woman who came from a family that struggled, as did so many, through the Great Depression. She had wanted to become a registered nurse, but she was forced to take a job at the local pharmacy to help support the family. In spite of her sacrifice, she felt that her family never acknowledged her contribution to their survival, and she resented them for it. She always believed that she had been cheated out of a real education and a chance to have a better life. To her credit, she even told her daughter of her mixed emotions of pride in Margie's success and envy over her opportunity.

Ultimately, Margie came to see how her concern about Keith's intelligence was really a projection of her fears of her own intellectual competence. As long as she was able to maintain that projection, she would not have to face her own fears. In some ways, Margie was doing just what her mother had done. Furthermore, as long as Margie retained her projection, she would not have to deal with her anger at her mother for constantly harping on Margie's inadequacies. Her creation would hold together, as long as she was able to be angry with Keith for not being smarter.

Once Margie took back her projection, the way was open for them to get their relationship back on track. In the end, Keith and Margie understood how Margie's projection was influencing both their lives; when last seen, they were well on their way to repairing their relationship. Margie was even developing a certain attraction to the cats and was learning to derive pleasure from them. (We'll have more to say about Keith's contribution to this relationship when we speak about the repetition compulsion in the next section.)

IT'S A CAT'S LIFE

Speaking of cats, here's another example of projection involving Fran; her boyfriend, Albrecht; and his cat, Rose. Fran was convinced that Rose was an unhappy animal. (Remember Donna in Chapter 2, "Let Sleeping Dogs (and Cats) Lie," who thought Angus the Irish Setter did not act like a dog because he just sat around waiting to be taken care of?) As Fran explained it, she brought Rose toys, which she seemed to enjoy at first but soon lost interest in.

Fran found Rose's behavior puzzling, but Albrecht said he did not think there was anything wrong with the cat. The situation was breaking Fran's heart, she said, but she had no idea what to do about it. Albrecht told Fran she was making a big deal out of nothing. In fact, Albrecht was right. Cats are slow to make new friends. Sure, they are curious, and when they see something new, such as a toy, they will take the time to check it out. That done, they will go about their cat business.

In spite of Albrecht's reassurances, Fran kept trying to engage Rose in play. She spent hours trying to coax the cat out of her hiding and resting places in an attempt to "cheer her up," as Fran put it. As a self-respecting member of the feline species, Rose was having none of it, which only made Fran more certain that this was one very unhappy cat. She even started yelling at the cat, trying to "snap her out of her depression."

Albrecht finally exploded, telling Fran that he was not worried about Rose's happiness. Instead it was Fran's happiness that he was beginning to worry about. This was a critical point in their relationship; Albrecht felt the cat was becoming an obsession with Fran and that their relationship had become focused on Rose's happiness instead of their future. The situation had become so bad that Albrecht was ready to break off their engagement.

It was at this point that I entered the picture. I asked Fran why she was so convinced that Rose was unhappy. She explained that Rose had been a wild stray cat when Albrecht found her, and she felt that the animal should be happier than she had appeared when Albrecht brought her indoors to a more secure and comfortable life.

I wondered why Fran believed a cat should show gratitude, which seemed to me more of a human emotion. I also wondered how Fran defined happiness for Rose and how she defined it for herself. A view of Fran's childhood answered some of my questions.

Fran grew up in a family in which everyone had to be thankful for their blessings. In itself, this is not a bad thing. But the not-so-unconscious message of Fran's childhood was that sadness was not a legitimate feeling. The children had to give part of their allowance money to the needy. Even if someone died, there was no room for sadness because the person was then "in God's heaven." For Fran, sadness could never be for herself; her only way of experiencing such feelings was to project them onto someone or something else.

Consciously, Fran regarded herself as happy. She had her health, a good job, and her relationship with Albrecht. He was attentive and nurturing and, until her obsession with Rose, never had any complaints about their relationship. In fact, Fran said she wished she could be as happy and content as he seemed. She did not feel unhappy, but she felt there was a lack of passion and excitement in her life. Finally, she blurted out that she loved Albrecht but was not *in love* with him.

Albrecht said that he had known Fran felt this way and had accepted it. Fran was both surprised and relieved to hear this. She told him she believed that she could grow into being in love as she continued to know more about him and let their mutual trust for each other build.

When Fran was able to admit to her own feelings of unhappiness, she could stop projecting them onto Rose. For her part, Rose continued to be her very own feline self—a contented cat.

.

Chapter 11

Different Needs, Same Result

OPHELIA, THE SENSITIVE ONE

There was nothing destructive about Ophelia, a Great Dane. She never made a mess or had an accident. Still, Angie insisted that she could not leave the dog alone—it was just too painful to think about, she said. Tom, Angie's live-in boyfriend, suggested leaving the television or the radio on, but Angie said that would do little to ease her worries.

Tom also suggested playing a cassette tape of Angie speaking or playing some home videos of Angie that might relieve Ophelia's loneliness. Yet Angie rejected all of Tom's suggestions because she believed that Great Danes were very delicate and sensitive; they needed to be tended to all the time.

In reality, anyone who owns a Great Dane will tell you that these are quite spirited and independent animals that can handle almost anything that comes their way. Ophelia was a beautiful and graceful harlequin, and she epitomized the classical Great Dane look. Majestic and well-built, she was content to be walked a few times a day and petted and scratched a little bit.

Tom liked Ophelia and could never understand why Angie could not leave the dog alone in the house for more than an hour or two.

It got to the point where Angie accepted only those invitations for Tom and herself that included Ophelia. Otherwise, most of their socializing consisted of having guests visit them. To say the least, Angie was very protective and possessive of Ophelia—well beyond the normal needs of the typical Great Dane.

To understand how Ophelia became cast in the role of supersensitive lap dog, consider this: Angie came from a traditional Hispanic family that was strong and protective with family members, particularly females. When Angie had wanted to get her own apartment, her mother, who by then was head of the family, refused to give her permission. Angie remained determined. Thus defied, her mother shifted from being angry to trying to make Angie feel guilty. She pleaded to know what she had done wrong to cause Angie to move out when she was not yet married.

No matter how much Angie tried to explain that, at 26, she was old enough to have her own place, her mother claimed that Angie was condemning her for having done something wrong in raising her. Angie moved out anyway, but not without a great deal of guilt at having separated from her mother. Adding to the difficulty was the fact that her father had died a couple years earlier, leaving her mother on her own. Her older brother and sister (Angie was the youngest of three children) had also left the family home, but they had done so to marry and start their own families, a reason her mother found more acceptable.

Having come this far in our discussion of the mysteries of projection, you may be able to recognize that Angie was using her relationship with Ophelia as a way of avoiding her guilt at having left the family home against her mother's wishes. By becoming so involved with the Great Dane and behaving as though the dog was completely dependent on her, Angie stayed with the dog in a way she hadn't stayed with her mother. She unconsciously created an imagined and false obligation to Ophelia, as a way of punishing herself for having hurt her mother.

Of course, nothing is free, even in psychology. While Angie was able to repress her feelings of guilt and anger by completely tying herself to Ophelia, she was not able to enjoy the autonomy and independence she had gained by moving out. And Tom was getting tired of having to plan his life around Ophelia.

What was the solution here? As with all our stories in this section, the answer was to help Angie see the difference between reality and her projection. Ophelia doesn't need Angie's undivided attention, and Angie doesn't need to tie herself and Tom down so completely.

THE OBEDIENT SAMURAI

Ned met Elinor in a dog obedience class. He was there with his Akita, Samurai, and she with a little French Bulldog. When they started talking, Elinor found out that Ned was always taking his dog to some kind of obedience class. He seemed to be oblivious to the fact that the dog was wonderfully obedient. In fact, everyone in the class said Samurai was so obedient that he did not seem to know how to relax.

Anyone who knows the breed knows that Akitas thrive on human contact and affection, and will do anything to please the people they love. Still, Ned never let the dog release from a command for more than 10 minutes before he would be giving Samurai another command. He seemed satisfied only when the dog listened to him, which had to be almost all the time. Samurai never got any time to just hang out and be a dog.

Elinor found Ned very interesting. He was funny, very intelligent, and attentive when they were together. Ned was a lawyer who had come up through the ranks and was soon to become a district attorney. He had a large professional staff and seemed to keep everyone very organized. In short, he was professionally on top of things.

At home, however, Ned was the exact opposite. His personal space was in disarray, and there was no order to anything in the house. Finding a matching pair of socks could become a two-week project. Dirty dishes and glasses where piled in the kitchen sink. Laundry was strewn everywhere. Leftover TV dinners and cutlery were scattered about the living room and the den. The bedroom looked more like a self-lock storage center than a place where a person lived.

Elinor offered to help Ned with his stuff, which worked out fine in the beginning. But as time went on, Ned had trouble deciding what he wanted to keep and what should be thrown out. After a while, Elinor made the decision herself simply by watching Ned's expression when she held an item up for inspection. If Ned flinched and looked like he would faint, she kept the item. However, if he looked as if he wasn't sure what the item was, out it went. It was becoming a standing joke between them.

What was *not* so funny was the demanding way Ned treated Samurai. Ned said he loved Samurai, but he complained that the dog was an uncontrollable animal. Nothing could be farther from the truth. Samurai was devoted to Ned and followed his commands. He was actually the quintessential Akita: alert, good-natured, and gentle. Despite this, Ned greatly feared that the dog would become completely uncontrollable if he did not constantly reinforce Samurai's training. Elinor began to feel uncomfortable with the way Ned was treating his dog. Eventually, it started causing friction between them.

By now, I think you know what was going on here. Ned's inability to keep order in his personal life was being projected onto Samurai. As a result, Samurai never got any doggy downtime.

What was actually going on with Ned? In therapy, he admitted that he feared spinning out of control and losing his mind the way his father did after serving in the Korean War and having his best friend die in his arms. For years, his father had suffered post-traumatic stress disorder, which was never diagnosed. All Ned knew is that his father had lost control of his life, and Ned feared that he, too, might suffer the same fate. But the fear was so strong that he projected it onto Samurai, who, in Ned's mind, was always on the verge of losing control. Poor Samurai!

SIMILAR, BUT NOT THE SAME

While a certain kind of behavior may indicate a particular problem, the cause of the problem may be quite different. And if the cause is different, so will be the solution. The key lies in defining what feelings are being projected, and why. Meet Paul, Adrian, and her dog, Chelsea.

Like Ned, Adrian was constantly giving Chelsea dog commands. It seemed as if the dog was never allowed any time on her own. Adrian demanded the dog's undivided attention, or Chelsea could expect a barrage of yelling and even hard smacks under the chin or on the rump. The discipline always seemed beyond whatever it was the dog had done.

Paul, Adrian's boyfriend, was dismayed by her behavior and often asked her why she was so hard on the dog. She replied that if she gave Chelsea an inch, she would take a foot. Paul felt sorry for the dog but was unable to do anything to change the situation, although it continued to bother him.

Paul knew Adrian's father was a control freak. All the kids in the family had had specific jobs to do daily, in addition to special weekend assignments. It seemed that there had been so many chores that Adrian and her siblings had often missed having a social life with friends. Adrian's mother had been terrified of her husband and stood passively by, feeling helpless to intervene.

Paul loved Adrian and wanted to marry her, but he was growing increasingly concerned with Adrian's treatment of Chelsea. Paul regarded Adrian's behavior as physically abusive toward Chelsea, and he insisted that she get help with what he saw as an emotional problem. Adrian thought Paul was making too much of the situation, but she agreed.

Adrian did not need much time in therapy to begin to understand how unconsciously angry she was at her controlling father. She also realized how much she had become just like him. By treating Chelsea as she had been treated, she had identified with her father to avoid experiencing her own anger. In short, Adrian was using her pet to demonstrate to the world how she had been treated.

That's the mysterious thing about projection: Ned was using it, through Samurai, to contain something he did not want to happen; Ophelia became the conduit for Angie's projection of unacknowledged guilt about defying her mother's wishes and leaving home; and Adrian used Chelsea to show the world what had been done to her. The same mechanism served different purposes. And that's why understanding a projection is only the beginning of working it through.

Projection is a very difficult thing to recognize in yourself. A therapist will be better able to detect it. But take a look at the following and see if you can answer "yes" to any of these questions.

> Are you demanding behaviors and reactions from pets that are far beyond what is normal for their species or breed?
>
> Do you sometimes get the feeling that your pet (or another person) is doing what you wish you could do? For example, do you get pleasure when your dog growls at someone you don't like, or when your friend argues with someone whom you find annoying?
>
> Do you believe your dog loves to watch horror movies or movies containing a lot of sex and violence, or you think your parrot likes it when you tell funny jokes? Then you may be experiencing projection.

The questions posed above may give you some sense of how projection can work in the real world. We all project all the time. Even when armed with the proper questions, it is nearly impossible to recognize our own projections. They remain unconscious, protecting us from the deepest pain, the greatest humiliation, and the most dreaded experiences. Attributing unwanted parts of ourselves onto people and pets will remain an unconscious action until some moment in therapy when the patient trusts the therapist enough to talk about the material hidden in the projection. That is the first, essential step. The next step is uncovering to which particular incidents these unbearable feelings are connected. It is my experience as a therapist that when a person is ready to feel and explore those connected issues, they find that experiencing the emotion is never as terrible as the investment of energy and sadness involved in using projection as a defense.

Chapter 12

Pets and the Mating Instinct

The thing about projection is that any feeling can be projected onto anything. It doesn't really matter whether the connections make sense in the logical world. Our pets can even get tangled up in our sex lives. Let's look at two examples.

A FISH STORY

Harold and Debbie had been married five years. They had been trying desperately to have a baby for the past three, without any success. They even had been to top fertility specialists in New York and Boston. Harold blamed himself because the doctors suggested his low sperm count was the reason he and Debbie could not conceive.

In the past year, Harold had begun to collect tropical fish. He became absorbed in learning the different species and had purchased a number of extremely expensive rare fish. In fact, he had become somewhat obsessed with the fish and had been buying more fish tanks and more fish as time passed.

At first Debbie thought it was wonderful that Harold was developing a hobby. But his hobby had progressed from having goldfish and guppies to purchasing paradise fish, rio pearlfish, and medaka. Soon he was even raising his own daphnia and tubifex worms at home for fish food. He spent a lot of time separating fish into different fish tanks to prevent the eggs and baby fish from being eaten by the adult fish.

Harold especially became interested in all the ways that fish reproduce. He talked incessantly about the differences between species—how his paradise fish built nests, how guppies bear their young live, and how medaka carry their eggs. He would talk about which species lay eggs in clumps and which lay their eggs individually. He then acquired a pair of very rare pencilfish that are extremely difficult to breed in captivity. He would stay up nights observing the fish and hoping they would conceive.

Debbie began to feel excluded from Harold's life. She was interested in his hobby and enjoyed watching the fish, but she never developed Harold's passion and enthusiasm for them. Judging from his obsession with breeding, Harold also clearly was not dealing with his feelings about being sterile. Whenever Debbie raised the subject of kids, he refused to discuss the topic. He rejected the possibility of artificial insemination or adoption. Instead, Harold projected his feelings about being sterile onto his fish. He could talk for days about the reproductive activities of his fish, but he could not spend two minutes discussing children in his marriage!

When I met Harold and Debbie, I suggested that his hobby now seemed more like an obsession. I asked Harold if mating fish might be related to his feelings about being sterile. He said he had thought of this but had decided there was no connection. I asked him how he did feel about being sterile, and he said he did not know. However, as he said this, he turned away and his face began to flush.

I said that sometimes a feeling of guilt that does not make sense intellectually nevertheless exists in the unconscious of many men and women who are unable to conceive. Harold was becoming visibly irritated with me. He pretty much told me I could keep my psychology hogwash to myself (except he used a different word). Then, from what seemed like out of nowhere, he blurted out, "And furthermore, I'm not raising someone else's load of DNA as my own." At that moment it was difficult to know who was more shocked, Harold or

Debbie. Then he burst into tears and talked about how he had always thought that having kids would be one of the prime accomplishments of his life—and here he was, sterile. The world seemed unfair and awful.

As we talked, Harold started to understand that true manhood was not a function of sperm count but of being able to make a deep emotional commitment to another human being. Although he was mourning his loss of the ability to parent his own child, giving to a child is a unique form of giving, regardless of whether the child has your genes.

Harold did not have to avoid his feelings. Besides feeling angry, he felt sadness and shame at disappointing Debbie. However, Harold learned from her that she loved him and that she understood how awful he was feeling. He talked more and more about being a father and what good parents he thought he and Debbie would make.

Ultimately, the couple was able to adopt two children from Russia. Fish mating gained a proper perspective in Harold's life when he stopped projecting his desires onto his fish. Interestingly, Harold has also become one of the world's foremost experts on mating pencilfish.

THOSE ROUGH-AND-TUMBLE FERRETS

Sam and Paula fought constantly about everything. One of their ongoing battles was over mating their ferrets, Chipper and Madonna. Paula had agreed to have the ferrets as pets without knowing too much about them. It did not take long for her to realize that ferrets can really stink. Paula was adamant about giving up the ferrets. Sam was not only unwilling to give them up, but he wished to mate the ferrets. The battle raged all the time.

When we met, Paula said she could not tolerate the idea of Sam's wanting to mate the ferrets. She cried as she described the ferret mating ritual. The male physically abuses the female for hours, Paula said. Often injured, the female ultimately submits. (Let me just interject here that while ferret foreplay is certainly not very romantic, Paula was exaggerating somewhat. The males do grasp and sometimes even bite the females on the scruff of the neck—and a little blood is not uncommon—but prolonged violence and serious injury are uncommon, and experienced breeders know to separate a pair that seems to be heading to that point.) In captivity, if the female conceives, the male must be isolated to protect the newborns. After birth, the mother, too, may kill the litter if she senses danger or is frightened by humans or other animals.

Sam looked completely annoyed with Paula and told her to toughen up. I asked Sam how he viewed the mating activities of ferrets. He called it a part of nature and said Paula was reading too much into the male's activities.

When Paula and Sam felt more comfortable talking in therapy sessions, I was able to ask them about their own relationship, including their sex life. Both said they were constantly fighting but loved each other. Paula explained that Sam had come from a home where his parents fought all the time. His mother had nagged his father a lot; his father would not respond, provoking her anger by forcing her to repeat everything many times before he answered. He had done nothing about the upkeep of the house and could not afford to hire people to make the necessary repairs. Sometimes he had become physically abusive toward his wife, as well as toward Sam and his two younger brothers.

As we talked, it became clear that Sam not only had issues about abuse, but also about women. He believed that his mother had provoked his father, who worked hard all day and came home to a wife who sounded unappreciative of his efforts. Sam admitted that he was secretly pleased when his father had struck his mother because she became silent and subdued. Sam had always wished that his mother could have been a softer, more gentle woman. I asked him if he thought she would have been different if his father had been more responsive to her.

Sam himself could not tolerate any form of violence and never watched anything violent on television or went to films containing violence. As Sam talked about his family, he connected the pieces about mating the ferrets for himself. He saw himself identifying with his father by blaming his mother. He also saw how the male ferret's mating behavior reflected his own confusion about the role of sex and aggression in human relationships. Sam acknowledged that his fear of viewing violence contradicted his fascination with mating the ferrets. He was willing to look at his own aggressive feelings, and he began to see how he set Paula up to fight with him. He also came to realize that his father had needed to provoke his mother to give himself permission to be abusive.

Paula pointed out how their sex life together was the exact opposite of the ferrets. Sam was totally passive and seemed to encourage Paula to make all the advances. Yet when she did, he rejected her attempts and left her feeling stupid and discarded. She told Sam that she would not mind him being aggressive as long as he was not hurtful. Sam seemed surprised to hear this and said that he was beginning to feel less frightened by his aggressive feelings as he and Paula began talking about the subject.

As Sam learned more about his projection, he understood how he had disowned his unconscious abusive wishes by focusing instead on the behavior of the male ferret, who was simply behaving like a normal ferret. He started to acknowledge his anger with both of his parents and his own feelings of aggression. He realized that he hated how his parents treated each other. Although he consciously knew he did not want to be abusive toward anybody, Sam also had unconsciously identified himself with his abusive father. This identification came to the surface via his fascination with the ferrets.

When Sam and Paula understood what was happening between them, they agreed to a couple things. First of all, Sam got the ferrets neutered, and there was no more talk of mating them. He also agreed to be more conscientious with their bath regime, which cut down a lot on the smell. For her part, Paula also compromised: She agreed to keep the ferrets, and she tried to get more involved in their routine care. And Sam and Paula both agreed to stop setting each other up for fights.

Chapter 13

Projection and Animal Abuse

::

As we saw in Chapter 12, "Pets and the Mating Instinct," projection can sometimes be tied up with violent feelings. We loathe the abusive impulses we see in ourselves, so we project them onto others. This can sometimes take a nasty turn.

SALLY, TED, AND A POODLE NAMED HOMER

Sally met Ted at a friend's dinner party. She liked his sense of humor and easy way with people. He liked that she thought he was funny, and he liked the way she laughed. They began dating.

Of course, there are few ointments without a resident fly. The fly, in this case, was Sally's Toy Poodle, Homer. Ted thought a small Poodle was effeminate, and he called Homer "faggy." Upset with the label Ted had put on Homer, Sally asked what made him think that the dog was gay. Ted said he did not think the dog was gay—only that he acted effeminate. After all, the dog pranced around and held his head up high and seemed a little contemptuous. Sally, who had failed Psychology 101, thought Ted was just being funny and commented on how much she enjoyed his sense of humor.

Then one day Sally saw him kick Homer. She was very upset and confronted Ted. He told her that she seemed closer to Homer than to him and that he was beginning to feel jealous. He did not know what had come over him—he had never been abusive toward animals—but nevertheless he gave her an ultimatum: If the relationship was going to go anywhere, she must get rid of Homer.

For Sally, this was a painful choice. She loved Ted and she also loved Homer. She did not want to give up either. She also felt that Ted's feelings toward the dog, and his treatment of the animal, suggested some deeper feelings at work. Rather than having to choose between her lover and pet, she asked Ted to go to a therapist with her. Ted agreed and presented his feelings about Homer in our first session.

Ted reported that the Poodle really annoyed him and left him feeling like he wanted to hurt the dog. He could not stand the way the dog wiggled his behind, or held his head up in the air, or barked or demanded attention. I asked Ted if I could meet with him alone for a session. I wanted to meet Ted without Sally because I believed it would be easier for him to talk about his sexuality without her present.

We talked a long while about Ted's feelings about Homer. He regarded Homer as sneaky and unsure of his sexuality. Then I asked Ted how he felt about homosexual people. He said that, unlike the rest of his family, he had no dislike of them as a group. He thought they were creative and smart. I asked him more about his family and found that both parents were alcoholics who had been physically abusive to Ted, and more so to his younger brother, Randy. When Randy had recently announced he was gay, his family disowned him. I asked Ted if he had disowned his brother as well, but Ted said he was the only one still in touch with Randy since he moved to Australia.

Not wanting to upset Ted—and wondering even more about his attitude toward Homer—I asked him if he himself had ever had a homosexual experience. He wanted to know why I was asking, and I explained to him that the news of his brother might be having an effect on the way he regarded Homer. I also wondered if his brother's announcement had stirred up anything inside Ted.

Ted said that he had been curious about his sexuality while he was in college, and in fact, had had a few homosexual experiences. He admired his brother for revealing his sexual orientation, but he also thought he was dumb for telling his parents, knowing how they would react.

I asked Ted if he still wondered about his sexuality, and he said he did. He reported that sometimes he was shocked to realize that he was turned on by some of the men in the Calvin Klein underwear ads, although he rapidly assured me that he was also turned on by the women in the ads.

I asked him if he had been physically abused as a kid, and he reported that his father used to make him drop his pants and bend over to be hit with a belt when he misbehaved. Ted did not think it was a big deal, since all the kids used to get paddled when they were bad. I pointed out that for many kids, getting hit or spanked was the only attention they got from a parent, and that negative attention became better than no attention at all. Ted said that his father was rarely home and never helped with the kids, except to discipline them.

I also pointed out that very often physical and even verbal abuse can be transformed unconsciously into sexual fantasies (in fantasies, events do not always follow the logic of the real world). I helped Ted to realize that his homosexual feelings were connected to the excitement of the sadistic relationship with his father. In fact, regular homosexual activities did not turn Ted on. I helped Ted to see that he had sexualized his pain and anger at his father's treatment of him. As a result, he experienced a kind of pseudohomosexual experience in which Ted was not sure whether he was gay. And Ted feared the possibility of being homosexual in a fundamentalist Christian family.

Once Ted began putting the pieces of his personal puzzle together, he was able to reclaim his sexual feelings and not project them onto little Homer. He was able to look at his worst fears and to deal with his father. Ultimately, Ted was able to confront his father and even received an apology from him. And Ted and Sally eventually became engaged.

ABUSE AND PROJECTION

A major reason for the existence of societies for the prevention of cruelty to animals is the vast number of people who believe that animals do not feel pain, or that animals are not entitled to the same care and consideration as any other living being. These include people from all walks of life, from the average citizen to a former President of the United States. Many in that group, often those whose business involves animals, don't even consider the possibility of pain in animals. This is nonsense!

All kinds of pets are subject to human abuse. However, the mistreatment of dogs is probably most widely recognized. Some dog owners abuse the pets unknowingly and unintentionally. For the most part, they do not understand that dogs are pack animals that need the companionship of others, or they think that it is okay to force them to spend their lives in solitary, guarding a junk yard or tied to a stake in all kinds of weather. Also in this group are people who fear that kindness and gentleness may spoil the animal, possibly allowing the dog to get the upper hand in the relationship.

Unfeeling as these people may be, others abuse their pets intentionally and beat their dogs into submission. Others isolate and torture these animals to make them fierce so that they can make them into fighting dogs or guard dogs. For some people, dogs are a commodity meant to perform a service and then to be discarded when no longer able to perform—the tragedy of racing dogs comes to mind here.

Widespread though this attitude may be, there is a growing consciousness about the true nature of animal behavior, including their emotional life. We are coming to understand that animals have true feelings and form real relationships with humans and other animals. They have emotional as well as physical needs that must be met.

Where does animal abuse come from? How does projection take the form of beating up on something or someone else? Keep in mind that a projection is placing a personal feeling, memory, or personal experience that is too uncomfortable or painful to bear onto something else. The trail from experience to projection can be a bit obscure, but it is there if you take the time to look. People who have been abused—whether sexually, physically, or even verbally—need to understand the psychological defenses that they may unconsciously resort to in their attempt to defend against further harm.

Dissociation is a major defense against the memories of the pain that follows abuse. It allows a person to behave as though he or she were not involved in whatever happened. Most typically, the person feels like an onlooker or observer rather than the one who experienced the destructive events. Dissociation can also involve verbal and physical reactions that appear to be totally unrelated to current events.

Many abused people do not easily trust others, are afraid of being controlled by others, and they frequently shrink from being touched. Often, people who have been seriously abused physically or sexually as children turn to pets as their only real source of comfort in what they see as a threatening world.

Again the question arises, what can be so traumatic as to make a person want to hide from his or her memory? Equally important, what can make someone hide from the feelings of anger and rage that grew out of it? To be abused as a child means having no control over your life or your destiny. Being overpowered by an adult is terrifying to a child; how does a small person defend against an assault from someone so much larger? That child has no recourse! If the abuser is a parent, the child suffers a double whammy because the parent is supposed to protect the child. When the protector becomes the abuser, the child feels hopeless and helpless in the most profound way imaginable. Can the abused child ever hope to trust humans again?

While the destruction of trust can be devastating to a child, so, too, can be the loss of control that is central to abuse. Often, people who have been abused seem to the casual observer to be out of control. Their lives may appear to be in disarray and often, if they have pets, it appears as if the animals have taken over their lives as well as their living space.

In other instances, things are quite the reverse. These people's lives seem totally controlled, with everything scheduled and in place. If pets are in their lives at all, they are obedient, often leading unnecessarily regimented lives. Their attempts at control may take the form of being very critical and judgmental, often offering an array of advice and suggestions. When you visit them, you may soon come to realize that every minute of your visit has been accounted for.

Many individuals who have been abused physically or sexually as children may have turned to pets as their only source of real comfort in the world. Many of these people learned early in life to keep their unhappy experience to themselves. Some of them tried to speak out and were not believed. For others, the non-abusive parent remained silent or refused to accept the reality.

For many abused people, the thought of physically punishing their pet may give them a sense of satisfaction, of power, of control, or a feeling of respect. Regret is often experienced after disciplining a pet (hopefully never physical discipline) for a real or imagined transgression. They wish the animal would forgive them for having disciplined it. The person will often report that the need to punish their pet had more to do with something inside them than with what the animal did.

When watching violent action—a televised wrestling match, a fight or argument in the street, a violent movie—abuse victims often feel compelled to keep watching even while expressing revulsion.

The recent French film *Baxter* is a powerful portrayal of how displacements, projections, and our defenses keep us locked within our own reality. It consists of three vignettes in which Baxter, a Staffordshire Terrier (more commonly known as a Pit Bull), narrates his own story of his three masters. In the first, an old woman adopts him as a replacement for her children who have grown and moved away. While she truly loves Baxter, the woman does little with the dog beyond petting and adoring it. When the woman dies, a young childless couple adopts him. With them, Baxter leads a more idyllic life, typical of what might be expected of new parents. Ultimately, the couple has their own child, and out of fear that Baxter's breed is too aggressive to be in a home with a child, they pass him on to an adolescent boy. The boy—who suffers from serious emotional problems and is probably capable of becoming a future serial killer—beats Baxter to death, then with great sobs tells his father how Baxter attacked him and how he beat him off to save his own life. In this final vignette the boy projects his vile, loathsome self onto Baxter, then symbolically kills off that part of himself. It is not hard to imagine how all the self-loathing parts of the abused self could be projected onto a pet. Almost anything a pet does that could be regarded as disobedience may be cause for punishment. Abused people report that the abuser often rationalized his or her actions as discipline or training. Many abused people believe that there was something terrible about them to begin with—otherwise, why would they have been abused in the first place? Considerable shame and guilt are attached to having been abused. There is always the feeling that if the abuse occurred, then in some way the person must have asked for it or must have done something to deserve what happened.

Chapter 14

Is It Real, or Is It Projection?

Generally, only the *symptoms* of projection show. To understand whether our behavior is a projection or a reaction to a real situation, we have to look *inside* ourselves, not outside. For example, are you somehow unconsciously showing hostility to the dog (remember Estelle and Fred)? And is your lover's dog really hostile to you, or is it just something you are projecting?

BEWARE OF DOG

Tony thought Marie's dog, Spike, was unpredictable. Sometimes, when Tony arrived at Marie's house, Spike greeted him in typical dog fashion by wagging his tail and jumping up on Tony. Other times Tony sat in the living room and the dog began barking with intermittent mild but noticeable growls while jumping backward.

Marie explained this as a form of play and said that Spike was trying to engage Tony in a tug-of-war game. While Tony tried to understand Marie's explanations, he could not get past his feelings of anxiety and sometimes panic over Spike's behavior. He would break out in a sweat, and his mouth would go dry as Spike began to bark and jump back. Marie's reassurances were of little help.

During one of our therapy sessions, Tony explained that when Spike barked, he was sure the dog could tear him to pieces without any warning or hesitation. He felt that the dog had never liked him and only pretended to be nice to Tony because Spike knew it pleased Marie. "I think he truly hates me and is capable of ripping me apart limb from limb," he said.

Furthermore, Tony said that he was terrified of the unpredictability of dogs. At the outset, this seemed puzzling because Tony was unable to remember any childhood incidents with dogs or any trauma upon which to base his fear. He added that he did not like Spike, but when the dog tried to engage him in play, Tony said he tried to get beyond that for Marie's sake.

I considered that Tony might be projecting onto Spike his own unresolved feelings of aggression, although at first glance his story seemed to suggest otherwise. Tony described himself as not being an aggressive person. He said he usually just let things go. Even more puzzling, he recalled nothing in his early family life that might reflect hostility and aggression within family relationships. His folks never argued in front of the kids. Certainly, like all kids growing up, he had many arguments with his mother, especially around the age of puberty. Many of them seemed inconsequential, such as wanting to wear jeans with holes in them because all the other kids wore them that way. That did not seem like the stuff that hidden hostility or aggression is made of. But there was more.

Tony's mother had died when he was 12 years old. He thought her death may, in fact, have drained his aggressive feelings and ambition. He said he just was not interested in doing anything competitive after her death. And therein lies the clue to Tony's true feelings.

On the surface, Tony appeared gentle and easy-going, which are the qualities Marie loved him for. She had grown up with a verbally abusive father, and she found Tony's patience and tolerance to be important in their relationship. Tony was not consciously aware of his hostile and aggressive feelings, but like so many children who have lost a parent, he became angry over what he felt emotionally as an abandonment. He had always felt guilty about his anger toward his mother, understanding intellectually that she did not die "on purpose." So

Tony covered up his childhood anger at being left without a mother and buried his guilt about this anger beneath fear and passivity.

To make the relationship work, Marie kept reassuring Tony that Spike was not going to devour him. That was true, but Tony was dealing with a projection of his own unconscious creation. Psychologically, it had become important for him to hold on to that projection and to keep his feelings of aggression bottled up in his unconscious at the same time that he externalized them in Spike. In this way, he did not have to experience his own feelings of aggression, which would likely frighten him. As long as Tony had Spike or a Spike-substitute in his life, he was *safe*. He never had to look at the angry part of himself because Spike could be angry *for* him. He never had to fantasize about tearing someone limb from limb because Spike would do that.

While this projection gave Tony some feeling of comfort, it was only superficial. His lack of awareness of the aggression within him was becoming more of an issue as he became increasingly passive in his relationship with Marie. At the same time, through his projection, he saw Spike as becoming more aggressive and unpredictable. His fear of Spike was ruining the time he spent with Marie.

But that was only one side of the story. As I've already noted, everyone makes a contribution in a relationship. In this one, Marie also tried to avoid confronting her growing frustration and resulting anger with Tony's passivity. She was beginning to complain to her girlfriends that he was content never to do anything but work, eat, sleep, and occasionally have sex. By not confronting Tony with her concerns, Marie reinforced Tony's belief that he was just not an angry guy. He was not forced to look at or acknowledge the aggressive and the unpredictable parts of himself.

MOZART, PETER, AND GEORGE: "DISGUSTING" MUSIC

To understand another aspect of projection, consider the story of Mozart, Peter, and George. Peter kept complaining that George's cat,

Mozart, showed no respect for his "master" (Peter's term). Mozart seemed to ignore George completely, and Peter considered Mozart to be rude, arrogant, and impolite. In fact, he thought the cat needed a good smack to shock him out of his arrogance. Mozart was just not a nice cat, in Peter's view.

For his part, George never noticed the things that Peter was complaining about in Mozart. He did know, however, that Peter had a real thing about being "nice" and "polite." Anything and anyone who was not being nice or polite was "disgusting," in Peter's view. When Mozart attended to the cat business of grooming by licking himself all over, including his genitals, Peter said the cat was too disgusting to watch, and George would have to shoo poor Mozart away. If Mozart pounced on his food bowl and walked around it as if stalking something, or if he smelled his food before deciding to eat or walk away, Peter claimed that he was involved in a "disgusting display of self-absorption." If the cat ate too fast, it was disgusting; if he ate too slow, it was also disgusting. Finally, George told Peter that there was very little Mozart did that he did not find disgusting and that all the things that offended him were basic feline behaviors. The friction over Mozart began to wear down their relationship. That's when Peter came to see me.

I asked Peter if there was anything he considered disgusting about himself. He thought for a while before noting that he found the perspiration stains that sometimes appeared on his shirt to be objectionable. Any stains on his underwear would absolutely mortify him. Sometimes he noticed a bit of food on his teeth after eating, and the thought of someone having seen it horrified him. In fact, he found almost anything related to normal body functions disgusting. Where did all this come from? Why was Peter so hypersensitive to such common, everyday occurrences?

In thinking back, Peter remembered that his mother had used the word "disgusting" often in speaking about his father and his older brother. He remembered that he was quite young when he consciously decided to be very aware of himself and what he was doing to avoid having his mother see something in him that she would not approve of and call him disgusting.

He was very careful about his appearance at all times, but as time went on he secretly and silently began to accept his mother's view of men as disgusting—and he extended that to include himself. No matter how immaculate he appeared to others, his mother's view dominated his self-image.

This secret, shameful, disgusting part of himself that he could not tolerate was being projected onto Mozart. In Peter's view, poor Mozart was disgusting no matter what, and that was that. The cat was the target of Peter's own unconscious self-loathing. He yearned to please his mother and be her favorite; he was unaware that most likely his mother did not have much use for males no matter what they looked like or did.

My task as a therapist was to help Peter reconnect to that cut-off part of himself, to recognize how far he had turned himself inside out to avoid being labeled "disgusting." To protect himself from being disgusting to his mother, he unconsciously adopted her view of men. I had to help Peter see how angry he must have felt with a mother who regarded men the way she did. In this way, he would feel free to form his own views of acceptable behavior. Peter is still in therapy, but Mozart and George are having a much easier life these days.

CANINE ESP

Miriam had been dating Stan for a number of months before she introduced him to her dog, Genghis. At first it appeared that the dog liked Stan and that they got on well together. But a few months later, Genghis was growling and snarling even before Stan entered Miriam's house. She told him she could not explain the dog's changed attitude.

As time went on, Genghis became more aggressive toward Stan. He growled and snapped so much that he actually began to foam at the mouth. Miriam, who was known for her calmness and patience, become increasingly concerned with the deteriorating situation between the dog and Stan.

Stan was even more perplexed. He liked the dog and could not see any change in his behavior that would explain the change in Genghis. Meanwhile, the dog's aggression escalated to the point where Genghis was charging for Stan's privates as soon as he saw him. In turn, Stan was so upset at the dog's increased hostility that he presented Miriam with an ultimatum: *It's either me or the dog.*

How many pet owners have been faced with that same awful choice? Maybe you're facing that choice right now and that is the reason you bought this book. Sometimes it seems those are the only two options. But there are always other choices. The hardest choice, but the one with the most satisfying and lasting results, is getting to the root of the problem.

When Miriam and I talked, she said that normally Genghis was a very friendly dog. She could think of only a couple people the dog had reacted to in a similar fashion, and she was no longer in touch with them. In fact, they were ex-boyfriends whom she had broken up with because she had suspected that they were unfaithful or because she had discovered their infidelity.

It became clear very soon after we met that the very quiet, demure Miriam had been very angry with Stan for quite a while, suspecting that there was another woman in his life. Although she was unable to tell Stan of her suspicions, Genghis had apparently sensed her unconscious hostility. As Miriam's suspicions grew, Genghis was reading her hostility and changing his behavior toward Stan. The fact that Genghis attacked Stan's crotch was not a coincidence!

As you probably know, animals are exceptionally intuitive. It is equally true that they can respond to the emotional states of their owners. They are known to comfort people when they feel sad or ill, and they are also known to transmit their owner's fear or hostility.

This is a particular form of projection. Miriam had unconsciously allowed Genghis to act out her hostile feelings toward a boyfriend she suspected of being unfaithful and toward past boyfriends she had suspected of betrayal. By not stopping Genghis' behavior, she effectively reinforced it, allowing Genghis to express the hostility she was afraid to express.

As it turned out, Stan was not at all unfaithful to Miriam. The real problem was her suspicion of every man she got really close to, and the real solution was to understand why she felt that way. Miriam's work had just begun.

BEYOND CATASTROPHE

Don went into a deep depression when an on-the-job accident left him permanently disabled. Barbara, his wife, accepted the news of his physical condition with good grace, in her typical stoic fashion. She had a job in her state's department of taxation that paid fairly well, and she assured Don that they could manage comfortably on her salary and his disability income.

Don and Barbara had a wonderful 9-year-old German Shepherd named Sheba, whom they both adored. But shortly after Don's accident, Sheba was diagnosed with cancer. It would be necessary to amputate her leg to save her life. They both agreed, and Sheba returned home in a fairly good state after the operation.

Still, Don was beside himself with fear and worry. He slept poorly at night and lost weight. All he could think about since his accident and Sheba's amputation was the day Sheba would either die or have to be put down. His dread continued to grow. Don said he could not accept Sheba's disability. Sometimes he began to talk about Sheba and burst into tears. Other times, as he petted the dog, he went into a full panic attack with the typical symptoms of labored breathing and tunnel vision.

By the time Barbara and Don came in for counseling, Don had all but stopped eating. He began to talk about the accident and allowed himself to express his fear that Barbara would soon get tired of being the main support of their family and would ultimately want to leave. The idea that this could become a reality was too much for Don to bear. His terror of abandonment and death were being projected onto poor Sheba.

Don had become so fearful that he did not notice all the ways Sheba was beginning to improve. She had learned to navigate her world on three legs, and in many ways she seemed stronger and happier than she had been for a long while before the cancer finally had been diagnosed. And because, from what we understand, dogs are generally not self-conscious about their appearance, Sheba was not feeling any of the anxiety about her disability that Don had projected onto her. Barbara reassured Don that she loved him very much and would not abandon him.

SUMMING IT ALL UP

In all these examples of projection, I have tried to show how any idea or feeling a person regards as intolerable might unconsciously be projected onto another person or an animal. If these feelings are projected onto another person, it is possible to get some feedback that something uncomfortable is going on between them; people do talk to each other. However, if the projection is onto an animal, no such feedback is possible. Only observation by another person may detect the projection. We have seen how this works in the stories told in this section about how a pet became an issue in the relationship.

- Barry projected his anger at Estelle onto their dog, Fred, claiming that it was Fred who missed his girlfriend after they moved.

- Tony could not deal with his anger and feeling of loss stemming from his mother's death. This translated into feelings of aggression, which he projected onto Marie's dog, Spike.

- Margie avoided her feelings of intellectual inadequacy by projecting them onto Keith, making him seem like the dumb one because he enjoyed playing with his cats.

- Fran projected her unwanted sadness onto Albrecht's cat, Rose, who was just enjoying the lazy lifestyle typical of a feline.

- Poor Mozart the cat was the target of all of Peter's feelings of self-disgust and self-loathing.

- Angie's guilt at leaving home and the emotional pain she felt at separating from her mother were projected onto her Great Dane, Ophelia.

- Ned's fear of going out of control, as his father had, was projected onto Samurai, his Akita.

- Not being able to sire his own child put Harold into deep feelings of despair, so he became obsessed with mating his tropical fish.

- Sam identified with his father's abusive behavior toward his mother and was not able to accept his own feelings of aggression. Instead, he became fascinated with the aggressive mating behavior of ferrets.

- Miriam's unconscious hostility toward Stan and his suspected affairs were sensed by her dog, Genghis, who became vicious with Stan.

- Don's fear of being abandoned by his wife, Barbara, after becoming disabled became completely fused with the illness of their dog, Sheba.

- Ted adored Sally, yet his ambivalent feelings about his own sexuality were being projected onto Homer, the poor Toy Poodle.

The common thread in all these examples is that these people harbored uncomfortable feelings in their unconscious. Projection became their mechanism for attempting to deal with the problems without actually feeling the emotional pain.

We all have parts of ourselves that we are not particularly comfortable with: jealousy, cheapness, sadistic feelings, rage, shyness, or dumbness—the list goes on forever. We may try to disown or deny those pieces of ourselves, but they remain lodged within us; everyone else may know about them but us. But if we admit to their existence and consciously try not to project them onto others, we have an opportunity to examine them and stop them from controlling our lives.

By now, you are equipped with some of the basics needed to begin working on your relationships from two new perspectives: displacements and projections. If you desire, you can make an attempt at answering some of the questions posed throughout the book, trying to be as honest as you can about your early childhood development and how you interact in you current relationships. Only you need to know your answers.

- Are there relationships, both pet and human, in which you suspect you may be displacing or projecting your own experience?
- Are you feeling in charge of your own life?
- Do you feel your relationships, both pet and human, are as fulfilling as you believe they should be?
- Is your career on track or is it derailed by displacements and projections?
- If you do not come up with many responses, you might want to think—shrink.

Part III

The Repetition Compulsion

Never-Ending Soap Operas and Old War Stories

Chapter 15

The Memories Linger On

Now we are ready to look at the next element of psychological dynamics: the repetition compulsion, which refers to the way we re-enact those old soap operas and war stories from our past. The unconscious keeps them alive inside our heads and tries to change the endings by re-enacting them in the real world. It reminds me of a couplet from Sir Walter Scott's *The Lay of the Last Minstrel*: "Oh, what a tangled web we weave, when first we practice to deceive." With that, meet the repetition compulsion.

At this point, we know that psychological and emotional development starts at birth and continues throughout life. We know also that at every stage of human development there is unfinished business—that is, developmental issues left over from previous stages of growth that can be at the heart of psychological problems. These issues usually take the form of receiving too little or too much affection, attention, stimulation, or whatever was needed at that developmental stage. As we progress through life from birth to death, these pieces of unfinished business keep reappearing in new forms.

Each time this unfinished business reappears, it comes in new guises, which makes it increasingly difficult to trace the steps back to the source of the problem. In a very real sense, we keep re-enacting updated editions of the past in our current relationships. These problems appear in relationships with our own children, other family members, even friends—almost anyone you come into contact with could spark a reaction. It is not unusual to recreate these issues with our pets as well. Sometimes we even create an entire lifestyle that reflects our unfinished personal business. Needless to say, these things can get complicated.

SETTING THE STAGE FOR UNCONSCIOUS DRAMA

Most people seem to find it uncanny the way two people are drawn to each other in some almost magical way. Psychologically speaking, the magic lies in the unconscious. On the surface, couples are initially drawn to each other by looks and other attributes. As the relationship develops romantically, it also evolves psychologically. Deeply rooted personality traits and unconscious defenses move in on the interaction between the couple. When the "honeymoon" phase of the relationship draws to an end, and as the two people begin to trust each other, they allow their less-than-perfect sides to show: She blows her nose into tissues left all around the house; he does not lift the toilet seat when he urinates—we all have foibles that annoy our mates. Inevitably, if all factors mesh, a relationship develops and the stage is set for playing out of the third element of our defense trilogy: the repetition compulsion.

To use another metaphor for the unconscious, dating can be seen as auditioning for roles in the next edition of the repetition compulsion follies. If your date is the individual with which you need to re-enact past traumas, the relationship blossoms.

How the unconscious organizes this phenomenon is beyond me, but after 25 years of practicing psychotherapy, there is no question in my mind that what I have just described is fact.

Almost any piece of unfinished business from an earlier part of our lives is subject to recreation or re-enactment in the present. Here are some clues to know if you are going through such an experience:

- In the middle of a situation, do you begin to have a clear idea of what the other person is going to say next?
- Do you know exactly how you will respond to what is being said before the person finishes speaking?
- Do you know the retort to your reply?
- Do you have a clear idea of exactly how the reenactment will end up?
- Do you have human expectations of the animals in your life? Should they know when you are feeling depressed or disappointed? Should they want to eat when you are ready to feed them? Are they supposed to understand and forgive when you come home late?

The cast of characters may be different from the original cast, but once again you have taken the show on the road, trying to tack a happy ending onto your never-ending play. The plot may thicken or thin, but the show goes on over and over and over. The compulsion to repeat keeps feeding itself. The gratification from acting out the drama keeps the repetition compulsion operating.

So what are those issues? Certainly, our earliest fears are about being abandoned. To be abandoned is not to be fed and cared for when we are too young to fend for ourselves. Later, not being loved and not having self-esteem are great fears, as are physical pain and, ultimately, death.

So why does so much of what unfolds in the repetition compulsion seem self-destructive? In attempting to master earlier trauma or create a new happy ending to past frustrations, the original suffering may resurface. While we may wish to master the traumatic situation, more often the end result is a kind of aggression turned inward on ourselves. Many people call this behavior *self-destructive*. Sometimes self-destructive behavior causes deep depression, or it may become externalized as antisocial behavior.

Frequently, the repetition compulsion takes on a life of its own and no longer operates with the goal of a happy ending or mastering a trauma. It truly becomes compulsive and self-destructive in seeking out both pleasure and pain.

Like displacement, the repetition compulsion is a defense against memory. It is an unconscious acting out of past experience instead of consciously remembering it. The acting out may be a carbon copy of the original situation, or it may be either a distortion or a new form of the past. The thing that keeps a person involved in this compulsion is the need to feel in control of his or her life. This is a natural desire. The wish for mastery over our personal life is within all of us and is natural; it is not limited to displacements and the repetition compulsion.

Memory and remembering are a big part of life. The importance of memory, to the psychologist, is not a question of dredging up facts relating to names, faces, and incidents, nor is it about chronology or locales. The importance of memory, to the psychologist, has to do with what you remember—and, even more, what you forget. Often it is more important to remember why you have forgotten a memory than to be able to recall the memory itself.

The task lies in being able to attach emotional significance to what has happened to you in the past. When you have managed that, you will have reconnected to those early experiences and integrated the emotions that come with them into your current life. Those parts of your life will no longer stick out like sore thumbs from the rest of who you are and how you experience yourself. This is what "working through" is all about.

Being consciously aware of your repetition compulsion helps you avoid letting it play a self-destructive role in your life. You can even learn to enjoy your repetition compulsion without having to act it out. This requires that you bring the repetition compulsion into your conscious world by reconnecting to those lost memories and feelings that are being acted out.

Unless the repetition compulsion is made conscious, each of us is destined to continually act it out. In the words of George Santyana, "Those who ignore history are condemned to repeat it."

Chapter 16

Couples Caught Up in Repetition

··

When couples realize they are engaged in repetition compulsion, they are often surprised at just how powerful the compulsion really is. Upon learning of their particular repetition compulsions, many couples thank me and leave therapy. To them, *just knowing* what the repetition compulsion is seems to be more important than resolving the problems connected to it. Unconsciously, they have a need to continue the repetition compulsion because breaking the cycle might be more frightening than just letting it continue to play out.

Repetition compulsions also involve a recreational aspect. Couples can experience ongoing excitement in trying to get what they believe they want from each other, and this constant cycle actually binds them together. Each is pursuing his or her own repetition compulsion, hoping to magically create through the other a happy ending to unresolved childhood problems.

Which couples have the best chance of staying together? My experience suggests that couples re-enacting parent-child relationships, sibling relationships, and sadomasochistic relationships lead the list. Trying to get the other person (or a pet) to change is a major force in continuing the drama within a relationship. "If only she would see how she tortures me." "If only he would understand what I am feeling, instead of walking away." "He is always criticizing me and telling me I am not good enough."

CAUGHT UP IN THE DRAMA

Remember Barry, his wife, Estelle, and their dog, Fred, from Chapter 9, "Getting Rid of the Unwanted"? Estelle was not interested in working on her marriage after she found out about Barry's affair with Yolanda. As it turned out, Yolanda and Barry split up as well. Estelle remarried, but her second husband was very similar to Barry because he was not able to acknowledge his anger. He, too, was involved in an extramarital affair. When last seen, Estelle was in the process of yet another divorce.

We can certainly see the repetition compulsion in action here. Now let's look at why it played itself out in the lives of Barry and Estelle.

Barry was the youngest of two brothers. His brother, Tyrone, was sadistic toward him for as long as Barry could remember. He was always getting Barry into trouble with their parents and with Barry's friends at school. Every year for Barry's birthday, Tyrone would give him a beautifully wrapped large gift that turned out to be a worn toilet seat. Tyrone would double up with laughter just thinking about how Barry fell for the same old thing every year.

Estelle, too, suffered at the hands of her siblings. Born a middle child between her sisters, Jeanette and Babette, she was blamed from above and from below for everything that went wrong in the sisters' lives. If a sweater was missing or a boyfriend broke up with one of them, there was always Estelle to blame. One of the more bruising incidents during Estelle's adolescence occurred when Babette, her younger sister, lured away Henry, Estelle's high-school sweetheart, and ultimately married him. The marriage was short-lived, but Estelle never got over the pain of that betrayal.

After Barry and Estelle were married, it became Fred the dog's turn to take the blame. Barry viewed many of his problems as if they were the dog's. Thus, it was Fred who missed his girlfriend, not Barry who missed Yolanda. As for Estelle, she usually took Fred's side, having grown up caught in the middle between her sisters. At the same time, she could alternate between blaming Fred and protecting him.

Fred, too, had a history consistent with those of his human family. He was a middle puppy in a litter of 11. He was always hungry and in need of constant attention. A puppy evaluator said he was the most verbal and was duly noted to have dominant qualities, sharpened by his need to compete for food and attention. Barry's brother Tyrone owned Fred's sire, Yuppi, and Tyrone had had his pick of the litter when the pups were born. He had offered the puppy to Barry. Because of the nature of Tyrone's earlier presents, Barry was very suspicious. But he took the pup anyway.

Both Barry and Estelle were caught up in their individual repetition compulsions. These dramas intertwined in some ways and were at odds in others. Sometimes they danced together in an unconscious tango in which both re-enacted their roles as victims of their siblings. Other times they had verbal battles in which Barry unconsciously experienced Estelle as Tyrone, and Estelle reacted to Barry as either Jeanette or Babette.

Estelle could not say anything against Fred without Barry protecting him as he would have liked someone to protect him from Tyrone. If she commented on the dog's muddy feet or fleas, it always managed to be her fault: She allowed him to walk in the rain, she did not bathe him enough, and so on. In this scenario, Barry got to be his brother and feel powerful like Tyrone, and Estelle got her old familiar role of being caught between Jeanette and Babette (in this case, played by Barry and Fred).

Estelle was always searching for a relationship in which she was not victimized. However, she has yet to understand that she unconsciously seeks out relationships that repeat the old drama. Nor does she understand her contribution in provoking the men in her life to leave her. Now that she is ending her second marriage, we can assume that her next relationship will likely end up the same way.

CAN A VIOLINIST HAVE CATS?

Let's look once more at Keith and Margie, whom we first met in Chapter 10, "The Tales of Two Cats." Margie was constantly worried about Keith's intelligence and often criticized him, suggesting that his love of cats indicated a lack of intelligence. If you recall, Keith came from a family of intellectuals. His interest lay in music, and he came to resent the idea that only thoughts had any value and that feelings were secondary (if they received any regard at all). No one in Keith's family cared about what anyone else felt. Any uncomfortable feelings were dealt with in the same fashion: "Get over it," or "Get on with it."

Keith thought Margie was different from his family when he first met her. She was as interested in his feelings as in his ideas. But, as their relationship developed, it began to feel more like one long IQ test. He stayed with the relationship anyway, trying to get her to accept his feelings.

When I pointed out these circumstances to Margie, she thought I was on Keith's side and wanted them to see someone else whom she felt would be more impartial. Keith felt that it was the first time anyone had ever put his predicament into words that made real sense.

When I asked Margie about her relationships with men, she said there had been many, but she always ended the relationships because she became *bored*. Slowly, as she became more specific about her past break-ups, it became apparent that they had less to do with boredom than with issues about intelligence. An old theme was replayed over and over: her mother's obsession with intelligence.

For his part, Keith reported little involvement in romantic relationships before he met Margie. He felt so free of his family's intrusiveness and intellectually over-bearing attitude that solitude was a relief. Cats, with their air of independence, seemed like ideal pets to him.

Keith and Margie brought their individual repetition compulsions to their relationship. That enabled them to hold on to their parents emotionally, while at the same time providing excitement in the form of disagreements. Keith knew he was angry with his intellectualizing parents, yet he believed they were correct about intellect being more valuable than emotions. Margie could not get angry with a mother who constantly complained about her lost childhood and adolescence, so she got angry at everyone else around her.

LOOKING FOR THE PERFECT BITCH

Let's look at another aspect of the repetition compulsion in action. Dave was unconsciously attracted to the most narcissistic, destructive, self-serving, aggressive women. He seemed to have a knack for zeroing in on women who were destined to hurt him just for the fun of it.

He would fall hopelessly in love with a woman almost before he knew her name. In turn, she would be attracted to his energy and good looks. All this sounds like a perfect situation. Unfortunately, the scenario kept playing to the same unhappy ending. The woman eventually jilted him; like all the others, she turned out to be mean and vicious beyond belief.

In homing in on these women, Dave reaffirmed his negative view of women in general. He was fond of saying that the only female he trusted was Lucy, his cat.

With therapy, Dave learned that all the women he was attracted to were unconsciously cast in the role of his mother and his older sister, Dora, who had hated Dave from birth. Their mother, Ravella, had a highly competitive nature that added to the flames of the children's rivalry. She demanded all the love of her children, with none left over for their father, Andre.

Dave's attraction to impossible relationships (his repetition compulsion) was a reflection of his unconscious attempt to recreate the old scenario, hoping that the ending would change and that he would finally receive love without any strings attached. At the same time, there was the excitement that came with re-creating the fury he felt toward his mother and sister.

Seigrid was a good example. She was annoyed with Dave because he did not devote enough time to her—according to her, anyway. She made that apparent on his birthday. Dave had not heard from Seigrid all week before the big day. He had expected her to take him out for dinner and a show, as she had the year before. Nothing happened. The next day she phoned and apologized profusely for not calling on his birthday, explaining that she had been busy with a dinner party she had given that day—obviously one to which he had not been invited.

Lucy was a shelter cat, and Dave had adopted her because he thought she needed company. Then he brought home Casius, a three-year-old male Maine Coon Cat, who outweighed Lucy by 20 pounds. Poor Lucy was humbled by Casius at every turn. They fought like cats and cats.

In bringing Casius home, Dave was recreating the rivalry between himself and his older sister. In Dave's scenario, Casius became a much stronger version of himself, one that did not let Lucy get away with anything. This was the way Dave wished things had been.

Once the repetition compulsion is explored in depth and is exposed, its hold on its victim is loosened. Dave was able to do that in therapy and began to seek out relationships with more nurturing women. He still sensed the old excitement and attraction of the repetition compulsion, but he did not feel compelled to act on it.

Finally, Dave ended up in a relationship with Kathy, who was gentle, giving, and sensitive to his needs. Lucy and Casius, too, seemed to sense a change in Dave. He had become quieter and more tranquil—as a result, they seemed more at peace with each other. Kathy moved in with Dave, who came to trust her enough to tell her about his repetition compulsion. She was able to recognize when it was affecting their relationship, and they could discuss it instead of reacting to it.

Chapter 17

To Repeat or Not to Repeat

Everyone has a repetition compulsion. The question is, what is yours? How do you know you have a compulsion to repeat when it operates in the unconscious? As mentioned in our discussion on projection in Part II, "The Role of Projection," it is not easy to bring unconscious feelings to the surface. Almost always, it takes someone to point out that you frequently seem to react to situations or events in an inappropriate way. You may even be aware of part of what you are doing, but you might feel powerless to do anything about it. Someone else may be needed to show you how to change.

To get to the heart of the matter, the situation must first be clearly defined. A repetition compulsion in action is a carefully orchestrated set of activities put together unconsciously. In treating it, you must first figure out which of the people in your life are assigned which roles. Once that has been established, you can start to dissect the issues of love, hate, and guilt that are part of the scene being acted out. Remember, any unconscious memory, thought, or feeling that is beyond recall can trigger a displacement reaction, a projection, or a repetition compulsion. Taken to the extreme, it can trigger an anxiety or panic attack.

The compulsion to repeat is also a defense against surrendering earlier behaviors for more mature ways of being satisfied. As long as displacement, projection, and the repetition compulsion operate, they prevent real emotional development from taking place.

THE TRAGEDY OF IT ALL

A kind of tragedy surrounds the repetition compulsion. As with all psychological defenses, if it is not dealt with, the repetition compulsion will continue to affect the victim's life. For instance, let's look at Amanda's unfinished business.

Amanda grew up with an exceptionally disturbed younger sister. When Amanda was 10 years old, her parents separated. The girls lived with their mother until one day she announced that she could not take it anymore and was leaving because the younger child was driving her to distraction. Their father, who was now living with another woman, took custody of the girls, and Amanda's mother did not return for three years.

Amanda hated her sister, believing that her behavior had driven their mother to leave. The experience made Amanda feel as though she had been "not enough" to keep her mother from leaving and that her sister had been "too much" to keep her from staying.

In an almost classical example of repetition compulsion, the adult Amanda got into relationships in which she was not enough for the man in her life. As a result, she always got jilted in the end. Her last lover told her, "I can't stand you anymore," would not tell her what it was he could not stand, and refused to talk to her ever again.

When Amanda was in a relationship, she was always number two to another woman; she often was jilted for the other woman. The men she was attracted to were also frequently unstable—at least two wound up in mental hospitals.

Amanda has two cats. Joey is dependable and always available for consolation. Bingo is aloof, as some cats are wont to be, and is always disappearing out the window or out the door of the apartment and wandering through the halls of the building. For Amanda, the cats represent the split in her life between what she wishes for in a relationship and what she gets.

Keeping a man in her life seemed a constant challenge. When Amanda finally found a guy who was very interested in her and who made her number one, he moved in with her. Their relationship had gone on for many years, and from outward appearances it seemed that their roles had reversed: Amanda started complaining that Harry was not enough for her! In spite of outward appearances, though, Amanda's repetition compulsion was very much alive in her unconscious. She ultimately left Harry to take up with her old boyfriend, Pete, who treated her as second best—just like the old days. When psychological problems are not dealt with, they will hang around and keep popping up.

SEBASTIAN, SYBIL, AND THE YAPPING YORKIES

Here's another side of the repetition compulsion. Sebastian never felt that he got his parents' attention. He had a manic depressive brother, and his parents focused most of their efforts on caring for his brother's illness. Meanwhile, Sebastian and his sister, Anne, were supposed to "understand." As a result, Sebastian experienced his childhood as one in which his parents never listened to him or affirmed his needs. In fact, his father was even verbally abusive.

At 38 years of age, Sebastian could not stand to feel unheard. No one listened carefully enough to him. The slightest distraction while he was talking was taken as a personal affront and often lead to a confrontation. He demanded that people implicitly understand his every word and nuance.

Sebastian was in a relationship with Sybil, who had two Yorkshire Terriers. Weighing in at three to seven pounds, Yorkies can be pretty agile and forceful. They can also be pretty yappy dogs—these dogs display a great deal of intelligence and don't mind being heard when they have something to express. Yorkies will also run 20 feet across the room to jump into the open arms of their owner or a guest.

Sebastian's relationship with Sybil began to deteriorate as he constantly complained that her dogs always seemed to be barking when he was trying to speak. Unconsciously, it reminded him of his childhood, where his father "barked" at him and his mother ignored him.

Sybil had her own scenario to replay. Her father was capable of great passion, but mostly about ideas rather than about people. He could easily lose his temper over something trivial and would rant for hours about discipline and respect. He paid little attention to getting to know his bright and sensitive daughter.

Almost any action on Sybil's part could label her for life. If she was late in meeting her father, she was "never on time." If she sent him a funny birthday card, she had a "wonderful sense of humor." Sybil was never defined in terms of herself. Instead, everything she did or did not do was a reflection of how it affected him.

Sebastian, too, found fault with Sybil. He was always blaming her for her "poorly disciplined" dogs. Like her father, he rarely acknowledged her for who she was as a person. Any time Sybil walked or fed the dogs, or took them to the vet or to the groomer, Sebastian would consider it an incursion on his time. He finally ended the relationship and was last heard of complaining that the woman he was presently dating had the "disgusting" habit of chewing ice cubes.

Both Sebastian and Sybil were replaying their childhoods over and over. Neither really had any sense of the dogs as separate beings; for both, they were just players in the never-ending farce of repetition compulsion.

WHICH ROLE IS WHICH?

Repetition compulsion comes in many guises, and it's not always clear who is playing what role in the drama. Polly, for instance, lived out a kind of a repetition compulsion in reverse. She believed that her father had cared more for the family cats than for his wife and daughters. Polly feared that people would also think she was the kind of person who related better to animals than to people. As a result, she resolved to have a family of her own in which her mate and children would be the center of attention.

To make sure this would happen, Polly married a man who did not even like animals. However, after the children were born, the family did acquire a cat, Perogi. Doug, Polly's husband, refused to allow the cat into their bedroom—he was absolutely adamant about it. One day he returned early from work and found Polly on their bed petting the cat. He was enraged, and Polly retorted, "At least I get more attention from the cat than I get from you."

I think you can see what was going on here. Polly was reliving her relationship with her father, only this time she was her dad and the cat was her.

And who was Doug in this drama? Polly was always concerned that she would marry a man like her father, a man who gained most of his understanding and intimacy from his cats rather than from other people. As it turned out, she married a man who was cold and unaffectionate, like her mother.

"I learned to see my father through my mother's eyes," Polly told me later. Polly's father had had an art studio and was doing modestly well when an accidental fire burned the place down. Polly's mother had insisted on asking her family to help him get work. They offered to send him to school to learn printing, the family business. Although he did well in the new business, Polly's father never again got the chance to express his creativity. Behind the mother's determination was a deep-seated insecurity about being without an income and a strong desire for a better lifestyle. And Polly's father never overtly expressed his disappointment and resentment over his wife's lack of faith in him and her unwillingness to help the family get back on its feet.

Polly and Doug were in the process of separating when they came to me. On the surface, the problem seemed to be Doug's attitude toward the cats in their bedroom and the lack of attention and affection Polly received from him. For him, finding Perogi in their bedroom was a gross betrayal of trust. Polly felt he had overreacted, behaving as if he had found her in bed with another man. (In fact, this had really happened to Doug when, as a child, he had discovered his mother in bed with a man who was not his father.)

As Polly told her story, however, other factors came to light. Polly recalled that in her mother's eyes, the worst thing anyone could do is have an extramarital affair—Polly's grandfather had done that, and her mother had seen how it had torn at the family. Polly's father certainly got the message, so although his wife was cold toward him, he chose Petunia, the cat, as the recipient of his affections. It became clear that the family cat had become a substitute wife, presumably with her father's unconscious hope of never again being disappointed.

When her father lost his studio, Polly had sided with her mother. She had felt pressured by her mother to hold her father in contempt. At the same time, she felt terribly guilty that she was not strong enough to stand up to her mother and defend her father. It was difficult for Polly to look at her anger at a father who did not insist that his wife help him, have faith in him, and not turn the kids against him. "My mother wanted a lot of attention, but she was not comfortable with affection and feelings," Polly told me. "My father used anger as a defense or protection. My mother did that, too, but she was much more cold and bristly. I always think my father would have been a lot more emotional and express his sensitivity if my mother was able to tolerate it more. My mother had such tension about it and was always pretty controlling about feelings. My father was more emotional when he was younger."

Like her father, Polly was struggling to release her creativity and affection, but she felt that her mother had stifled those feelings in her. After many sessions and a lot of work in therapy, Polly came to realize that she wound up with Perogi instead of the husband she wished for, just as her father wound up with Petunia instead of the wife he had wished for.

Chapter 18

A Tangled Tale of Rage

I have purposely separated displacement, projection, and the repetition compulsion so that you can get a sense of how each operates. Unfortunately, these defenses rarely, if ever, appear separately. It is so difficult to figure out what's really going on unconsciously between people and pets because we combine displacements, projections, and repetitions with other defenses and then throw all these into our childhood stories to end up with some pretty complex dramas. Let's meet Peggy, Maria, Fatima, Zeus, Randy, and everyone else who was unconsciously drawn into a play with texts and subtexts aplenty.

Here we will see the interplay of displacements, projections, and the need to repeat unfinished business from childhood. We can also see some components of jealous rage and revenge, which we will look at in greater depth as we continue with this adventure.

Peggy had met Maria at a women's conference four years ago. They had become fast friends very quickly and found themselves moving toward a romance. Peggy lived in Boston, and Maria lived in Denver with a large Siamese cat named Fatima and a huge Belgian Malinois dog named Zeus. Zeus had belonged to Maria's former lover, Jimmy, who was now living on the island of Jamaica.

Maria, Fatima, and Zeus arrived in Boston and took an apartment not far from Peggy. The women's relationship continued to develop, and Peggy made plans to help Maria financially so she could return to college and complete her degree in anthropology.

The one roadblock in the relationship was the dog. Peggy complained about Zeus constantly, although she did not have to live with him. First of all, he was too large for her liking. Zeus was a good watchdog, but Peggy took that as a sign that he could not be trusted. She saw him as a dog that would easily attack someone, if provoked. She also claimed that he soiled Maria's books and bed and terrorized Fatima when Maria was not looking.

In reality, since moving to urban Boston, Zeus was not getting enough exercise. Maria would run him around the block four times a day, but that hardly came close to the good hour and a half a Malinois requires. He did have times when he was excitable or destructive, but this was just because of all the excess energy he had pent up.

Peggy could not see Zeus' keen intelligence behind his black face-mask and ears. She interpreted the dog's air of confidence as arrogance. Most of all, it seemed to Peggy that Maria adored Zeus much more than she did Peggy. Peggy began to complain to her friends about Maria's "obsession" with Zeus. She would ask her friends how they saw her relationship with Maria, and if they knew how humiliating it was "to be less loved, appreciated, and protected than some damn dog."

When Peggy asked me what I thought, I reminded her that she often spoke of her humiliation at being a girl in her traditional Greek family, where boys are the valued children. I asked her if Maria's attentiveness to her male Belgian Malinois pressed any of her old family buttons. She acknowledged that only the men in her family were considered important. She knew there was a connection, and she had discussed it with Maria. Why wasn't her lover being more attentive to Peggy's needs than to her dog's?

In Maria's family, she was always the one to give in. She basically had been raised by her paternal grandmother, whose view of the world was extremely pragmatic: Do what you have to do.

Maria had been raised by her grandmother because hers was a very dysfunctional family. Her mother had been a professional actress who had always been on the road. Her father had stayed home to have flings with other women. Despite being away frequently, Maria's mother was insanely jealous of her father's affairs and tried to get even by having affairs of her own. One day, during a rare stay at home, Maria's mother, in a fit of jealousy, shot and killed her husband and his girlfriend. She was arrested and tried and is still in prison in Colorado.

Maria was always afraid of her own feelings of jealousy and resentment, and believed that she, too, could be a very vengeful person. Knowing this, she was afraid to get close to anyone in a relationship and make a deep commitment, for fear of having the relationship turn from intimacy and trust to distrust and jealousy. It was important for Maria to keep her emotional distance in human relationships. But this was not the case with her animals, whom she loved without reserve.

Ultimately, Peggy presented Maria with an ultimatum: her or Zeus. As we've seen, this either-or choice is often the result of friction over the animals in a relationship. Because Peggy was paying for Maria's education and expenses, Maria had little choice; she had to give up Zeus. She found friends in Florida who were willing to take Zeus, for a fee, which Peggy was more than happy to pay. She silently believed that she had finally won a victory over the males in her new family: Goodbye Zeus, hello Maria.

Life went well for Maria, Peggy, and Fatima for a number of years. Maria completed school and was becoming recognized in her field. It looked like everything was in place for the relationship to continue to grow and flourish. Then, quite by surprise, Peggy's old friend Randy visited from Montreal.

In one instant, one moment in time, Maria and Randy connected to each other in a way that seemed nothing less than predestined. At first Peggy noticed nothing—perhaps because Randy seemed somewhat annoyed with Maria and kept asking Peggy if Maria reminded her of his first wife, who had abandoned him. Peggy said she did not see any resemblance and went so far as to tell Randy that she hoped he would get over his displacement of feelings about his ex-wife and get to like Maria, because she was very important to her.

Months after Randy left, Peggy realized that he and Maria were having a long-distance relationship. When Peggy found evidence that they were also having sex, she confronted Maria, who had no trouble owning up to it. (When you want someone to know something, you make a point of telling one way or another.) Maria told Peggy that she had never forgiven her for being forced to make a choice between her and Zeus. She now even seemed gleeful in revealing that she had taken some of the money Peggy had given her for tuition and used it to pay off some old debts. Maria plunged the knife in a little deeper when she said that the therapy Peggy had paid for had made her aware of her resentment about the dog, and she was just waiting for her moment of revenge. (Before you blame me, I told Maria in therapy that becoming aware of a feeling was not a good reason to act it out.)

In a fit of rage, Peggy shot Maria with her father's game rifle, wounding her slightly. Maria collapsed in terror, and Peggy fled, believing that she had hurt Maria quite seriously. Despite her terror, Maria had the presence of mind to telephone and warn me that she believed Peggy was either going to confront me or else head north to Montreal after Randy. (I told you we repeat old soap operas, didn't I?) Luckily for Peggy—and perhaps me as well—she had a flat tire. The time she spent stranded on the road was enough to cool her down a little and bring her back to reality.

Maria had been questioning her sexual orientation in therapy, and now she understood that her choice of lovers had to do with her fear that competing with her jealous, vengeful mother for the love of a man was tantamount to death. As she worked through these issues in therapy, Maria had left Peggy out of the equation. Her own narcissism got in the way of understanding how she had discarded Peggy and other people in the same way her parents had devalued and discarded each other.

Peggy brought her own piece of personal history to the relationship. In the tradition of her culture, the men in the family were considered more important, and Peggy's mother had always made sure her husband came before the kids. On the flip side, her father had always had affairs and made sure his wife knew about them. Her mother loved her father but felt trapped; she could not bear to stay in her situation, nor could she leave her husband. For her, the solution was alcohol. Peggy could rarely remember a time her mother was not drunk.

Psychologically, Peggy unconsciously identified with the men in her family. For Peggy, relationships were about power and competition. The women led lives of weakness and subservience, so in choosing a relationship with another woman, Peggy could identify with power and feel herself to be powerful in the relationship. Providing financial support was another way to reinforce her powerful position.

However, in her relationship with Maria, Peggy was left thinking that the males still came before her. Zeus symbolically represented her father and all the other men in her family who had priority over her. But even with Zeus gone, Peggy still got the short end of the stick. When Randy appeared on the scene, he betrayed his friendship with Peggy, and he and Maria left her with nothing.

In their relationship, Maria became her vindictive mother, wanting revenge for having to give up Zeus. Symbolically, Maria came to realize that Zeus represented her grandmother, the only constant figure in her childhood. Zeus was also the only male she felt she could trust and love. When she felt pressed to give up Zeus, she was symbolically surrendering the only constant source of nurturing in her life, other than her grandmother. Just as her mother sought revenge on her father by taking lovers, Maria entered into an affair with Randy. And she waited for an even better way to take revenge.

Although the events that occurred in this relationship made it impossible to save, both Peggy and Maria walked away much wiser about their psychological issues and the unfinished business from their pasts. Zeus and Fatima played big roles in this complex drama. Peggy was displacing her childhood belief that only men were important. She did not think Fatima was important to Maria, who did not seem very upset whenever Zeus would chase the cat. Once again, for

Peggy, the male was getting away with murder; all her projections about men were now being directed onto Zeus.

Maria displaced her feeling of having been discarded by her parents onto Zeus. Like her grandmother, he, too, would remain faithful and not betray her. However, Maria, like her mother, finally chose her career over Zeus, Maria's symbolic child.

So much is laid on animals that does not belong on them! People drop the parts of themselves that they do not want to look at onto their animals. People exclude parts of who they are in relationships with other people, but they include all those parts with their animals. People unconsciously use animals to re-enact old dramas and soap operas. And all this time, the animals are just being themselves. The key to resolving these problems is to take these issues out of the people/pet relationships and bring them back to people/people relationships, where they can be resolved.

Part IV

Unburdening Your Pet and Yourself

If the Pet's Not the Problem, What Is the Solution?

Chapter 19

Influences from the Past

So far, we've looked at three basic concepts in psychology: displacement, projection, and repetition compulsion. These are all related as forms of *transference*, or imbuing other persons, our pets, inanimate objects with characteristics of people from our past, or even part of ourselves. We've also seen how these transferences can express themselves through a variety of emotions, such as anger and jealousy.

These defensive mechanisms can raise hell with our current relationships. They keep us stuck in earlier chapters of our life as we try to rewrite their original outcome. Sometimes it is just a matter of trying to tack on happy endings, or it may be a question of trying to stay connected to our family members, even if they are long dead. Sometimes things get even more difficult—mastering the traumas of childhood and adolescence is very tough for most people. The difficulty about trying to master a trauma, particularly on your own, is that you usually traumatize yourself all over again in the process, sometimes without recognizing what you are doing.

Defenses that worked for us as kids—and that probably helped us survive childhood—no longer do the job as effectively as they once did. Still, our unconscious defenses keep operating to connect us with people and situations that encourage our search for happy endings.

The end result is that we cheat ourselves out of real awareness, reality, and happiness.

Through a variety of examples of how psychological defenses keep people stuck in the past, we have seen that there is always some interplay between the past and the present. There is also always interplay between the unconscious and the conscious, and between what we believe to be real and reality itself. Finally, there is an interplay among the displacements, projections, and repetition compulsions and everything else that makes us human. These complex, subtle interactions are what keep us from living fully in the present.

TRIANGLES AND MESSAGES

The pets in our lives—ours and other peoples'—are most often just being the animals they are. They may have quirks and behavior problems or special personality features, but those characteristics are all part of their species' makeup. Anything else we attribute to them is a result of our personal displacements, projections, and the need to include them in our dramas and old soap operas.

Why do we do this? Psychologists call it *triangulation*. Very simply, a triangle forms when one of the parties in a relationship brings in a third party as a catalyst to allow a drama to unfold. Movies and operas are mostly about triangles with love, intrigue, and power. One might even say that triangles and the repetition compulsions behind them are what really make the world go round.

Anyone who has seen a little girl fawning over her father while ignoring her mother has seen the beginnings of triangulation. Every child at least partially solves the triangles of childhood, and the solutions are age-specific. A solution for a four-year-old is not necessarily a workable solution at 24 years old.

When triangles are part of the repetition compulsion, they carry on throughout our lives. How many of us form triangles as a way of gaining energy and control in a threatening emotional situation? Do you search for an ally to aid you in defeating the threatening person?

How many of us have used a pet instead of a person in forming this triangle? Do we use the pet to keep others away or to draw others into helping us? There are as many forms of triangles as there are types of relationships.

IS ANYONE LISTENING?

Sometimes you listen to someone talking and start to feel irritated or hurt or frustrated for no obvious reason. The person is not saying anything that should make you feel that way, yet here you are experiencing unexplainable feelings that do not seem to make sense.

Two levels exist for any message: One is the *content* of the message, which is the words actually being said; the other is the *intent* or purpose of the message, which is what the speaker intends it to convey. For example, one woman might tell another, "My, you look nice today." The *content* sounds like a pleasant compliment, but the *intent* of the message may be more like, "You could not be more out of style than if you dropped in from another century."

So, content may not always be the same as intent. To make things more confusing, content can be misinterpreted, as can intent. What someone says may not be what he or she means, and what you think that person means also may not be what he or she means.

CAN WE CHANGE?

If you are reading this book with the intention of changing someone else, forget it now. No one has ever changed anyone but him- or herself as a result of reading a book. If you thought this book would arm you with the information you need to prove to someone else that whatever the problem is, it's not your fault, forget that, too. Psychology is not about fault and blame: It's about understanding how little power we had as kids and how we developed defenses to help us believe we were more powerful than we felt—hearken back to those childhood games we played in which the heroes were so clearly powerful and right, and the villains were obviously not. It is about reconnecting to the feelings of childhood that were so unbearable because our defenses, thought processes, and emotional systems were not fully developed and were not operating at adult capacity.

When we were kids, we truly believed we would die if we were rejected or felt disappointed. As adults, we usually find out that is not the case. But fear of rejection is still a powerful motivator, even when the rejection comes from a stranger. It is amazing how many single adults will not attend any singles events or strike up a conversation with someone they would like to know because they fear rejection and disappointment. The fear of feelings that were overwhelming in childhood continue to keep many people from having the life they wish for.

There is a twofold purpose to understanding your individual defenses. One is to be able to identify the defenses that have gone beyond simply defending you and that are instead causing you pain and problems. A good example is when you dig in your heels and become spiteful or stubborn. That probably helped you to get through some pretty tough situations as a kid. As an adult, though, these same reactions hardly ever get you what you want or need, and leave you feeling lonely and often unable to pick up the pieces after a dispute.

Second, you need to see how many of your reactions are connected to dramas and old stories left over from childhood. How many times do you respond in your adult life the same way you did in your childhood family?

But even this is not enough. Unless you can get a real handle on these behavior patterns and their effects on your current relationships, understanding may amount to little more than the frame for a pretty picture. The missing part of the picture is the role you, your significant other, and your pet play, and the roles all of you have been unconsciously (or even consciously) assigning to one another. Doing the work of solving the puzzle can lead to more fulfilling relationships with the pets and the people in your life.

What brings the old defenses and re-enactments to the forefront? Well, certainly any situation producing feelings that you felt keenly in childhood can unconsciously trigger old reactions. When normal

childhood feelings were not permitted to be experienced, for whatever reason, they will eventually become disconnected from conscious
emotional experience and move into the unconscious, waiting to
emerge in the guise of some other emotion or defense. The old
defenses and patterns return to interfere with us most often when we
feel rejected, disappointed, unloved, or not in control. As adults, we
have the freedom to express our feelings in words without acting
them out. However, if we never learned how to express our feelings,
we may still be responding to situations the same way we did as kids.
It's almost as if the old patterns have lives of their own and want to
survive within us, even if it means killing us off in the process.

THE MYTH OF THE PERFECT FAMILY

After years of practicing psychotherapy, I have come to the conclusion
that there is no such thing as a family without problems. Just think
about it for a moment: When two people get together, each brings a
distinct view of the world from a different family; each may or may not
be in similar positions in his or her family's hierarchy; each comes from
families with a unique repertoire of defense reactions and soap operas.

At best, two people coming together will have explored their personal issues and are at least aware of them when they deal with each
other and with the world at large. This is the best possible scenario for
a good relationship, with or without pets or kids.

It is amazing how many people come into therapy talking about
unhappiness and even depression, yet they describe "ideal" childhoods
full of fun and pleasure. I eventually have to ask, "You had a great
childhood, and what happened? What went wrong, and when?" We all
need to idealize our childhoods to some extent. Certainly, everyone
wants a Brady Bunch family, but then the bubble bursts and we learn
that this exists only on the screen.

Defenses against this reality often appear to be operating on
the person's conscious level, but that is a distraction; the heart of
the defense lies always in the unconscious. We are sometimes able to

recognize the superficial aspects of the problem and mechanically set about counteracting them. Sometimes we even use the right words to describe the problem without really understanding their deeper meaning. We may desperately want to avoid repeating an aspect of a parent's life, so we transform our life into something quite the opposite. Put another way, acknowledging the existence of a psychological defense can, in itself, be a defense against experiencing the emotional content underneath the defense mechanism. Whew!

One patient of mine described a wonderful childhood, and in his telling it really sounded great. Leland's parents truly had both liked and loved each other. Dad had a steady job, and Mom stayed home with the five kids. But when Leland was 16 and his mother was pregnant with her sixth child, his father died suddenly. Leland's life changed dramatically.

Suddenly he became the acting father, the "man of the house." He had to put his high school social life on hold while he helped his mother take care of the other kids. The family faced limited finances and had received meager Social Security payments. The money from his father's insurance policy barely got the family through the first year. They went from being relatively comfortable to being poor. Christmas consisted of hand-me-downs from friends and relatives. Being the oldest, Leland found himself spending a lot of time caring for Brian, the new infant.

This experience had a powerful effect on him. Leland decided that he would never marry and that he did not want kids. He moved to New York and became an aspiring playwright. By day he was a paralegal, and he spent his nights writing and meeting friends for dinner and drinks. Leland also took writing classes, where he met Claire-Marie. They grew close, but Leland would not make a commitment to anything beyond caring for Claire-Marie's cats and birds when she visited her ailing father.

Leland's decision to avoid commitment was a conscious one, but it had the unintended effect of breaking his repetition compulsion. He said he feared dying at an early age like his father and had decided not to marry or have children—as if this decision would prolong his life! When Leland was 38—the same age his father had been when he died—he spoke often of his fears. "I feel too young to die, because there is so much I want to do. Yet my real sense of my life is one of having been burdened with the role of a parent at an early age. I am aware of my resentment now, but it still does not get me over the hump to go on with my life. Perhaps if I live through this year, things will change for me."

Leland did live through the year, and he finally dealt with the loss of his adolescence and the unfair demands of early family responsibilities. He wrote a fictionalized account of his experiences, and that story made him a successful writer. He also realized that caring for cats and birds was not such an odious task as an adult as caring for children had been as a teenager. He and Claire-Marie now are thinking about taking their relationship to a more serious level.

On some level, pet ownership and people-pet relationships are often stepping stones to intimate human relationships. Having a pet may be a kind of a dress rehearsal for the responsibilities of parenting, for instance. I believe that in receiving different forms of unconditional love from pets, people learn to be more patient and trusting in their personal relationships. In addition to the T-shirts that say things like, "I trust my cat more than I trust humans" (you can plug in dog, horse, hamster, piranha, or whatever), there should also be T-shirts that say, "My cat (or dog, horse, hamster, or piranha) taught me to trust people."

WHEN CHILDHOOD MEETS ADULTHOOD

So what do we bring from our childhood family to our personal relationships? We bring a combination of positive and negative baggage holding our displacements, projections, repetition compulsions, and other defenses. It all has to be sorted out, selecting what to keep and what should be jettisoned.

Almost any influence you can think of will affect a person's development. Influences start before birth with sensations of your mother's moods, as well as her health. Excitement, joy, sadness, and so on all make themselves known to the prenatal infant. Even mom's choice in music is sensed.

Early on, we identify with our parents; they become the model of how a person operates in the world. In childhood, we accept our parents as whole beings, all-knowing and perfect in our idealization of them. As we mature and develop, we begin to realize that they are not perfect and that we can, in fact, pick those qualities we wish to hold on to and discard the rest without harming the real-world relationship we have with them.

So, to be ridiculous, if your mother was a serial killer, you may not want to remember her for that aspect of her personality, but you may still admire her fortitude to climb water towers and her ability to get in touch with her anger. If she was kind to children and had a good sense of style, you might want to keep that part as well. She does not necessarily have to know that you disapprove of her murderous tendencies. And so it is with friends and acquaintances. We may enjoy one person's company and friendship yet be particularly irritated by his tendency to be a little cheap.

The childhood influences that give rise to displacement, projection, and the repetition compulsion originate during the very early growth stages, from birth to possibly the early teens. A valuable perspective regarding early adolescence, which is noted for its turmoil, can be gained by considering just how many of the issues facing teens are really new editions of earlier childhood issues. It is during adolescence that the first dramas and soap operas from earlier unresolved conflicts start to play out.

For example, developing sexuality begins in early infancy as we learn to touch our genitalia to comfort ourselves when mother does not instantly appear. The self-touching and the touching that accompanies diaper changes evolves into masturbation in late childhood or early adolescence, and flowers into full sexuality by late adolescence and young adulthood. Accompanying sexual development are the early issues of little boys secretly loving their mothers while little girls move from having their mothers as the primary person in their lives to secretly (or not so secretly) adoring their fathers.

All of these "triangles" unconsciously submerge (become repressed) around the age of seven years, so that learning can effectively take place. By the time kids are in their early teens, the same early-sex issues arise at a point not too far away from where they were left in early childhood. The difference now is that they are displaced and projected onto adolescent romances. These displacements and projections are part of the new editions of earlier issues. Later editions of the same issues will appear in adult relationships in the form of repetition compulsions as well as in displacements and projections.

The psychological self is not just about displacement, projections, and repetition compulsions. Many other mechanisms come into play. Where do fault and blame, sibling rivalry, meanness, verbal abuse, double messages, control, stubbornness, spite, triangulating, and that all-time favorite—denial—come from? The fact is, the triggers are so numerous and complicated that it is impossible to generalize about their origins. Nevertheless, these mechanisms have important effects on our relationships.

Bear in mind, too, that all people are manipulative and controlling, if only on an unconscious level. Also bear in mind that manipulation is not necessarily negative. Strictly speaking, manipulation comes about when we feel powerless, when we are not in control of our lives. Contrary to appearance, manipulation is not so much a desire to control other peoples' lives as it is a need not to be controlled by others. Remember, when you are being manipulative, the other person's unconscious picks it up even if that person is not consciously aware of what is going on. Depending on how devious and how sophisticated your family members were in manipulating and controlling each other, you have come into adulthood with lessons well learned about how to manipulate others.

UNCOVERING YOUR OWN PAST

If you have a problem in your relationship that centers on a pet, by now it should be obvious that the pet is probably not the problem. With the exception of real behavioral problems, pets are just being animals. But when we pull pets into our relationships by engulfing them in our psychological defenses and power plays, we turn them into porters destined to carry our emotional baggage.

If your relationships continually derail or seem never to leave the station, it is time to look within yourself, not your pet. Here are some questions that may help shed some light on your situation:

- What were the realities of your childhood?

    Did you feel you were a wanted child, or an accident?

    Did your parents marry for love or out of necessity?

    Were you adopted or a foster child?

    Were you a lost middle child?

    Were you forced to be the responsible oldest child?

    Were you the baby of the family, not to be taken seriously or not allowed to grow up and separate from your parents?

    Was early independence forced on you, or were you coddled and not allowed to emotionally separate from your parents?

- What was your parents' relationship like?

    Were they warm and tender with each other?

    Were they emotionally involved with each other?

    Were they optimists, pessimists, or a mix of each?

    Did they talk about feelings?

    Were they curious about each other's experiences?

    Did they argue all the time?

    Did they never argue?

Did the family spend much time together, emotionally as well as physically?

Were family members excessively dependent upon one another?

- Would you like a relationship like the one your parents had?

  If the answer is yes, is it because you really enjoyed their connections with each other and with you, or do you idealize your parents' marriage and your own childhood?

- Did your parents stay together although you hoped they would separate?

- Did your parents separate or divorce?

  How did it affect you?

  With whom did you live?

  How did each parent handle the breakup?

  How did they regard each other afterward?

- Did a parent die during your childhood?

  How did that affect you?

- Did any illnesses or hospital stays separate you from your parents and family?

These are some key events that can shape a person's early childhood experiences. But, as you can imagine, the list of possible childhood influences is endless, which accounts for much of our individuality. And it is a continuum; the influences change over time, and so does your development.

WHY GIVE UP OUR DEFENSE MECHANISM?

If displacement, projection, and the repetition compulsion are such valuable defenses against emotional pain, why does therapy urge us to give them up? Don't these defenses give us comfort and protection against those unconscious assaults from an earlier time? Wouldn't it make sense to hold onto them? Do we *really* want to give them up when we seem to expend so much effort maintaining them?

We hold onto those defenses because they are comfortable, because they feel familiar. At some point, though, we need to recognize that we are in an emotional rut; those defenses are not giving the relief we need. Until that happens, we unconsciously keep turning to them over and over again.

Giving up defense mechanisms takes work. It means taking a chance on the future. It means consciously recognizing these mechanisms for what they are and stopping ourselves before they go into operation. Once you have consciously recognized a defense that no longer serves you and decide that a better one is needed, you are well on your way to surrendering it; your unconscious begins replacing it with a more effective one.

Displacements are fairly easy to accept once they have been brought to the conscious level. They are recognizable and detectable. Displacements can be verbalized instead of being acted out. For example, saying, "You remind me of my Aunt Sylvia, who always fed us tuna fish sandwiches instead of a nice dinner at Christmas," is very different than going into a rage if someone serves you a tuna melt.

Projections are considerably more difficult to resolve because it means accepting all those thoughts and feelings that are difficult to acknowledge within ourselves, such as mean-spiritedness, revenge, envy, jealousy, hate, and violence, just for openers. Few people are willing to admit that they have such unacceptable feelings and thoughts.

The **repetition compulsion** is something else. At first glance, it would seem that no one would want to give it up. To the extent that it is familiar, no matter what problems it causes, no matter how good or bad the feelings are, no matter what the consequences are, the repetition compulsion is comfortable. However, when you keep winding up with the same old unhappy ending, you begin to realize that the old defenses and the old roles you find yourself replaying do not leave you with what you want.

The repetition compulsion, in particular, is a bit insidious because it always carries with it a feeling of excitement, a buzz of energy. If you have devoted a large part of your life to your repetition compulsion, what could you possibly replace it with that would feel as exciting and at the same time would defend you against the harshness of a childhood reality?

So a conflict emerges: Do you hold on to your repetition compulsion and its fruitless search for the happy ending, or do you gamble on being able to get what you really want and need as an adult? Many people are so tied to the protection of their repetition compulsion that they go to extremes to protect it. They often leave therapy when they learn about their repetition compulsion, claiming it is a hopeless cause to try to change it. For many people the energy and excitement of their life is wrapped around their repetition compulsion. For them, life without it would be flat and boring—and perhaps even depressing. (I have found that for some people, a repetition compulsion is specifically a defense against a deep childhood depression.)

The decision to give up a defense is always yours to make. Therapy does not demand that you change—it asks only that you look and examine. Whenever we are stuck in the past, it is because we are holding on to defenses from former chapters of our lives, chapters that keep us from maturing as complete persons. Unless we somehow modify our defenses, some emotional parts of us will never keep up with the changes that go along with maturity.

Chapter 20

Jealousy, the Complex Emotion

··

Jealousy is far from a simple emotion. It includes elements of fear, happiness, grief, sorrow, and rage, and it can be very painful. We all experience jealousy at various times in our lives and in some of our relationships, but for most of us it does not become a serious issue. We recognize it, master it, and get on with whatever we are doing. For some people, however, jealousy becomes a preoccupation that takes over a large portion of their lives. It can be an intense emotion! When jealousy involves a pet, it can be just as devastating to a relationship as when another person is involved.

One of the more dramatic cases of jealousy I've encountered in my practice involved Gary and Cynthia. No one in their crowd was surprised when Gary shot Cynthia—they only wondered whether he intended to kill her or just to frighten her into paying more attention to him. One thing was for sure: He had long accused her of being more interested in horses than in him. Over their 12 years of marriage, their relationship had become increasingly strained because of Gary's jealousy.

The couple had always loved horses and enjoyed their free time together riding Western-style at various ranches. Cynthia's expertise had developed to the point that her riding friends came to her for advice. Her friend Rene, who was part of the English-saddle set, asked for her help in rehabilitating a horse that had a back injury. Cynthia paid a lot of attention to the horse.

At the same time, Cynthia and Gary were very involved with their own horses, but not with each other. Cynthia loved Sultan, her gelding, and Gary loved his mare, Betina, but they were not doing well as a couple. The horses had become a diversion from the problems of the marriage, which was rapidly disintegrating.

Both Cynthia and Gary came from broken families. Both were young when their parents divorced and never were exposed to the love and affection that parents normally show for each other. They grew to adulthood without any exposure to adult love. This is not to say that Gary and Cynthia did not love each other in their own way—they did. They just did not know how to express that love to each other.

Gary showed his caring and love by being jealous. Cynthia accepted his jealousy as an expression of love and often created incidents that she knew would get a jealous reaction from her husband. It seemed that all their physical expressions of love and devotion were reserved for their horses, Sultan and Betina. For both Gary and Cynthia, horses unconsciously became their real mates, the beings they could trust with their true love and affection.

Each also had a compulsion to repeat the history of their parents, and there was an unconscious pull toward separation and divorce that become stronger with each passing year. It is astonishing how often people unconsciously repeat their parents' lives as a defense against the adolescent pain of becoming individuals. It is as if the child is symbolically saying to the parent, "See how much I love you? I will be just like you."

As complicated as it seems, the psychological truth was that beneath the facade of caring for the animals, both could not endure the unconscious guilt associated with the feeling that they trusted their animals more than they did each other. Each defended against and covered over guilty feelings differently: Cynthia by trying to get more distance from Gary, and he by having excessively jealous reactions. The final blow to their relationship, and the one that brought them into therapy, came when Cynthia announced that she was no longer interested in riding Western-style and now preferred to ride with a group devoted to riding English, a completely different group of people and activities. In effect, she told Gary that she no longer preferred his company. His jealousy was ignited.

Cynthia seemed somewhat taken aback when I asked how old her parents were when they divorced. She raised her eyebrows in surprise and said, "Oh my God! I am the same age my mother was: 33." Gary, concerned only with his own feelings of jealousy, did not see the connection. But Cynthia certainly did. The unconscious keeps track of time in uncanny ways, always remembering numbers, dates, and anniversaries.

Let's take a moment to take stock of what had been going on in Gary and Cynthia's life. Cynthia had given up her job as an office manager and was now going to the stables every day. According to Gary, she was hardly at home at all. She either was down at the stable grooming Sultan or else was riding him. Cynthia also spent almost every weekend at shows and auctions. When she started riding English saddle, she traveled with a new crowd—in many ways a much more socially and culturally sophisticated crowd than the couples' old Western-riding colleagues.

Gary was jealous and told her so. He was angry at her being away so much. She told him he was welcome to join her, knowing that he could not see himself as part of the English crowd. Gary also blamed some of the problem on Sultan. He felt Sultan was the wrong horse for Cynthia and that she had chosen him merely for his striking good looks. He felt that her attraction to Sultan was almost sexual, and he said so. A horse lives between 15 and 30 years, so Gary realized that things would not change any time soon. He felt that he could not put up with the existing situation much longer.

Pathologically jealous people are driven to irrational acts. One New Year's Day, he drove out to Sultan's stable. For Gary, Sultan was the essential element in his problem with Cynthia and therefore held the key to his shaky marriage. Knowing that Cynthia could never give up her horse, he brought his 22-calibre pistol to Sultan's stable and planned to wound the horse just badly enough so that Cynthia would no longer be able to ride him. As he took aim and squeezed the trigger, Cynthia stepped out from behind Sultan, whom she was grooming.

Gary was devastated to be caught in the act. As he rushed to Cynthia, he tried to explain that he only wanted to wound Sultan so that he could recapture her attention. He begged her forgiveness, but all she had to say was, "You son of a bitch! You tried to kill my horse!"

TOO HOT TO HANDLE

In this relationship, the fatal love triangle consisted of Gary, Cynthia, and the horses. But for these two, jealousy was far from a simple matter. It involved each of their repetition compulsions and became an all-consuming part of their relationship.

The important thing to remember about jealousy is that it can involve the whole gamut of emotional responses: sadism, revenge, masochism—almost any human reaction is possible. Statistics show that about 35 percent of homicides in the United States and approximately 85 percent of spousal abuse cases are related to issues of jealousy and infidelity.

Jealousy may be a part of more than one psychological dynamic. It could be connected to displacement reactions, projections, or a repetition compulsion. While always related to your own history, jealousy can also stand on its own as a reaction to a real-life situation. It is also possible that a lack of any apparent jealousy in an obviously jealousy-inducing situation on the part of an individual can be a defense, possibly related to unacknowledged sibling rivalry or even love itself.

When it comes to emotions, the greater the intensity of the emotion, the greater the obsession with the object of the emotion. With jealousy, the more intense it is, the more likely it is to be masking other kinds of feelings. These may range from fear of loss and abandonment to rage and the wish for revenge. Certainly, Gary could not tolerate the loss of Cynthia and their life together in the Western riding group. Jealousy is often a response to a fear of loss. That loss could be something denied to you or experienced as unattainable, yet something you continue to deeply wish for. As bad as the jealousy may feel, it may not be as bad as facing the underlying fear of humiliation or rejection. For some, the experience may be so intense and deep-seated as to be devastating to any relationship.

Some psychologists argue that jealousy is a part of love. Others regard it as a disguised demand to possess another in both the physical and the emotional sense. (In jealousy, the other person is often regarded as property to be possessed rather than an object of love.) In extreme cases, the desire to possess can be so encompassing that it amounts to demanding total control. And because even that would not satisfy the basic fear of loss or abandonment, it would not be enough—a far cry from love as we understand that emotion.

EIGHT PAWS IN FOREPLAY

Just to get the flavor of how jealousy works, here's a case in point. My Labrador Retriever, Troll, was the catalyst. But first, a little background.

My friend Jody is also a psychologist. She and I participate in a peer study group and have done so for years. Many psychologists use this method of reviewing how they handle their cases to make sure that their own emotional needs are not influencing the way they treat their patients. Understandably, such a group becomes close-knit as the members come to know each other's personal issues and how they affect each other's lives. Of the group, four of us had established a particularly close friendship. Besides Jody and me, this little group included Mary and Rick.

Unfortunately, Jody's husband, Hershel, became quite jealous of the close friendly relationship his wife and I developed through our participation in the peer group. It did not seem to matter to Hershel that the friendships developed in the group were just that: friendships. Nor did it matter to Hershel that I was involved in a much more intimate relationship outside of the group—such is the blindness of jealousy.

At any rate, Troll and I were out walking one evening when I decided to stop by Jody and Hershel's house to borrow a book. At their invitation, I stayed a while for a drink and some pleasant conversation.

During the visit, I noticed that Hershel was becoming increasingly agitated and openly hostile. When I looked around, the cause became obvious. Troll and Molly, their Irish Water Spaniel, were humping. Hershel's temper got the best of him, and he started screaming that my dog was disgusting by trying to rape his dog—and in her own house (he did say that). He ordered us out of his house and told me never to bring "that filthy dog" back. Hershel's parting words were that I should have Troll neutered before I become responsible for "ruining someone's life!"

Quite obviously, Hershel had blown things totally out of proportion. However, this did not seem like a good time to discuss his projection, so we left. Once again, a pet took the brunt of someone's anger, just because he was obeying his natural instincts.

Fortunately for our otherwise good friendship, Hershel is normally a very level-headed person, and his wife was able to help him see that it was really jealousy and not Troll's behavior that was upsetting him. Hershel called the following evening to apologize.

While Hershel's behavior was a clear-cut instance of jealousy, something else was at work: a desire to hurt whomever had caused the jealousy—in other words, revenge. Bear in mind that implicit in jealousy is a sense of denial: The victim believes that he or she has been denied something desperately wanted. It might be something once possessed, or it may be something the person always wanted to have. In either case, the jealous person is frustrated, and the emotional pain can be unbearable. The response is to want to punish whoever or whatever is getting in the way.

In my example, Hershel was not able to hit out at me directly, so he took his hostility out on Troll, whom he knew I adored. Drastic as that may have been, it was nothing compared to what someone in the grips of jealousy is capable of.

In part, jealousy may be influenced by cultural expectations. Hershel had great difficulty accepting the idea that his wife could be closely connected to another man without it involving sex. It works the other way, too. Usually when a man wishes to be emotionally understood, he will turn to a woman for friendship rather than to another man. But women often have jealous reactions if their men have close women friends. It is important for the primary woman in a man's life to understand that men, too, can have woman friends. These relationships can be prime targets for jealous reactions, but they needn't be.

ENTER REVENGE

Revenge is a conscious reaction to a hurt. Revenge can be driven by feelings of jealousy, or it may have a life of its own. In the next story, unfortunately, an animal bore the brunt of an owner's jealousy in a cruel act of revenge. While you are reading, don't be too quick to point the finger of blame. Very rarely are any of the participants in a troubled relationship guiltless; everyone contributes in some way.

The cast in this story includes Tom, Margo, and a prize-winning Standard Poodle named Irving de la Favorie, whom, you might say, brought them together.

When I met them, Tom and Margo had been married 11 years. It was the second marriage for both. They had met at a dog show, where Margo was showing Irving de la Favorie and Tom was looking to buy a dog for his daughter. One thing led to another, and they were married a couple of months later.

The couple moved to a small village in upstate New York, where they built a kennel business around Margo's show dogs, particularly Irving de la Favorie, her much-desired stud. All went well until Tom received an anonymous call from a woman (they never found out who) who claimed that Margo was having an affair with Glenda, their dog groomer. Tom went ballistic. The idea that his wife preferred *anyone* to him, much less another woman, drove him into a fit of jealous rage. On the surface, the problem seemed a simple one: Margo was denying Tom her company and giving it to another. In psychological terms, however, the implications were much deeper. Here's what happened.

Margo admitted that it was true, but she assured Tom repeatedly that her affair with Glenda was only a fling, that she still loved him very much, and that she had no wish to end their marriage. Tom, however, could not forgive her.

The more he thought about that fling, the angrier and more jealous he became. He found himself having revenge fantasies. He became fixed on the idea that if it were not for the dogs, Margo would not have met Glenda. In addition, he saw the dogs as the most important things in his wife's life. Obviously, the best way to get back at Margo was through the Poodles.

Tom's plan for revenge was exquisite in its simplicity: While Margo was attending an out-of-state dog show, Tom had her prize stud Irving de la Favorie neutered. To him, that was certainly poetic punishment for Margo's infidelity. Margo's affair had hit Tom where it hurt the most; he hurt her where he knew she would feel the most pain.

Before going further, let's step back a bit and try to look at this situation. Tom and Margo were in what seemed to be a comfortable and successful marriage. However, for reasons as yet unknown, Margo had become involved in an extramarital affair with a woman.

Now jealousy reared its ugly, destructive head in Tom's life. Not only had his wife shared her affections with another person (in effect, taking something away that he valued dearly), but she had challenged Tom's masculinity by having that affair with a woman. The need for revenge became all-consuming in his life.

Another man might have just buried the pain and gone on. But for Tom, this affront demanded a more drastic response. Simply leaving Margo was not enough for him: Margo had damaged what was dear to him—his trust and masculinity—so he would have to do the same to her.

At this point, we do not know how Tom really felt about the animals, but with the ogre of revenge in control, it would have mattered little. The dogs became the path through which Tom could get back at his wife, and that was all that mattered.

The events so far in this relationship raise many questions. Why did Margo have that affair? Is the fact that it was with a woman related in any way to her marriage to Tom? Why was Tom's reaction so drastic? Is there a message in the fact that he chose to castrate the dog? Is it significant in any way that they chose to live in a remote village? Whose idea was it?

When we met, Tom was so wounded emotionally that he was not sure he could stay in the marriage. Perhaps that is testimony to what may be the most vexing aspect of revenge: It rarely satisfies the desire to punish its object. One of the more immediate needs in this couple's therapy was to help Tom explore whether he wanted to stay married. An essential element here was that he could not trust his wife to remain faithful, even though Margo insisted that her feelings for him had not changed.

Both Tom and Margo had no trouble recognizing that jealousy and its accompanying demand for revenge were behind Tom's actions. I explained to them that jealousy is a very difficult emotion to get to the bottom of and that people who are inclined to jealous rages cannot easily be reasoned with during their episodes. Tom amplified that observation, saying, "You cannot even come close to imagining how terrible it is to be immersed in that moment of jealousy when your entire body is tingling with rage over having been cheated on, betrayed, and abandoned."

That was quite a strong statement from Tom, one that revealed a deep torment. Margo, while still claiming to understand the role of jealousy in Tom's actions, tried to shift the responsibility for her affair to Tom. She explained that she had been complaining to Tom for a long time that he no longer paid any attention to her. They had very few conversations and hardly any sex. Margo said she felt completely taken for granted and saw herself as being one step above a house maid and a kennel keeper. She also complained about Tom's drinking habits. How long, she demanded, did he think the two of them were going to live in an isolated village with no real friends and no family since their children had left?

Hearing this, it is easy to see that Margo, too, was suffering from jealousy. Had Tom not denied her something that she cherished: the fullness of their marriage? Could her affair with Glenda have been revenge for that denial? In her mind, Tom had replaced sex with alcohol.

Tom *was* beginning to drink more and more, as he forced down his own anger about the turn their marriage was taking. Margo spent more and more time on the show circuit as her dogs began to take more shows and move on to their championships. She was away every weekend, showing all over the country, usually accompanied by Glenda. Tom did not enjoy being on the road with her when she was showing her dogs, so he remained home feeding and caring for the remaining dogs, showing potential buyers their stock and responding to telephone inquiries. Margo had not realized the extent to which she had turned Tom into a "kennel boy."

Whatever communication they had in the early days of their relationship, whatever qualities they shared, everything certainly seemed to have broken down. Why and how did this happen? And what about that isolated village life? Was it really so isolated? Whose idea was it, and after living there long enough to raise children and build a business, why were there no friends?

Tom explained their isolation as his way of trying to avoid the jealous fits that plagued him. Being safe in this isolated place, he reasoned, he would not have to deal with the uncontrollable emotions that accompanied his jealousy. Something must have happened before he met Margo to raise that fear in him. His desire for emotional tranquillity also explained why he avoided friendships. But he had never told Margo about his rages.

Tom was reluctant to speak of his history. As it turned out, he had a long history of jealous fits, the most recent of which was with his first wife. Their marriage ended in a jealous rage when he caught her in bed with another man. He had lost all reason and, not even thinking about the fact that he was enraged with a man twice his size, he threw himself at the man and was severely beaten up and hospitalized. Adding to Tom's pain, during the scuffle his wife bit Tom, a wound that he could never forgive or forget.

At the beginning of their relationship, Margo and Tom lived and worked together. Margo was seldom out of his sight, and Tom had little cause for jealousy. In fact, it had been so long since he felt that terrible hurt that he believed such emotions were no longer an issue for him. But then came Margo's affair with Glenda. The jealous rage that had descended over Tom frightened him, to say the least. It also reminded him of his first wife.

Exploring Life's Ups and Downs

As I mentioned earlier, all parties in a relationship contribute something. If there is a problem, all parties play a role. With this in mind, I asked Margo if she also suffered from jealousy. She thought a bit before saying no. But then she added, "I was jealous of my older sisters when I was growing up, but that subsided as I got older and started enjoying the same privileges they had."

With that in the open, I asked Margo how she felt about being the focus of Tom's jealousy. She loved the attention, Margo said, but she went on to emphasize her anger over Tom's abuse of her dog. Margo was not sure if she could forgive his action. She explained that she had spent years developing her breeding line. Irving de la Favorie was her top stud dog, and without him there was little future for the kennel or the reputation she had almost single-handedly built for Tom and herself. Of course, she still had Evita and Madonna, her top-producing bitches, but finding another stud dog of Irving's quality was going to be difficult.

I changed the subject to the symbolism in Tom's projection onto Irving of the feelings he was so afraid of. In plotting his revenge, Tom said he felt impotent in dealing with his jealousy, and castrated in being unable to win Margo from Glenda.

"If that was the case, what kept you from telling Margo about your obviously strong feelings, instead of sending the message via Irving?" I asked. Tom said, "I wanted her to experience some small part of the pain I was feeling. Margo would have dismissed my message. Even now, with Irving castrated, she is still saying that her fling with Glenda was no big deal."

Margo's response? "Why couldn't you just tell me how angry you were? It really scares me that you do not have better control of your emotions. Maybe if I had been around when you found out about Glenda and me, you might have killed me instead of punishing Irving." Tom burst into tears and finally told Margo about the way his first marriage had broken up. At last she understood the disconnectedness that had been an undercurrent in their marriage. Jealousy was part of Tom's repetition compulsion; by trying to isolate himself from it, he had unconsciously pushed Margo to the brink.

Tom was willing to go into individual therapy to work on his problems. Now that Irving was no longer a stud, Margo could not show him. The dog was able to retire to a life of comfort by her side, and she loved him dearly as a companion and a pet. Tom became more attentive to the people around him, and Margo eased up a bit on her show career so that they could spend more time together. In a sense, you might say that Irving brought them back together.

SO WHO IS JEALOUS AND WHO IS NOT?

At the heart of that feeling of loss that we call jealousy is a terrible feeling of inadequacy, a feeling that we are no longer enough and that somehow we have lost the ability to please—and because of that we are being replaced! It always hurts. The question is, why do some people become so consumed with jealousy, while others find it just one of many emotions to be experienced as a normal part of living?

In time, we may learn that there is a gene for jealousy that some of us come into the world with—scientists now believe they have uncovered one for worry. Meanwhile, almost anyone who has siblings has at one time or another felt jealousy as brothers or sisters seem to replace them in their parents' eyes. Most of us get past it. Getting knocked off the throne as a kid can be a terrible experience, but usually it's no more terrible than plenty of other life experiences. For most of us, where there has been a loving family, time is the consummate healer.

I believe some people with serious jealousy problems are driven to act out their feelings because words fail them, or because they are incapable of containing their jealous fantasies. Their earliest experiences of jealousy usually occurred before they had words to describe their emotional experiences. That is, they were very young, and at a stage where they still acted out every feeling.

As we have learned, jealousy is based on the jealous person's belief that he or she has been denied something strongly desired. The key to a solution is finding how the person came to that conclusion. In other words, is jealousy the feeling of being denied based on reality—or is it a creation in the person's mind?

One fear regularly reported by jealous people is that the significant other in their life will become bored or disillusioned with who they are. Often, just getting to the truth of that fear can bring some relief.

It is an awful feeling to believe that you are fraudulently seducing another person into believing that you are very funny, or very deep, or very spiritual, or very sensitive, or very profound and knowledgeable, or very whatever. The way this fantasy usually goes, after you have made the first impact, you begin doubting whether you can keep up whatever the positive trait is. You start to wonder how long it will be before your partner finds out that there are limitations to your "specialness." When that happens, you think, your partner will either drain you of whatever your expertise is and leave you, or will simply leave you. Small wonder that jealousy lives hand-in-hand with anger and revenge!

Consider the effect on a child growing up in a family where other siblings seem to be more valued. The child would constantly hear things like:

> "Jimmy always goes to the store for me without complaining and always gets everything right."
>
> "Helga always gets such good grades and wonderful reports from all her teachers, and I am proud of her."
>
> "Mark can fix anything and is so ingenious in figuring out how to put things together. He is amazing!"
>
> "If there is a way to get into trouble and embarrass me, George will figure out how to do it."

Who might be the most jealous person in this family? Actually, they may all be. Each time someone is praised for some quality, there is a suggestion that the others are somehow lacking. While this is definitely not a guarantee of a future emotional problem, a steady diet of hearing how everyone else in the family is better than you could be. As a psychologist, I say, by all means compliment those who do well, but find something to praise in everyone.

THE LOOK OF LOVE

Here's another example of how seemingly small experiences during childhood can have a lasting affect when constantly repeated:

Mark told me the first thing that attracted him to Arlene, his wife, was her eyes, the way she could focus on him and leave him feeling as if she had entered his very being. He also told me there was nothing about his family dynamics that would explain why he was insanely jealous of Arlene's relationship with her dog, Paloma, a little Papillion. Mark had almost killed two men on different occasions because he had suspected that Arlene was interested in them. She did not even know one of the men that Mark suspected. Mark said it was the way she had looked at the man that set him off.

We worked for a very long time trying to figure out why Mark's jealousy was so violent and so powerful. It was quite by accident that we found out. Mark had gone to see the film *Secrets and Lies,* a story about an adopted black woman in search of her birth mother who finds her, only to discover that the woman is white. At first the mother denies their connection but then remembers her one and only experience with a black man. There is a moment where the mother realizes that this lovely woman is indeed her daughter whom she gave up, sight unseen, at birth. She turns to give her daughter a look of love that fills the screen.

Mark recalled that the mother's look in the film was the same look his mother always gave to his baby brother, but never to him. He had buried his jealousy and rage all these years. When Mark made the connection, he had a big *ah-hah* experience. In fact, we both cried together at the childhood loss of his mother to his brother. The depth of his sadness was overwhelming.

Mark said his mother's gaze had affected his entire life. He feared getting into relationships, lest he again lose the gaze of his beloved. He said the first thing that always attracted him to a woman was her eyes. He never took his eyes off people when he was talking with them. It was her look that had originally brought Arlene into Mark's focus. Mark was jealous when Arlene gave Paloma the same wonderful gaze he wished was reserved for only him.

It took a while, but Mark finally understood that, unlike his mother, a person can love more than one being without denying anyone. He understood that Arlene could have the same look for Paloma and for other people, including him. It did not have to be reserved solely for one.

SADISM AND MAYBE SOME REVENGE

Being able to consciously fantasize and verbalize what you would like to do to the competition is very helpful in working through the more violent feelings of jealousy. Believe it or not, no matter how bad an artist you think you are, finger-painting is a great, safe way to express a lot of the blood and gore you might like to shed.

Often an element of sadism is connected to jealousy. Sadism is a complicated mechanism because it operates on many levels of consciousness. It is generally regarded as a projection of one's own suffering and hurt onto another person or pet. I believe sadistic impulses can be a reaction to loss or a response to trauma and abuse. In fact, sadism can be an element in all kinds of psychological stuff.

As a case in point, meet Frank. After his third date with Liz, he knew he wanted her to be his wife. The trouble was, he saw her Sealyham Terrier, Fritzy, as competition. Frank decided to do something about it—immediately. Liz lived in a condominium on the 18th floor. The windows run nearly from floor to ceiling and swing out from the window frame, much like doors. While Liz was getting ready for their date, Frank picked up one of Fritzy's favorite toys and threw it a couple of times for the dog to retrieve. Frank's last throw of the little white Snoopy doll was out the window, and after Snoopy went Fritzy.

When Liz came out, Frank told her what had happened and how awful he felt. Frank was a sadist *par excellence* who could be exceptionally charming, intelligent, and seductive. Because Liz had no reason to believe that Frank had an ulterior motive—and after all, *it was an accident*—she forgave him.

You may think Liz was letting Frank off too easy, but you have to understand that while growing up, she had watched her father's drunken rages. He frequently threw her mother around the living room, and on two occasions he knocked her down the stairs. Her ability to use denial ("This bad behavior never happened") was profound.

Here's another example. When Nelson was 13 years old, his father sat on his parakeet and crushed it. It really *was* an accident, but Nelson, an only child, never forgave his father. He had loved the bird, who was almost as old as he was.

When Nelson was in his 50s and his father was dying in a hospital, Nelson found a moment when there was no one else in the hospital room. He pulled the plug on his father's respirator. The wish for revenge had remained with him for nearly 40 years.

CRAZY JEALOUS

I have always been amazed at how little psychotherapists know about how to alleviate the anguish of jealousy. Once started, jealousy takes deep root and is difficult to tear out. I know that I cannot reason with someone at the height of a jealous episode. If I discuss the jealous incident and reaction after the fact, I am met with a lot of agreement. The jealous person agrees that I am making perfect sense. The person can repeat verbatim every word I said on the subject. But it soon becomes apparent that whatever I am saying in moments of calm is of no use to the person when the jealousy button is reactivated. In those moments, that person is crazy-jealous and remembers nothing I have said. At best, I can teach some coping skills that hopefully will be of some value in preventing physical outbursts next time.

While it is difficult to work directly with the feeling of jealousy, it is possible to deal with the way those jealous feelings are expressed. I have found that the best way to work with someone engaged in destructive jealous behavior is to focus on the people involved in the situation.

It is important to help the jealous person separate fact from suspicion and fantasy. An astonishing number of jealous beliefs are based only on assumptions. Just the process of slowing the jealous person and asking him or her to think about what is fact and what is only suspicion is very helpful. Being able to make that distinction means the person is able to focus enough to recognize how far he or she has gone.

Jealous people are always suspicious in ways that leave them feeling miserable. So many of the excessively jealous people I have worked with are always going through a loved one's wallet or purse, a desk drawer, an underwear drawer, or the car's glove compartment. They are always alert to offense (real or otherwise) and always in emotional pain. Suggesting that the person just ask or confront the object of suspicion usually gets a short, "Why bother, how can I believe the answer?" Imagine the pain of never being able to trust those you love!

WHEN YOU CAN'T TRUST THE EVIDENCE

The workings of jealousy can be devious, indeed. Sonya was convinced that Sam was having an affair with her best friend, Maureen, who lived a few blocks away. She believed their dog, Tootsie, was the instrument of Sam's fidelity, and she began to think that Sam and the dog came back from their evening walk smelling of Maureen's favorite perfume.

Sonya went through Sam's wallet almost nightly, and through the pockets of whatever he wore that day, without ever finding evidence of an affair. Her search through Sam's clothes closet, his workroom, and his car was equally unrewarding. But her suspicion remained just as strong.

Luncheons with Maureen were just as frustrating because they turned up nothing. Maureen was warm and friendly and invited Sonya and Sam to dinner with her and Norman, her husband. Nowhere could Sonya find any support for her suspicions. And she successfully hid her torment from Sam.

Like so many jealous women, Sonya also blamed herself. She truly believed that if she had done something differently, she would have been able to get more attention from Sam. She considered having breast reduction surgery and a nose job, and the cellulite in her thighs removed, too, but she never pursued it. She also blamed herself for not joining a gym with Sam when he asked her to.

Norman and Maureen did join the gym. Strangely enough, Sonya was not concerned about that possibility of a rendezvous between Sam and Maureen at the gym. She knew that Maureen went in the afternoon, and Sam went first thing in the morning.

But that did not diminish Sonya's jealousy. The questions and the suspicions continued, still unverbalized. One of the things about the emotional problems besetting us is that there is usually a recreational quality attached to them. In essence, Sonya got some unconscious pleasure from the amount of time she spent each day running through her jealous thoughts and explaining to herself why she really had no reason to worry. As the worry seemed to develop a life of its own, it was possible to see the connections to Sonya's repetition compulsion. I see jealousy as a form of obsessing—that is, continually repeating jealous thoughts, regardless of their justification.

Sonya ultimately became so crazed with jealousy that she believed if there was no dog in their lives, Sam would have no excuse for going out in the evenings. And she acted on that belief. One day she removed the dog's I.D. tags and drove Tootsie to a shelter a few towns away. She told the folks there that she had found the dog along the road and left it with the shelter people. When Sam came home in the evening she put on an excellent act, crying as she told Sam that Tootsie was missing. She said she had reported their loss to the shelters throughout the county, but so far there were no replies.

She hardly anticipated Sam's reaction. Instead of sharing her apparent distress, he told her he was tired of her crazy and her groundless suspicions, her searching his drawers and possessions for evidence of what existed only in her mind. He said there was no one else in his life, but she had made their life together impossible. When Sonya finally acknowledged what she had done with Tootsie, he told his wife that he felt there was nothing left to their marriage, and he wanted a divorce.

Constructed Reality

Sam rescued Tootsie and did indeed divorce Sonya. As Sam and Sonya (and Tootsie) learned only too well, jealousy exists whether it is based on reality or a fantasy.

In jealousy, we often alter realities or construct new ones about what we believe others are thinking and feeling about us. Even if what we believe is true but has not been confirmed, it is still a constructed reality. Whenever we do not examine our suspicions, we remain in a constructed reality. There is no real benefit to being suspicious unless you try to confirm those suspicions. If you do not, then you are just acting paranoid.

A WOMAN SCORNED

In jealousy, the need to prevent something or someone from being taken away is very powerful. When Dirk threatened to break up with Theodora, all she could think about was that he had found another woman. She never considered the possibility that she, herself, might have been the reason.

A former model and talented architect, Theodora might have been every man's dream but for one flaw: She was capable of jealous rages that turned her into an ugly shrew, quite different from her outward appearance. And her jealousy was not limited to relationships with other people. She could not tolerate anyone around her achieving any kind of distinction; it always led to a tantrum. Dirk, however, never had to deal with her venom directly.

To all outward appearances, Theodora was a clinging vine with Dirk. No matter where he went, she wanted to know who he met and what they talked about. It didn't stop there, though. When Dirk adopted a dog, a pedigree-challenged bitch he named Shoshana, Theodora saw the dog as competition for Dirk's affections. Shoshana seemed to be everywhere Dirk was, and she never let him out of her sight. Theodora was convinced that Dirk had adopted Shoshana to offend her. Her jealousy of the dog got to a point that their friends said that if Dirk had brought another woman home, it could not have been worse in Theodora's mind than having Shoshana around.

On the surface, Dirk was attractive in a rugged way, with an almost European manner about him. He was suave, sensuous, and extremely gregarious. Beneath the surface, though, he carried tremendous guilt over the loss of his sister, Tamar, who was killed by a bus. A few hours after the accident she was brain-dead, and the family had had to make the terrible decision to disconnect her life support. Dirk had always felt that if he had spent more time with

Tamar, she would have learned to be more careful and might not have died.

Such is the irrationality of guilt. In this case, Dirk suffered what is called *survivor's guilt*. As with survivors of any trauma, there is guilt at having survived while others have perished.

Theodora's revenge, which grew out of her jealousy, turned out to be vicious and just as irrational as her suspicions. Dirk was an Israeli who had come to the United States on a student visa but never returned home after completing his education. He was an illegal immigrant without a green card, but like so many others, he had somehow managed to get lost in the crowd. Because he was intelligent and articulate and had mastered the English language with only the slightest trace of an accent, no one ever questioned his origins. Everyone assumed he was an American citizen who had emigrated from Israel a long time ago.

Of course, having lived with Dirk and Shoshana for a number of years, Theodora knew the truth. Periodically, she threatened to turn him in to the Immigration and Naturalization Service if he tried to leave her. Her threats started as a kind of joke but soon became quite serious. When Dirk did indeed decide to leave, she reported him to the INS. And all this because Dirk had wanted a dog!

Gender Reactions to Jealousy

Psychological research indicates that the jealousy reactions of men and women are different. Women trying to deal with their jealousy often (but not always) blame themselves for failing to hold on to their man. In attempting to deal with their jealous reactions, women are more likely to try to hold on to their partner by using guilt and tears. Studies also indicate that women are more upset if the man is infatuated with another woman than if the man is just having sex with another woman.

Men, on the other hand, rarely see themselves as responsible for their jealousy, often react to real or suspected infidelities with rage and violence, and are more physical in actively pursuing the one they think is the "other" person (or pet). Put another way, my friend Connie says that a woman wants to be the last with her man, while men want to be the first with their women.

Many psychologists believe that jealousy is almost invariably an accompaniment of love. Having some jealousy in a love relationship can be healthy, the theory goes, because it forces you to examine your love for the other person. Some element of jealousy is needed as an expression of the other person's value. Without it, these psychologists say, the other person may as well be interchangeable with anyone else. In addition, it often takes jealousy to make us aware that we, in fact, do not own the other person. But when the jealousy begins to incorporate possessiveness, control, and physical or emotional harm, that is a different matter. This is definitely not healthy, and it can have serious consequences for all involved.

DEALING WITH A JEALOUS PERSON

If someone you care about seems jealous of your relationship with your pet, it's important to focus on making that person recognize that there are different kinds of love relationships. Explain that a person may love more than one person without denying or limiting another. Thus, we love our children without denying love to our parents or our mate. The way we love a helpless infant is different from the way we love an adolescent, in terms of expressing both verbal love and physical affection. Similarly, loving a pet does not in any way take anything from a human relationship, nor does it suggest in any way some strange or unnatural relationship with the animal.

As my friend Alan says, "Love is love." There are many ways of expressing it, depending on whether you are speaking of your mate, child, pet, or parent. But the love itself involves the same emotions of warmth, passion, trust—the list is long. Feelings such as passion, desire, and sex seem to confuse the issue. Yes, they are part of what we call love, but they can also exist without love—anyone remember those teenage hormonal surges?

Friendship can grow to become entwined with love, or it can remain a close bond. And for the jealous person, a sense of wanting to be number one is often confused with love.

One helpful hint in dealing with jealous people is to look for facts to substantiate their accusations—or to demonstrate that there are no facts. Jealous people tend to engage in recreational obsessing. Psychologists agree that obsessing is a way of not having to get to more difficult feelings regarding the subject of the obsession. I further believe that, in a strange way, while obsessives complain of the pain and emotional drain that comes from obsessing, there is also an unacknowledged pleasure that comes from this activity. As much as they claim to hate the great amount of time spent in jealous obsessions, it does help people to avoid finding out what else they may be feeling. In general, obsessing is a way of keeping ourselves from knowing what we are feeling. It is also an unconscious statement of not really wanting to change—obsessives always want the *other* person to change.

Because jealous people engage in so much obsessing, they tend to treat their suspicions as facts. In doing so, they may work themselves up into states of fury in which they become enraged with themselves or others.

Helping a jealous person who is enraged (turned inward) or outraged (turned outward) only works after the person has cooled down. Trying to be rational with someone at the height of jealous, angry feelings only invites him or her to become more entrenched in what he or she feels and believes to be the truth. So, take a time out, go to neutral territory, and when things have cooled down, examine the facts together. It may help.

Chapter 21

Control Issues: Who's In and Who's Out?

....

The basic premise of this book is to show how our relationships with pets and significant others become catalysts for bringing out our own unresolved psychological issues. I made the point early in this book that many times our annoyance with our pets has little to do with their behavior—the animals are only doing whatever is natural to their species. And behavior includes maneuvering for control of their environment, or pack. We humans should not feel like we are that much more advanced, either, because we, too, maneuver for control of our environment.

Different animal species have their own ways of determining leadership. Scientists who study pack dynamics refer to the pack leader as the *alpha* and the second in the pecking order as *beta;* then there's all the rest. In elephant herds, the alpha is always a female. Among lions, the strongest becomes the alpha male. Seals also give way to the biggest and heaviest. Anyone who has had a pig for a pet knows how much time this animal engages in alpha tactics, taking over family members.

When a "pack" extends to humans (and your pet's pack includes you, whether you want it to or not), it is necessary for our peace of mind to be the alpha pack member. Unfortunately, this is not always the case. (Remember Judy, from Chapter 5, "Animal Actors," who let her dog Buster control her, even after consulting with numerous trainers and dog behaviorists.)

Often the animal that appears to be alpha is not. Animals are quite capable of being very devious. Being the most prominent, the most verbal, or the most aggressive does not necessarily indicate alpha status. As in human society, sometimes the alpha stays in the background and lets the underlings take the spotlight, as long as they acknowledge who the real leader is.

The demand for control is probably an innate part of a newborn human's survival equipment. The new infant has little choice but to control the environment he has been thrust into. He cries insistently, and often pitifully, to attract attention to be fed, to be cleaned, and to be comforted. As he gets a bit older and becomes more aware of his surroundings—still without the benefit of speech and with only minimal control of his actions and functions—he learns to do the things that get attention. He teaches us how to care for him. That bundle of new life learns to gurgle and smile because those actions get us to relate to it. All parents, particularly new ones, can bore you silly with stories of how their *wunderkind* makes himself understood. Let's face it, parents, you are being trained (controlled) by this little thing that can't even talk or program the VCR.

Okay, so we accept the fact that an infant (animal and human) knows instinctively that his survival depends in large part on his ability to train the adults in his life to tend to his needs. That infant must control his environment if he is to survive.

By the time children are physically developed enough to be toilet-trained, they know quite a bit about control. They become aware of how complying with or defying toilet training can be used as either a gift or a punishment to the parents-in-training. Where did they get that knowledge? Why, we taught them, of course, by showing different reactions to bowel activity.

Animals coming into our human habitat are in much the same position as the human infant. They, too, come equipped with instincts and traits peculiar to their species, none of which have much relation to life in the big city or any other human habitat. Each generation of domesticated animals still needs to be trained by humans. Thus, a battle for control is mounted. It is three-way conflict with humans at one point, the animal at another, and society at the third.

We readily accept control from our children, but are we equally accepting when it comes to our animals? How often have your friends asked whether you or your pets control the household? How often have they chided you about the way your dog barks or pushes you with his nose or paw to get you to pay attention or do something? For that matter, how often have you had to fight your 80-plus–pound Bouvier lap dog for your favorite easy chair? I do it often! And, lest you feline fanciers start feeling superior, how often have you been woken from your warm, cozy sleep by your cat walking on you— sometimes on your head?

Our pets know all too well how to get our attention, and it's often debatable who is in control. Do you remember the story in Chapter 3, "The Siamese Code," about Pete and Jackie and their Siamese cats? It wasn't until the couple regained control of their household that they were able to attain a measure of peace and tranquillity in their relationship.

We hear a lot these days about what's in control and what's out of control. People say the system is out of control, a person is out of control, the house is out of control, the pets are out of control, and even, "I'm out of control." Whether we are dealing with our children, other adults, pets, or complete strangers, feeling in or out of control has become a huge issue in our society.

We hate to feel out of control. What we cannot deal with, cannot solve, and cannot get rid of, we rename. I was once invited to a conference for the "chronologically challenged." After a week of pondering what this could possibly be a euphemism for, I telephoned the conference sponsors and found out it was about the elderly. It's as though we can change reality just by changing its label. So, the next time someone cuts you off while you're driving your car, just think of that person as driver-education challenged.

Despite our need for control, many people who insist on having their own way are uncomfortable making absolute statements, so they couch their complaints by speaking of what is "appropriate" and "inappropriate," hoping, perhaps, that not speaking in absolutes will take the onus off their push for control or perhaps keep us from noticing their maneuvers.

The wish for control is not always subtle, though. Think about how often you have heard one person tell another that all-time infamous line, "Believe me, I know you better than you know yourself." That might be followed by, "You are being selfish and just thinking about what you would like instead of what's best for the dog, to say nothing of what is best for us just starting out together." Now compare these to the more subtle, "I know you won't be happy if you bring this dog to live with us in the cramped apartment in the city while you are at work all day. We both know Fido will be happier staying with your folks in the 'burbs with their fenced-in backyard now that your dad is retired." That sounds a little nicer, but it's still control.

IF YOU REALLY LOVED ME . . .

Here's another side of control—and a very subtle one. Somewhere in the last few decades, we have become romanced by the idea of unconditional love. As a term, *unconditional love* was coined by Carl Rogers, a well-known psychotherapist who had an amazing capacity to understand and empathize with his patients, who then felt completely understood by him, both intellectually and emotionally. Rogers' success had much more to do with who he was as an exceptional human being than with the therapy technique he developed.

Unconditional love embodies the idea that, while I might not always like your behavior, nothing will diminish my love for you, no matter what! Sounds great, doesn't it? Trouble is, relationships grow and are affected by all the emotional baggage the participants bring to them. In our relationships, we often hurt each other, whether purposely or unintentionally, consciously or unconsciously. Sometimes we do things that cause our partners to love us less. Sometimes we all just change. To insist on unconditional love is a nice idea, but it is not realistic—except maybe for infants, puppies, and kittens.

If two people can survive the loathing and contempt (either expressed or implied) that exists within all relationships, there is a good chance for the relationship to continue. Yes, true love allows for rough spots, but it has its limits.

People in relationships do not have the same agendas, and there is always some level of conflict. Because people commit acts that do not support unconditional love, no one should be made to feel guilty about not unconditionally loving. In other words, if you act like a jerk, don't expect me to unconditionally love you without telling you that you are a jerk and how I feel about it.

RIGHT AND WRONG

Melinda was furious because Boris refused to get up at 6:45 AM on weekends to walk their dog, Shakespeare. Boris felt that on weekends he should be able to sleep late (at least until 8 AM, and sometimes even to 9 AM). For Melinda, that was outrageous and insensitive because it would upset Shakespeare. Boris said the dog would be fine because he usually walked Shakespeare later in the evening when he planned to sleep in the next morning. He also felt that a three-year-old dog should be able to control himself for an additional hour and a half once in a while without splitting a gut.

Melinda disagreed with Boris, saying he was wrong for upsetting the dog's schedule, wrong for thinking the dog would know what day of the week it was, and wrong for believing the dog was not suffering terrible discomfort. Melinda ultimately would walk the dog on weekends when Boris slept late, but she claimed it interfered with her own plans. Melinda had no desire for a career of her own, nor was there any need for her to work; Boris's income was more than enough for their lifestyle.

Owning a dog was not Melinda's idea; Shakespeare had been Boris' dog when they married. Actually, Melinda had no real objections to the dog. In fact, she cared for the animal all week long, but she felt that dog care should be Boris' responsibility on the weekends.

Melinda also wanted Boris to take the dog for obedience training classes. She said it would be a bonding experience for them both and that it also would help Shakespeare feel more secure with Melinda's presence. She tried to get the trainer to press Boris to take classes, which only made Boris more stubborn in his refusals.

Have you already formed your opinions of these two people? Discussions of who is right and who is wrong usually go nowhere. After a very demanding workweek, Boris just wanted to sleep a little later; this does not seem like too much to ask. Melinda, however, felt she was being taken advantage of. She felt that with Boris home, she should be relieved of some of the dog-care chores. Whenever she said this, Boris became furious because Melinda did not work outside their home.

As long as both parties are convinced that a dispute concerning a pet—or anything else, for that matter—has a right and a wrong position, we have entered into a court of law and have left the realm of mutual understanding and communication.

In looking at real issues involving pets and people, we need to know a lot more than just the facts—we need to know what the feelings of the parties are as well. In court, feelings are inconsequential; what is significant in court are the facts. What is significant in relationships is a combination of the feelings and the facts, put together in a way that enables us to explore their interaction. This holds true whether or not the relationship includes pets.

Let's look at Boris and Melinda: When Boris said he was going to sleep late on Saturday mornings, he annoyed Melinda, who then felt that she had to postpone or interrupt her weekend plans. The problem here was that the two of them had never discussed the issue; as a consequence, Melinda had developed a great deal of resentment toward both Boris and Shakespeare. This, of course, did not go unnoticed by Shakespeare.

By the time Boris and Melinda came to see me, they were just about ready to divorce. Boris could not live with his wife's constant nagging, and Melinda was finding the loneliness of Boris' work schedule unbearable, even on the days she was spending six or seven hours at the gym.

Meanwhile, Shakespeare had begun urinating on her dirty laundry. Melinda felt that Shakespeare was running her life. With Boris at work, she had to walk and exercise the dog. Even though she jogged as part of her daily exercise, Melinda resented the responsibility of having to take the dog along. Where did all this come from?

Melinda had been the unwanted child of two adolescent parents obliged to marry. As far back as she could remember, Melinda had heard what a burden she was and how her mother could have been a great musician had she not become pregnant. When not complaining to her daughter, her mother blamed her father for whatever else was wrong in her life. Her mother's complaints had been her way of controlling the family, silencing them with rantings calculated to make everyone feel guilty. There was no room for Melinda or her father to do much beyond avoiding this woman.

Now Melinda found herself in a relationship in which she was acting like her controlling mother and blaming the dog for all her problems. Ironically, she did not want children because she feared that she might become like her mother.

Boris, on the other hand, came from a family with a powerful work ethic. Unlike his mother, who never complained, never had any needs, and always seemed satisfied, Melinda constantly verbalized life's problems. Perhaps Boris' silent, stoic mother left him yearning for more interaction and excitement between husband and wife than he had seen in his parents' life. In a strange psychological twist, Boris' weekend habits may have been an attempt to goad his wife into putting some excitement into his life, although it was not quite the variety he hoped for. His dog was being labeled the problem, but he suspected it had little to do with Shakespeare.

Melinda did ultimately realize that she had become her mother and had turned the dog into the child she feared. She told Boris that she loved Shakespeare but hated her husband's absences, exhaustion, and silence. Boris now understood how he was using the issues about Shakespeare to gain Melinda's attention. He agreed that weekends should involve more time together. They started planning their weekends around mutually enjoyed friends and activities, which almost always included Shakespeare. This gave Melinda time to take care of dog business while still spending time with Boris.

When Melinda and Boris stopped focusing on who was right and who was wrong, their relationship changed from one in which control was the major issue to one that embraced cooperation.

PET PROPHETS AND POWER PLAYS

Sometimes I am amazed at my own naiveté about the connection some people make between pets and control. Some feel weak and helpless—not in control of their own lives—and become new people once they acquire a pet. I am not talking about those people who have pets for the pleasure and comfort they offer. Many people are driven to pet ownership by their need to control something in their lives.

Suddenly, it seems, these pet owners gain a sense of power and self-esteem. Usually—and it appears to happen overnight—these individuals become experts. They know exactly what the animal needs, what is going on in the pet's head, and how to handle any pet-involved situation. Their expertise and authoritarian pet views leave the listener speechless.

Breeders of dogs, cats, birds, fish, horses, or what have you are no exception. It is astonishing what a litter or two of puppies can do to create an instant expert. Often this self-proclaimed expert and power broker is a weak, powerless individual in his or her human relationships. The self-esteem plug was pulled long ago, and it is as if these pet prophets have finally found a niche for themselves—a niche that's high up on the wall. An observer gets the feeling that such a person feels obliged to control every experience of the animal.

THE REALITY OF CHAOS

Like every psychological mechanism, control rarely appears in isolation. Remember the story of Marguerite, Tom, and now alto-barking Irving de la Favorie, in Chapter 20, "Jealousy, the Complex Emotion." Jealousy was definitely a factor in their lives, but control lived right alongside it.

Tom tried to control his jealousy by moving to a remote village where he and Margo were always within sight of each other. While that gave Tom a measure of relief, Margo suffered because she felt totally controlled by him. To make matters worse, he rarely communicated with her.

As usually happens, Tom and Margo were repeating the power issues of earlier years. How we see power, how we respond to control, and how we attempt to control are all connected to our early history and our unconscious choice of our defenses. Holding on to who we are while remaining in a relationship and developing intimacy stirs up old questions of who is in charge and who is in control. The end result is what I call new editions of early sibling and parent-child struggles.

Like all of us, Tom and Margo wanted to believe that they are in control of the important components of their lives. The reality is that they, like the rest of us, have almost no control over most situations and people in our lives. Despite the innumerable aspects of order in the universe, much of what occurs daily in our personal lives is subject to randomness, if not complete chaos.

The best description from chaos theorists that I have been able to comprehend involves taking handfuls of sand and building up a mound by letting the sand fall between your fingers. At some point, the hill of sand collapses from the one falling grain of sand that changes the entire composition of the form. Chaos is the randomness of how the hill will change and not knowing which grain it will be.

This example is an interesting illustration of the illusion of control. You have a hand in the construction underway, but there is no way of knowing whether or when that control will give way to chaos.

Tom and Margo each had their own form of control: Tom had his controlling silences, and Margo had her controlling absences. Neither was able to simply live with the randomness of the world around them.

I LOVE YOU TO DEATH

Another form control can take is intrusiveness and over-concern. Just as an individual can have an intrusive parent, so, too, are pet owners seemingly obsessed with every nuance in their pet's behavior. (Remember Chad, Diana, and their dog, Heidi, in Chapter 6, "The Pet in the Middle"?) Let's look at Monty and his attention to detail regarding his rabbits.

Monty never wanted to go anywhere. Paying attention to his rabbits was a full-time preoccupation. He even weighed their feces, hoping by some calculation to determine if they were getting enough to eat. Unless you are a scientist conducting a controlled research experiment, measuring a pet's nutritional intake to this degree is a demonstration of extreme control, not careful husbandry.

Too little control can be as much of a problem as too much. For some of us, not knowing where the boundaries are and how far we can step in expressing ourselves intellectually, emotionally, and physically can severely hamper the variety of our reactions. As with kids, if we do not offer boundaries to our pets, they can also become confused about how to please their human pack members. They may also overreact, causing fear and worry.

I have seen dogs who have attacked and bitten other dogs on the street solely because they slipped out of their collar or have got loose from the leash. The animal was so shocked by the unexpected freedom that he reacted to his fears by becoming aggressive. I have also seen extremely possessive bitches growl and become physically aggressive with any female, human or otherwise, who comes too close to their male owner. This also happens with male dogs that belong to women.

Control is saying, "I will never let anyone determine how I will lead my life, the way my parents did when I was a kid." As a child, Lenny could not do anything without his father's permission. His mother was terrified by his father and pleaded with Lenny to be good so as not to upset Dad. Coming from a strong fundamentalist Christian background, the first thing Lenny did as soon as he was able was to was join the Hari Krishna movement. His mother reported that his father had practically foamed at the mouth when he learned what Lenny had done. Some years after learning of his father's death, Lenny left the movement and returned to his hometown in Mississippi.

There he married Regina, and together they started a carpet-cleaning business. Regina brought her Andalusian Shepherd dogs with her.

Lenny loved the dogs and spent a lot of time telling Regina what she was doing wrong with them. In fact, he told her what was wrong with just about everything she did. It did not matter what the activity was—he insisted on deciding when they would shop, what they would buy, what brands, and how much. Regina not only had to account for how she spent her time and money, but also whom she met, to whom she spoke, and what was said.

Lenny's need for absolute control was pathological and extended to the dogs as well. They had to urinate and defecate on command. People were amazed that he could have such exquisite control over such matters. The dogs loved him the way an obedient slave, not knowing differently, loves a master because he supplies food and shelter.

Regina could not bear Lenny's need to never allow the dogs a moment's rest. This is similar to the story of Elinor, Ned, and his Akita, Samurai, in Chapter 11, "Different Needs, Same Result." You'll recall that Ned took Samurai to a never-ending string of obedience classes; he was projecting his fear of going out of control (the way his father did) onto stoic Samurai.

Lenny refused to surrender any control whatsoever. He justified all his actions by saying that his way was the right way, or the most efficient way, or the most economical way of doing things. He claimed to have information to back up his position, so there was little room for argument. Something as simple as washing the dog's dishes could evoke tremendous rage in Lenny. The aluminum dishes had to be soaked in boiling water before liquid soap was applied to them. They then had to be flushed with hot water seven or eight times to ensure that all the soap was removed, because even a spec could cause diarrhea. How to wash, when to walk, when to feed, how much to feed, which TV programs to watch, how to open the newspaper and carefully return it to its original form, how to drive, the best route to get somewhere, how much sleep, the opening and closing of windows, the best room temperature—these were all potential arguments.

Lenny was always a bully. Many people said he got it from his father. When Lenny was a child, sometimes his father yelled at him about some insignificant thing that Lenny did or did not do. Either way, Lenny had had to listen to the screaming until his father wore himself out. Sometimes when his father was particularly upset about something, he got abusive with Lenny. Lenny told himself that when he became an adult, no one was ever going to get the upper hand again.

And, as an adult, Lenny spent a great deal of his time making sure that he had the upper hand over everyone else around him. On the job, people hated him because he was so domineering. He was very good at what he did and believed that everyone tolerated him because he was so accomplished. But his coworkers avoided him at all costs, which was more than Regina could do. It was as if Lenny was showing his wife and their dogs what it was like for him growing up with a sadistic father and a silent mother.

Lenny had become everything he hated about his father. He knew it, but he felt compelled to control everything anyway. In psychological terms, he *identified with the aggressor*, something victims often do in attempting to master childhood inequalities.

BEYOND OUT-OF-CONTROL

Control relationships need a cast of characters; no one can be controlled without some level of collusion. An unconscious magnetic pull keeps people trapped in controlling relationships. This is part of the bigger picture of emotional sadomasochism (I'll say more about that soon). There is an energy in these relationships that has a beginning, a middle, and an end. The control scenarios may be different, depending on what is affecting the individuals, but the amount of emotional energy expended is pretty much the same from relationship to relationship.

Generally speaking, a control episode might be pictured as the classic bell curve. At the beginning, the situation gains energy from the participants. As the interaction grows in intensity, its energy content grows to some maximum level, whereupon it falls off to its original level. There is a sense of relief in those involved, and life goes on until another curve begins.

Adolf and Gert's married life typified this control curve. They had been married a long time. In fact, they had been married three times—twice to each other. Gert's first husband, Bob, died of liver failure five years after they were married. Adolf's first marriage ended in divorce when his wife, Trixie, ran off with another man.

Two years after Adolf and Gert married each other, they had a child named Kevin. Adolf was then working hard as a TV and radio repairman, but was barely making ends meet. He was taking courses in air conditioner repair to expand his skills.

Part of Adolf's economic difficulty was of his own making. He could not hold on to his clientele because he would not tolerate any form of criticism. He was known for his temper, and it did not take much to set him off. Even when customer complaints were justified, Adolf became abusive and showed little desire to control his temper. Adolf was one of those transparent people; you could see the steam rising in his face as his eyes became little slits and his skin turned red. His body would shrink like an accordion until his neck disappeared.

Usually he managed to maintain enough self-control not to get physical with his customers, but their property was something else. In his rage, he would fling objects—often the TV sets waiting for repair—around the shop until the customer fled in panic. Needless to say, this was not good for business.

Adolf's abusiveness was by no means limited to his business. He verbally abused Gert, demanded that she clean the house in a particular way, and insisted that food be served piping hot within 15 minutes after his return home in the evenings. If he felt that something that belonged on the table was not there, instead of asking for it he turned the situation into an inquisition by asking if Gert knew what was missing—salt, ketchup, or whatever. It did not matter whether Gert said yes or no. Adolf would inevitably fling his dinner against the wall, yelling "Clean it up, bitch," and storm out of the house, returning well after midnight.

Adolf tried to excuse his actions by explaining that they were part of a nervous condition sparked by a virus he had contracted in the South Pacific while on submarine duty during World War II. Gert believed him. But, as we will see, much of the couples' dilemma came from their respective repetition compulsions.

Gert remained with Adolf, just as her mother could not leave her highly critical and verbally abusive father. Gert's mother had found her escape only when she eventually faded because of lymphoma. Her disease was an apt metaphor for someone invaded by a mate whose meanness ate away at her. Adolf, too, had had a physically abusive father who beat his wife and children regularly, believing he was keeping everyone on their toes and in their place.

Not a Happy Heritage

This was the family Kevin was born into. At age three, the seeds of his own repetition compulsion were being sown. Adolf's need to control his son was as strong as his need to control Gert. He demanded that Kevin refer to him as "sir" and insisted that "thank you" or "no thank you" be used all the time, even at this young age. Kevin knew how to say "sir" before he could say "daddy."

During one of his calm periods, Adolf returned one evening with a 10-week-old Rhodesian Ridgeback puppy, which they named

Farfel. The little puppy was timid and retiring. Adolf's idea of training this little dog was to scream at him and hit him across the face with rolled newspaper. He had no idea that animals, as well as people, are able to perform tasks only when they are ready developmentally. It is not possible to think about teaching a puppy even simple tasks much before the age of five months—canine comprehension and frustration tolerance are just not in place yet.

For Adolf, Farfel was another candidate for his sadism. While pet owners enjoy the love and attention that most pets give, Adolf enjoyed hearing the dog's cries when he was being abusive. It was similar to twisting the arms of his wife and child when he was engaged in a sadistic episode.

Gert was reluctant to leave, believing that, in time, Adolf would get better. Of course, that was only a dream. To avoid having to ever face her rage at her own parents for a miserable childhood in their emotionally dysfunctional family, Gert allowed her own life to follow the same path. As long as she accepted her parents' way of life, she need not look at their effect on her. In order to reject Adolf's sadism toward her child, her dog, and herself, she had to first come to grips with her own repressed childhood and acknowledge the rage at her parents that she had bottled up.

Sounds simple, doesn't it? The fact is, something like that is excruciatingly difficult to do. In Gert's case, it took an act of faith and courage. Finally, after an evening of Adolf's plate flinging, wall punching, and limb twisting of his wife, child, and dog, she screwed up her courage and fled. Then she filed for divorce.

Gert, Kevin, and Farfel moved to Mexico and established residence there. After the divorce was finalized, mother, son, and Farfel returned to Gert's family home in New Jersey. Through mutual friends, Adolf learned that his ex-wife and son were back in town. He found where they were living and followed Gert to work. With tears in his eyes, he told her how much he missed them, begged for forgiveness, and promised, on his knees, that he would never raise his voice or hands to them again.

In her own loneliness (that bell curve was beginning to ring), Gert began meeting him for dinner, and within two months they remarried. Her parents were devastated. Kevin and Farfel seemed glad to see him. For a long while there was no obvious sign of Adolf's problems. But they were there, just beneath the surface.

Soon, Adolf took to having Farfel run with him when he went jogging. The trouble was that Farfel suffered from advanced hip dysplasia and was arthritic. It was obvious to everyone that the dog could not handle the long runs. People along the jogging route would stop Adolf to tell him that he was killing the dog. His reply was that the dog had to toughen up. Gert and Kevin pleaded with him to leave Farfel home. The dog was getting on in years, but Adolf would not relent. Then one day, in an argument over Farfel, the old Adolf surfaced. He flung Gert against the wall, he threw Kevin against the wall, and he flung Farfel against the wall.

Gert did not have the emotional strength to leave Adolf again, and she could not bear to see Farfel tortured anymore. She took the dog to the vet and, explaining the circumstances, pleaded with her to put the dog down rather than having him die a terrible death. The vet agreed, and poor Farfel paid the ultimate price for Adolf's sadism and repetition compulsion.

THE DOG OR ME

Adolf's behavior was obvious and extreme. But often the power behind control is quite subtle and actually comes from the victim. Jamie and her fiancé, Sol, had been living with his parents since they became engaged two years ago. She had brought Mitzi, her four-year-old Lakeland Terrier, with her. Mitzi liked Sol and slept in their bed, usually lying across Jamie's chest like a cat.

The first hint of the controlling future came one night when Sol rolled over in bed and was startled to see the figure of a man trying to come in their bedroom window. Even more startled was Mitzi who, in the ensuing confusion and panic, bit Sol on the nose. Jamie rushed him to the hospital, and the wound required many, many stitches to repair. Jamie said later that there were more stitches than nose!

Lakeland Terriers have powerful jaws but are not mean-spirited or aggressive. As a breed, they are well-known for their endurance and courage. When they returned from the hospital, Mitzi would not come into the house and stayed outside all night. It was as though she regretted having hurt a member of her family. Mitzi had never been nasty before, and they figured that this event had just frightened and agitated her enough to react by biting Sol.

Sol said he understood the situation but was still afraid of Mitzi. Jamie pleaded with Sol to try to make friends with the dog, but he did not want her around and wanted Jamie to give Mitzi to a shelter for adoption. Jamie pleaded that the dog was just as confused as the people were by the attempted break-in and had reacted intuitively to a threatening situation. Jamie was upset enough to challenge Sol with, "A mature adult would have been happy if a dog reacted this way with an intruder. Confusion is not a good reason to give up a dog."

Jamie's best friend, Myra, asked, "If you give up this dog before you are married, I wonder what else he will ask you to give up?" It was a fair question. Jamie told Sol that he was asking a lot of her to give up Mitzi and said that it was not fair to her or the dog. Jamie suggested putting Mitzi in a dog crate at night.

But Sol's mother was now insisting that she, too, feared Mitzi. Living in her future in-laws' house made it difficult for Jamie to oppose Sol's mother. And the situation was getting more intense as time went on. Sol was now questioning whether they could have children with such an "unreliable" dog around. He warned Jamie that if anything happened to their future kids, he would hold her responsible.

Sol moved into complete control mode when he began insisting that Jamie must love Mitzi more than he loved her. Jamie said that she would do whatever it took to ensure the safety of any future kids, and she reminded him that Mitzi would be a lot older when the kids were born. However, Jamie was beginning to question her future in this relationship. She was finding it very difficult to stand up for herself, and Sol was not willing to give her suggestions a try.

Jamie regarded herself as unseen and unheard by her fiancé and his family, in very much the same manner that she had been treated in her own family. Her relationship with Sol was rapidly becoming a carbon copy of her childhood years. It took all her strength, but with a broken heart she ended the relationship. Giving up Mitzi would have been her personal tragedy, but she knew that marrying someone whose need to be in control came before her feelings would have been even worse.

Sara Whalen, who runs Pets Alive, a no-kill animal shelter in Middletown, New York, told me that she receives an unbelievable number of calls each week from people who want to bring their pets in because a parent or mate has demanded that the person make a choice between the pet and the significant other. As if to illustrate this point, Sara received a telephone call as we spoke from a young man asking if she could take his nine-year-old cat. His father was letting him move back home because he had lost his job. The only condition was that he could not bring his "disgusting" cat with him.

MORE GAMES PEOPLE PLAY

Sometimes competition and control get intertwined. What starts out as a contest can easily turn into a show of control if the winner believes he or she gets all the spoils. The difficulty in trying to deal with control issues and control freaks is that neither are very clearly defined. Both control issues and control freak behaviors are so intertwined with other issues and other behaviors that it is difficult to single them out and to be able to define, describe, and deal with them. Adolf, for example, who was so obviously a control freak, was also caught up in a repetition compulsion.

However, one clear way this plays out for couples is through the old game of "Who is the better parent?" Lots of couples have a problem agreeing on how their pet should be treated, but the argument probably has more to do with what is lurking in their own backgrounds than with anything about the pet.

On the surface, disagreements can arise about whether the pet is allowed on or off the furniture, in or out of the bedroom, and even in or out of the bed. Most pet-owning families come to grips with these and many other disagreements. But when the owners are using their pets to respond to something in their own lives, the pet issues seem to take on exaggerated prominence.

However the pet arrives at the household, it is usually welcomed and loved. While everyone loves the pet, sometimes one person develops a stronger passion for the animal than the other. With Craig and Emma, it was Emma who developed the strongest attachment to Potampkin, a purebred-challenged Poodle-Terrier mix that Craig brought home from a shelter. Soon, Emma started spending a lot of time in deep conferences with the veterinarian, the dog walker, and the groomer, and having extended discussions with the trainer concerning training techniques. Despite Craig's objections, Emma even hired a dog nutritionist to advise her on which ingredients should be in Potampkin's food.

Whenever she was not discussing canine health and nutrition issues, Emma was devoting inordinate amounts of time to determining the best leash and collar to use, the best brushes and combs for Potampkin's type of hair, the safest toys for him, and so on. As far as Craig was concerned, there seemed to be no room for discussion on any of these Potampkin-related subjects. He found himself excluded from all pet parenting, as Emma took total responsibility for all of Potampkin's needs.

One-Sided Pet Parenting

Emma began to treat Craig as though he was unable to so much as walk the dog safely. She frequently scolded Craig, saying that he played too roughly with the animal, that he fed him table scraps, that he walked the dog without his raincoat and booties. It seemed there was never a day when Emma did not find something to scold Craig about concerning Potampkin.

While Emma's focus appeared to be on Potampkin, it really was a reflection of what was going on with her. Emma was obviously doing her best to control her environment, using her total control over the dog to also control Craig.

In these parenting contests, the best way to win is not to play. What Craig and Emma needed to do was get to the root of Emma's control problem rather than argue about how to take care of Potampkin.

Proving who is the better parent may be a form of competition that reflects a person's own parents and how he or she was parented. It is amazing in American culture how the mother becomes the all-knowing child-care "expert" and the father is reduced to novice, either by choice or by default. By this I mean that in traditional families, the mother is regarded as supplying the nurturing, while the father supplies the discipline and experience about the world. While this view remains a tradition rather than a reality, it is astonishing how many people still believe that is the way things are supposed to be.

In an age of house-husbands and men who know as much as women do about nurturing and developmental issues (whether they pertain to humans or pets), it is possible that both can be good parents. To me, the greatest value of having two caregivers is that each relieves the other of the stress of care taking, and each prevents the other from transferring too many of his or her issues onto the kids, or pets, or both.

THE ILLUSION OF CONTROL

Remember Rachel, Bert, and his cat, Beauregard, from Chapter 2, "Let Sleeping Dogs (and Cats) Lie"? Rachel had grown up with a depressed mother who was in and out of hospitals, so Rachel had spent some time with aunts and cousins before her father returned home from the Army. While she seemed to come out of her shell after he returned, Rachel never really worked out her problems concerning separation and abandonment in her relationships. As do all unconscious conflicts, Rachel's emerged as an unusual form of control.

After she and Bert were married, they acquired a Briard puppy named Frenchy at about the same time they had a baby girl, Aviva. Frenchy required monthly professional grooming. Rachel insisted on remaining at the groomer's while Frenchy was groomed, and she thought Bert and the groomer were being insensitive by telling her it was better for the dog if she did not stay. Rachel insisted that Frenchy would be traumatized if he were left alone with strangers

Clearly, Frenchy was the object of Rachel's projection. Rachel was left alone with strangers as a child, and she was projecting her feelings of fear and loneliness onto the dog. Strangely enough, while bending over backward to protect Frenchy from separation anxiety, Rachel regularly left their daughter, Aviva, in child care. So while Frenchy was carrying Rachel's projection of abandonment fears, Aviva was being left, so-to-speak, with the "aunts and cousins"—the same childhood that Rachel had lived. I'll just remind you again that nothing in psychology is simple!

This behavior is a kind of splitting in which components of a person's life that represent a conflict are split by being projected onto different recipients. So, Rachel projected her fear onto Frenchy and lived out her repetition compulsion through Aviva.

In situations such as this, control is an attempt to avoid those emotions connected to past events.

THE WARNING SIGNS IN OTHERS

What are some warning signs that you may be signing up for life with a control freak? Nothing is cut and dried, and anyone worth his or her salt can *appear* thoughtful, concerned, and caring. Also, control freaks may not be consciously aware of what they are doing.

After many years as a therapist, I have developed a list of warning signs that will help you recognize this quality in others—and in yourself. Naturally, I am talking about excesses of behaviors, not the bits and pieces that we all exhibit occasionally. While some of these warning signs are a bit tongue-in-cheek, they are still worthy of consideration. Beware of people who

- Are excessively orderly in dress.
- Rarely have pets (certainly never ones that shed) or plants, unless they are cacti.

- Say they are easily distracted and subject to changes in the weather and sound levels. They are always demanding that you change something: Could you lower the window, close the door, turn on the ceiling fan, turn up the air conditioner, turn down the stereo, not tap your pencil, not swallow so loudly—you name it.

- Tell you about everyone's fatal flaw and are desperately searching for yours. They also may try to summarize your entire life in one sentence.

- Don't like the way you laugh.

- Don't like any of your friends.

- Think your glasses make you look a little nerdy and eventually suggest contact lenses.

- Watch Court TV more than an hour a day.

- Tend to look at you with a somewhat constipated facial expression. This takes time to recognize. The facial constipation comes when the person almost never says up front and directly what is bothering him or her.

- Always speak of being afraid of hurting you, yet always make unilateral decisions involving the both of you.

So, how do the symptoms of the control freak play out? Here is one example.

Lydia took care of Hans' dog, Torval, because Hans worked late hours, and she could not stand the dog being alone without being fed and walked. While the couple had dated steadily for four years, they were not married. Lydia believed that as soon as Hans' divorce became final, they would move in together. As it turned out, she was fooling herself.

That became evident when Hans asked Lydia if she wanted to keep Torval. To her, this was an indication that Hans had no intention of pursuing the divorce, moving in with her, or ultimately marrying her. Hans had been able to sound very convincing about their future, but now that his divorce was closer to reality, his plans for a life with Lydia were becoming more and more vague.

When Hans and Lydia spoke during therapy about their relationship, neither of them looked at each other, nor did they respond to what the other was saying. I asked if they were aware of this and what they thought these behaviors indicated. Hans was unsure. Lydia said she was afraid of making him angry. "So by not looking at Hans, it is as if you are not having a real discussion, and therefore there is no need for anger or a confrontation?" I asked. Lydia said, "Yes, I think Hans gets angry and I never get what I want anyway, so what's the use?"

Lydia went on to say that she believed she could never be happy or get what she wanted out of life because she did not turn out the way her father had wanted. She also thought she was somehow being punished because she had had an abortion as a teenager. When I asked how her father wanted her to be, she quickly replied, "I should be married to a well-connected man by now and have children by him. Instead, I am sitting here talking about a relationship with a man who is neither interested in marrying me nor in having children."

Lydia did not seem to notice that her great wish to please her father covered her feelings about an absent father she had not seen from the time she was 10 years old until they had reconnected again in her mid-30s. The fact was that she barely knew her father, much less what he wanted or did not want for her. Lydia had long ago lost contact with what she truly wanted for herself.

Lydia may sound very passive, but make no mistake: She was a control freak. Her method was to whine, nag, complain, and generally wear the other person down. Lydia also found an outlet for her control in Torval. She assumed she knew exactly what he needed, and gave it to him—whether he wanted it or not.

Hans went at it in a different way. He, too, wore the opposition down, but with rationalizations, ambiguous explanations, and passive-aggressive postponements. Torval suffered at both their hands because they were so involved with their control issues that they had little time left for him or anyone else.

Hans loved animals but was not very interested in the everyday business of caring for them. He would have more dogs if he knew someone would care for them. For him, Torval was a child, and pets and children were women's work in Hans' mind. This was much like his mother, who adored his father and had children to please her husband. She had not wished to put much effort into their emotional needs and mental development. Rather, she saw children much as did Rousseau, the great French philosopher: Children were flowers needing only water and sunshine in order to thrive.

Hans did not want to pay anyone to walk or care for the dogs, and he regarded people who did have professional help as uncaring, like his mother. Having a girlfriend feeling sorry for the animals and becoming totally responsible was his solution. In the past, he could always get his girlfriends to do what he could not get his mother to do: Take care of the children. And that suited Lydia perfectly. She finally found a simple, effective way to "please" her father.

Hans kept the scenario going by constantly thanking Lydia and presenting her with gifts, but without much promise of anything else. He *knew* how to compliment and give gifts, including the gift of gab that kept Lydia reaching for the carrot at the end of the stick.

As you can see, the drive for control is usually not an obvious one. No one is standing there holding a gun to your head. The tools of control are more likely to be subtle and insidious.

So, now you have an idea about what a control freak is and how to identify one. The question is, How do you maintain a relationship with a controlling person? Again, from my experience, try these tips:

- Do not ask a control freak for advice.
- Do not ask a control freak to help you choose anything, from a dress, to a car, to a dog, to a CD.
- Do not ask a control freak if you were right or wrong about anything involving you and another person—ever!

- Never ask a control freak to walk your dog, feed your cat, or clean the birdcage. Always sound bewildered and helpless, and wait for that person to volunteer. In other words, be more controlling than the control freak.

SOME SIMPLE SOLUTIONS

Many couples solve their control issues over pets very simply: They bypass them. Ida and Trent are one such couple. They had been married 19 years and had two dogs, a cat, and a well-educated pigeon.

Ida, a highly regarded forensics expert, was in great demand at conferences and often traveled for business. Her husband was a successful corporate lawyer. Both valued their careers and agreed early on in their relationship not to have kids. Sounds idyllic, doesn't it? It wasn't.

When Ida was away, Trent refused to take care of the dogs. He would watch and feed the cat and the bird, but he refused to feed or walk the dogs. His refusal appeared especially strange because he enjoyed the dogs as couch companions. Ida solved the problem by hiring a dog walker, who also fed the dogs while she was away.

Trent understood that his refusal was related to his contempt for a mother who always allowed her dogs to come before her husband and son. Nevertheless, he was not interested in modifying his behavior. In all other respects, the couple had a good marriage. They were able to remain together without resolving their differences over the dogs.

The reason this relationship remained peaceful is that Trent did not extend his desire for control to other issues, Ida accepted the limits he set, and there was an easy solution to the practical problem of who would feed and walk the dogs.

Paul and Christine took a different tack with her mixed-breed dog, Penté. Christine had rescued Penté five years ago from a shelter. That was before she met Paul, who did not get along with Penté.

Christine and Penté had a special bond, and she could not even imagine giving up the dog.

Penté sensed right away that Paul did not like him, and he behaved aggressively toward him. Paul could not go near Christine's bedroom without Penté baring his teeth and growling—they definitely had a hate-hate relationship.

Christine refused to choose between them. Instead, she sent Penté to friends who had a country cottage and loved taking him along. The dog spent Thursday night to Monday morning in the country, when Christine and Paul cohabited. Paul thought the arrangement was just fine and even agreed to accompany Christine when she reciprocated the favor by baby-sitting for her friends.

Christine and Paul managed to avoid turning her dog into a major issue because neither expressed a need to control the other. Paul didn't insist that she give up her dog, and Christine didn't insist that Paul change his feelings about dogs. Instead, they found a concrete solution that worked for both of them—and for Penté.

CHANGING IS HARD TO DO

Can a control freak change? Of course, but not without help. If you want someone in your life to change, you have to help. Just saying, "I would like him to *understand* me," "You should be more *attentive* to me," or "You should be more *sensitive*," is not enough. That's just describing the end result you would like to see. What you are really looking for is a change in behavior.

One good idea that can help someone learn to give up control is for each person in the relationship to suggest three ways in which the other person can change his or her behavior. Write them down if you feel uncomfortable saying them—and keep them positive, not negative. For example, don't say, "I want him to stop being so annoying." That's just a criticism in disguise. Rather, say, "I want him to tell me more often when he likes what I've cooked or what I'm wearing or the way I've done something." That's a positive suggestion.

After you've each made your three suggestions, the other person must pick one and try to do it. That means both of you—don't forget, in any relationship *everyone* is involved.

For example, let's take another look at Tom and Margo from Chapter 20. Tom was extremely jealous of his wife's affair with their dog groomer, and he castrated their prize stud Poodle for revenge. Margo was beside herself with fury over Tom's behavior, but there was much more to their story. She could no longer tolerate Tom's excessive drinking, his negativity, and his passive behavior. In fact, it was her husband's drinking and lack of communication that led to her infidelity.

I asked Tom and Margo each to come up with three suggestions for behavioral changes for the other. Margo offered: He should not drink before cocktail hour; he had to begin each sentence with a positive statement; and he had to lift the seat and flush the toilet when he used the bathroom.

Tom's three were Margo was to make breakfast as a symbol of her love for him; she should spend an hour or two a day walking through the woods with him; she should invite him to join her when she attended dog shows (even if he did not want to go).

Tom, in no hurry to reduce his drinking, chose to change his toilet habits. Margo chose the walks, feeling that they would both get exercise together and could use that time for conversation. It was a start.

What is interesting in this kind of exercise is how few couples actually do change their behavior. They may both agree to pick a behavioral change, and they may even discuss how they are going to implement the change, but all too often that's as far as it goes.

Many couples report that they could not remember their selections and waited until their next session with me to ask again. (All of a sudden they could not call me on the phone!) Many more couples say they implemented the changes and things went well until the week was almost over. But then they started slipping into old habits. Rarely do couples actually implement and maintain the behavioral changes they seemed so ready to agree upon.

Why is this? Well, we are in no hurry to surrender the displacements, the projections, and the repetitions that have made up so much of our lives. How could there possibly be any real excitement left in the relationship without the old familiar baggage? Getting people to see that there is life after behavior changes is pretty hard to do. It is easier in therapy, and even easier in individual therapy. The reasons why are pretty technical—just trust me on this one.

ARE YOU A CONTROL FREAK?

Are we talking about you? I've said earlier that it is extremely difficult to recognize defense mechanisms in your own self, and it is dangerous to try to analyze yourself, but here are more clues that may point you in the right direction:

- Do you often mention that you have not missed a day of work in the last 12 years?
- Do you take more than 22 vitamins and mineral supplements every day without fail, and without a doctor's recommendation?
- Do you videotape your favorite TV programs if you know you will not be home, and *have* to watch them the *same* day?
- Do you share dishes and culinary articles with your pets?
- Do you generally react to people in authority by being compliant?
- Do you generally feel defiant when people in authority give you instructions?
- Do you often find yourself wanting to do the exact opposite of what people are asking of you?
- Do you generally give people what they want, but only when you want to give it rather then when they ask?
- Do you often find yourself responding to peoples' questions with a "yes" followed by a "but," after which you explain

your thoughts or feelings about what you are being asked?

- Did you decide long ago that you were never going to let anyone tell you what to do again?

- Do you believe that people need to be taught how to behave by your example rather that by expressing your thoughts?

- Do you prefer to entertain at home rather than visit friends or relatives?

- Do you wait for others to put fun and excitement into your life?

- Do others depend on you to help them get organized, repair things, or build something?

- Do you have to have the final word in arguments?

- Does shouting and being loud mean you are winning?

- Do you interrupt during discussions?

- In an argument, do you name-call and swear in order to be emphatic?

- Do you demand obedience from your animal?

- Do you punish pet accidents physically?

THE RESULTS?

I'm sure a number of these have a familiar ring, and you can probably recognize them in yourself. No, that doesn't mean that you are a control freak. However, if you answered yes to a large number of these questions, you might want to take notice.

Fifteen or more "yes" answers, and you may be a Superstar Control Freak. Ten yes answers suggests that you are fairly obsessive and possibly well on your way to becoming a controlling person (only because your way is the right way). More than five suggests that you can go either way. Less than four "yes" answers would pretty much rule you out of this category. However, with less than four "yes" answers, you might wonder if you are attracted to control freaks, because opposites often attract.

HOW MUCH DO YOU NEED TO CONTROL?

If you see yourself in some of these stories and in the questions just posed, you're probably feeling somewhat uncomfortable. Remember, most control freaks rely on obsessive defenses. They intellectualize, rationalize, and insist on doing things according to their own schedule, which means they always seem to be putting everyone else on hold.

The intellectualizer can explain away everything he or she ever needed to know about anything because it is a good way to avoid experiencing his or her own feelings. Rationalization is another obsessive defense in which almost anything uncomfortable can be explained away without having to emotionally experience it.

If you are in the control freak range—or come close to being there—there are probably very good reasons for it stemming from unresolved childhood issues. Many controllers are really trying to tell the world what it was like to have been controlled as a kid. They may also be saying that they will never let anyone get the upper hand again. If you feel that this may be you, you might begin to explore how much power you had as a kid.

We all grew up with control issues. Some of us took them in stride. For others, these problems may have felt like life and death issues, particularly when they revolved around physical, verbal, and even sexual abuse. Threats of abandonment and real punishments can leave us with lifelong control issues.

If you are consciously aware of your displacements, your projections, and your repetition compulsion, then you are well on your way to *really* being in control of your life rather than just maintaining the illusion of power and control while having these mechanisms control you.

Do not forget that there's a real price to pay if you want to be a control freak. You must make everyone in your life dependent on you. Once you become the boss, everyone waits for your decisions. They seem to have lost all motivation and initiative. Soon you will regard them as burdens—self-imposed, of course, but nevertheless, real burdens. In doing so, you create for yourself a lifetime of resentment both on your part and from everyone else. Demanding such obedience, you have taught everyone to lean on you in order to know what to do.

I've said often in these pages: All the psychological mechanisms I talk about here are a normal part of maturing. It's when they keep us from getting what we want and need that they become troublesome. Knowing what it takes to make things happen the way you want is a healthy form of power and control. Setting short-term and long-term goals and making them happen is as important as knowing the impact your actions will have upon others.

You can accomplish your goals without manipulating, threatening, throwing tantrums, instilling guilt, sinking into stubbornness, or acting out of abuse, spite, or force. The trick is to know accurately what is possible, given all the circumstances and the resources and abilities you have available to you. It also means knowing how to negotiate, knowing what the other people will and will not respond to, and having a plan that clearly defines the goals you want to achieve.

Chapter 22

Custody Cases: Now He's Mine

The drama and the power of love and fury in custody cases over pets in a failed marriage or a failed relationship are no less than those found in custody cases over children.

Some time ago, I was a guest on a TV talk show and discussed with couples how they dealt with custody of their pets when they separated or divorced. One of the couples found the shared visitation rights they had set up after their divorce intolerable. Separations from Muffin, their tabby cat, were very painful for both of them. In all other aspects of their divorce they were at each other's throats as well.

Another couple discussed their imminent separation before a studio and a million viewers. She complained that he paid more attention to their dogs than he did to her. She could not stand not being the center of attention. The woman was wonderfully attractive, and the audience (especially the men) were convinced that he must be pretty crazy to prefer time with the dogs over time with his wife.

The husband grew up in a family in which he did not receive much attention, and he saw their relationship as an extension of his early life. After the show was over, we talked for a few minutes, and I asked him if he was trying to get his wife to feel what he felt growing up. Because he did not have words for his early wounds, he could only show her through his treatment of the dogs what it was like for him. He had an *ah-hah* experience. He became teary-eyed and said he had never thought about that, but he realized when I said it that it was, in fact, the case.

Another participant, a lawyer, had spent tens of thousands of dollars in a custody suit over the couple's Fox Terrier. He won complete custody of the dog through sheer fortitude and financial strength. He was obviously happy about his success, but his total victory over his ex-wife may have had as much to do with his own control issues as his love for the dog.

GOING TO EXTREMES

Animal custody cases can be just as extreme as child custody cases. When Dan found out that Madeline, his significant other, was sleeping with another man, he could barely contain his rage. Divorce was the only solution. Somehow, they managed to work out all the details, except who would get custody of their Otterhound, Pele. Because they were both moving to other states, joint custody was out of the question.

Madeline solved the problem by having Pele dognapped from Dan's backyard. Dan hired a private detective to try to find them, but without success. Pele and Madeline were never heard from again.

In custody cases over pets, as in custody cases over children, it is difficult to determine how time should be worked out. When Joanne and Ray broke up, Kipper stayed with Ray because he was Ray's cat before Ray met and married Joanne. Although she initially agreed to this, Joanne found herself missing Kipper and asked Ray for time with him. Ray refused, and Joanne went into a fury. She phoned the local society for the prevention of cruelty to animals and reported that he was abusing the cat. The SPCA visited a number of times before Ray slapped Joanne with a harassment suit.

As you have seen in so many of the stories in this book, there was much more to this situation than there appeared on the surface. Ray actually forced Joanne to see a therapist with him by offering to drop the suit if she did.

We talked a little about their relationship before the breakup, and I asked Joanne if she considered getting another cat of her own. She said Kipper was special and that she could not imagine another animal being just like him. I asked what his specialness was about, and without hesitation she replied that Kipper was the child she and Ray never had together.

Ray said he had never realized how Joanne felt about the fact that they'd never had children. Why hadn't Joanne told him what Kipper represented for her? She said she was too furious about his refusal to have children. Every day, she said, Kipper was a comfort to her.

This came as a complete surprise to Ray. He offered to work out a different solution for Kipper, permitting Joanne to have some time with him.

CALLING KING SOLOMON

In pet custody cases, one cannot judge who loves the pet more. So how do you determine who gets the pet? Certainly, if one person had the pet before the relationship began, it would seem appropriate for that person to retain custody at the time of separation.

If the pet was acquired together, and if both want the pet but not each other, it is much more difficult because pet custody cases are rarely determined by law. In fact, under the law pets are treated as material possessions. Legally, there is not much difference between owning a pet and owning a car. The law sets the value of a pet at its purchase price.

If the pet was mutually acquired, perhaps one of the main considerations in determining who keeps it would be who the pet connects with more. If there really is no difference, the next question might be who has more time to spend with the pet, followed by who can handle the finances of keeping the pet.

Of course, pet custody cases are rarely resolved in such a rational manner because there are so many emotions involved in people-and-animal separations. No matter how terrible the people relationship has become, it is almost always difficult to separate and call it quits.

DO'S AND DON'TS IN CUSTODY CASES

If you're involved in a pet custody situation, first acknowledge to yourself how you feel emotionally since you split up. Being able to do so, and knowing how each of you has contributed to the breakup (and it *always* takes two!) helps to keep you from turning this hurt, anger, and pain in on yourself. Very often when people overlook anger, they unconsciously turn it inward on themselves. This is one of the main causes of depression. Just because you cannot put a finger on the source of your anger does not mean that you should blame yourself.

Try, if you can, to see the relationship in its true light. No one in a relationship is all right or all wrong, all good or all bad. This can be hard to see when you are hurting, but remember that there had to be a time when the relationship met some need for you, or you would have never gotten together in the first place.

It is easy to be in touch only with the negatives about the other person, but this is a guaranteed expansion of your host of unresolved unconscious problems. Above all, if left unresolved, these issues will affect your concerns over custody, be it pet, child, or anything else in your lives. They are sure to be waiting to interfere with your next relationship. Even though the negatives may outweigh the positives at this point, try to hold on to a total picture of your ex. Avoid the blacks and whites, and try to integrate the grays.

Give yourself time.

If you are totally furious and cannot imagine even having a dialogue with you-know-who, try writing a letter laying out all your thoughts and feelings. If you are not completely mired in anger, putting it on paper (even if you don't mail it) can help you to get perspective back. If you want to mail it, remember that you still need some kind of working relationship to maintain a custody agreement. Ask yourself how mailing the letter may affect what you want for yourself. Most people discover that they do not need to invest in a stamp.

Give yourself time.

Be prepared for the false accusations. People often falsely accuse one another of having committed terrible things in child custody cases, and this also happens in pet custody cases. The husband of one of my clients accused his wife of attempting to have sex with their horse. Another client's ex-wife accused him of beating their dog. Knowing both clients well, I knew these were not true.

Give yourself time.

Remember that as you go through the process of ending a relationship and as each of you tells your side of the story to your friends, you can expect 25 percent to side with you, 25 percent to side with your ex, and 50 percent not to give a damn either way.

Give yourself time.

Stay away from non-pet people while you are dealing with pet custody issues. The last thing you need is an unsympathetic ear to your very real plight. You do not need anyone telling you that you are nuts.

Give yourself time.

Talk to people who have resolved their custody problems, and learn how they arrived at solutions.

Consider joining a support group or getting some short-term therapy to deal with the pain of separation and loss (it is a form of grief, you know). If you do not admit to the pain and loss of separation—particularly in a really bad breakup—you are bound to carry the unfinished business into your next relationship. Few things are worse than unloading your garbage from a previous relationship onto a new partner.

Give yourself time.

Don't give way to stubbornness and spite. Don't reject compromise. When we are hurting, one of the main ways of holding onto ourselves is to get stubborn. Once that happens, you are locked into isolation, and your thinking processes get clouded over by your hurt. It is more likely that you will lash out with verbal abuse (and, in some cases, even physical abuse) if you stubbornly hold on to your stubbornness.

In custody battles, stubbornness becomes a way of life—it can cloud all reason. It is difficult not to fall into this trap because this was one of the main ways we protected ourselves as children. Like many other things that worked in childhood, but don't work for us as adults, being stubborn knocks you out of any possibility of effectively negotiating for what you want.

Resist the temptation to force others to listen to how you are being victimized by a heartless ex-lover, spouse, or lawyer, unless you are on a fast-moving train with strangers. Most people—often even your friends—are not interested in hearing again and again the blow-by-blow descriptions of what is happening in your breakup and your custody situation.

If you feel the necessity of unloading all the time, consider a round of therapy. Remember, therapists are not only paid to listen, but they are paid to listen in a special way that helps you get to the deeper meanings of the issues you are dealing with.

If all else fails and you are left petless, do not run out and immediately look for a "replacement." Read Chapter 23, "Grief and the Loss of a Pet." Then give yourself six months to a year to experience the loss of your pet and your relationships (human and animal) before replacing either. If you immediately replace your pet before giving yourself time to adjust to your loss, you will be placing unconscious expectations on the new pet to be just like the old pet. Not only will you be doomed to disappointment, but you also will not give yourself a real opportunity to get to know your new pet.

That goes in large part for your ex as well. Don't go running out to replace your ex with someone who appears to be the total opposite of what you left behind. You are bound to find that the opposite has almost the exact same drawbacks of whatever you could not tolerate in your relationship.

Give yourself time.

Chapter 23

Grief and the Loss of a Pet

Losing a pet can be very difficult for everyone in the family. Be it animal or person, the grief that goes with death is the same. To be sure, some people who have never had pets will try to comfort you by saying things like, "It was only an animal," "You can always buy or adopt another one," or "It's not like it was a person." Stay away from these people! They don't mean to be cruel, but they do not understand that when you lose a member of the family, it hurts just as much regardless of whether it had two legs, four legs, fins, or wings.

Another thing to keep in mind is that very often when you are first hit with loss, you experience a kind of numbness. If people ask what you are feeling, you might very well reply "nothing." This nothing is actually a flooding of feelings that makes it impossible to separate out and identify specific feelings. This is quite truly a numbness to all feeling. Often people report guilt and not being able to feel anything when, in fact, they are flooded with feelings.

Making time to mourn a death is an important part of recovering from that loss. Religions perhaps universally recognize the pain of family losses. In Jewish tradition, there is a seven-day mourning period called *shiva,* observed directly after the death of a loved one. During this period, the grieving family remains quietly at home to experience their loss as a family, while friends and relatives stop in to bring food and offer their condolences. This tradition has lasted thousands of years.

Many other religions and cultures also have customs designed to give the mourners time to accept their loss and get past the pain. The wake, memorial services, the wearing of black, and the unveiling of the tombstone are all markers in the process.

While most religions do not extend mourning to animals, the ancient Egyptians did revere cats, and there are thousands of mummified cat remains in Egyptian tombs. Other cultures, including Native Americans, show similar animal reverence.

In one sense, the loss of a pet is different from the loss of a person because there are fewer memories to disconnect from. I don't mean that you don't remember much about your pet, but rather that most animals do not live as long as humans do. So, while you may spend 50 years with a spouse and all your life knowing a parent, you probably have about 10 years or so of memories with a pet.

It is difficult, if not impossible, to replace a departed relative or friend. But with pets that may not be so. Many people suggest replacing the pet immediately to fill the vacuum. Personally, I have some problems with this position, for a couple of reasons. Having been there more times than I care to remember, I know that taking the time to grieve one animal before obtaining another allows the process to proceed in a natural way. It takes about six months for a person to integrate (emotionally digest) the loss. Then he or she may be ready to take on another pet.

IT TAKES TIME

In general, I believe that people need time to mourn. When loss involves a pet, it is sometimes just as difficult as mourning the loss of a person. As a culture, we Americans seem to be constantly reducing the time we allow for mourning. Perhaps this is part of our growing emphasis on business needs, at the expense of experiencing our emotions. While there are growing indications that we recognize the need for mourning, the time allotted for it seems more a matter of convenience than an expression of understanding and compassion for the griever.

In 1927, Emily Post put the formal mourning period for a widow at three years. By 1950, that period had shrunk to six months. And in 1972, Amy Vanderbilt suggested that widows should be back on their feet within a week or two. In contrast, psychologists know that the grieving process consists of a number of stages that can play out over a period of three to five years, sometimes longer.

A 1980 study by sociologist Louis Pratt reported that 90 percent of American businesses granted three days as the official leave for bereavement, and that was only for the closest of loved ones: parents, children, or spouses (some more enlightened employers included grandparents). That period remains the standard today. Many employers expect mourning employees to use vacation time.

Caught between the needs of the economic world and their cultural and religious backgrounds, people in mourning must find ways of satisfying their need to grieve.

WHAT CAN NEVER BE REPLACED

Loss is permanent, and you should try not to think about "replacing" one pet with another. To think of replacement is to place an unfair expectation on the new arrival to be as much like the lost pet as possible, or sometimes to be as opposite as possible. This is a terrible burden, even for an animal, and it diminishes the relationship that was. The healthier concept is the idea of succession. You had one dog, and now you will have another, different dog.

The wish to replace a loved one and bypass grief can go to extremes. Recently a couple made headlines when they donated $2.3 million to Texas A&M University to have their pet dog, Missy, cloned while she still lived. Dr. Mark Westhusin, head of the cloning project, said he believed the owners were sincere in wanting a copy of their pet, although they realized it might not work.

Dr. Westhusin began the project because he wanted to gain information that might be helpful in breeding animals with a particular talent for being rescue dogs or guide dogs for the blind. It might also provide data for new methods of contraception and sterilization.

Whether or not Missy can be cloned, most scientists agree that you cannot recreate an individual through cloning. The personality of every creature is the sum of its genes and its life experiences. Genes shape personality but do not entirely determine it. And because no two beings—human or animal—can ever have exactly the same experiences, the Missy clone may look just like Missy but will not be her.

This is an extreme example of seeking to avoid the experience of grief. From the standpoint of emotional health, recovering from grief means placing value on experiencing those difficult emotions. Unfortunately, grieving people find many ways to avoid dealing with the pain of experiencing their emotions. Some who have lost children have attempted to avoid dealing with their grief by having another child or substituting a new pet.

EXPERIENCING YOUR EMOTIONS

Somehow, regardless of the depth of grief, many people cannot bring themselves to deal with the feelings about and the connections to the deceased. Grief-stricken people can become obsessed with the dead pet and focus every bit of their attention on the animal. Often they become overly attentive and protective of the pet's memory, to the point of driving every one else crazy. In effect, becoming obsessed with the pet is a way of avoiding coming to grips with their grief.

As a case in point, recall the story of Chad and Diana in Chapter 6, "The Pet in the Middle." The couple lost their first child, and one of Diana's reactions to her grief was to kidnap her friend Betty's Bernese Mountain Dog. We learned then that the kidnapping was an unconscious attempt to replace the lost child. Here is a digest of our discussions during therapy sessions:

> Diana: "When my first child died, I did not mourn, but I
> did not work for a week. Soon after I returned to work

and to graduate school, we got Heidi, our Bernese Mountain Dog. I became obsessed with her. I spent hours just looking at her and petting her and adoring her. I even took her on vacations. When she would just sneeze, I took her to the hospital, where I spent a fortune on her. She still goes to the best doctors.

My husband, Chad, said I was really crazy and that there was nothing wrong with Heidi. Any time the dog's nose felt hot, we jumped into a cab to the Animal Medical Center. This might happen a few times a week."

Chad: "I know that getting Heidi had something to do with the loss of our first child. I remember the first time we took Heidi to the cemetery—it seemed as though she could read Diana's mind. She found the child's grave, seemingly on her own."

Diana: "I think of Heidi as my lost son, Edward. She fulfilled the gap and became the child that I did not mourn. She became my child. Sometimes I have to stop myself and remind myself that she is a dog and not Edward."

Diana and Chad's reaction to their loss is not unusual. For many couples who have lost a child through miscarriage or as an infant, the thought of having another child and possibly losing it is too painful to bear. Other people find they cannot conceive another child. Either consciously (which is usually the case) or sometimes unconsciously, they invest those loving feelings into a pet.

What I find particularly annoying are those insensitive people who feel compelled to note that such-and-such a couple has a pet as a "substitute" for a lost child. Such statements are usually made in an all-knowing tone of voice that has a certain edge of criticism—as if the couple was not already painfully aware of their circumstance. We've all heard those comments:

"Of course they love that cat as if it were their child. You do know Greta had a miscarriage and could not have more kids?"

"She never married, but she is so good with children that I guess that bird of hers is a substitute for a child."

"They divorced after the baby died, and now he has that Belgian Malinois that he treats like a child."

At the risk of being overly repetitious, when it comes to loss and grief, never mind those rules that measure the mourning period. The rule should be this: Whatever helps you through, go for it, as long as it is not self-destructive.

This is as true for a lost pet as it is for a lost person. In addition, when you have lost a pet, stay far away from non-pet people as possible. If you just put down your hamster, do not get weepy around someone you know who hates rodents. Instead, save your grieving for private moments and for when you are with people who can really be there for you and understand.

WHEN YOUR MATE DOESN'T GET IT

What if your mate does not understand why you are so broken up over your loss? There are a couple of possibilities here: If your mate is a pretty decent person in all other areas of the relationship, he or she will be as comforting as possible, simply because you are so upset. Console yourself by knowing that no one in your life can ever be there for you the way you need them to be 100 percent of the time.

There are legitimate reasons why a person might not be as comforting after a loss as you might want. Your significant other may just not have experienced loss before and may not know how to deal with the situation—or may not want to deal with it. One man I worked with found his girlfriend's apparent indifference to the loss of his cat intolerable. As he told me more about her background and I learned that she was raised on a farm where animals are viewed differently than pets, we both realized that for her, the loss of an animal is handled in a much more matter-of-fact way.

DOING WHAT YOU NEED

Don't be embarrassed to consider the possibility of having a memorial service for your pet. Formally burying or cremating your pet is just as important as it would be to properly and respectfully dispose of the remains of a relative or friend. The people in your life who liked your pet and who care for you could be invited to say a few words about their experiences and feelings. If you lost a dog and were part of a social network of dog people who knew your dog, you might consider inviting them for some type of service or gathering. I've done it, and it helped tremendously.

When my Lab, Troll, was diagnosed with lymphoma, his vet, Dr. Stephen Cole, agreed to come upstate to my cottage to administer the injection that would put him to rest. A grave was prepared by "his" river, and Troll was given a last meal of all his favorites, from blue cheese to filet mignon. A number of close friends and animal lovers attended.

Kathleen, a spiritual director and a close friend, prepared a memorial service afterward. Many friends got up to talk about Troll. Some remembered him for his playfulness and strength. Some recalled what a pain in the neck he was when he thought he was a lap dog, although he weighed in at 150 pounds. What followed was a feast of great food and wine among good and caring friends who were there to be supportive and loving.

I also think that, as painful as it sounds, it is helpful to wait at least a period of six months before getting another pet. Unless you experience the grief, the new animal will be destined to be a disappointment, and you may never get to see who and what the new animal is really like. Troll all but lived in the river near the cottage nearly every waking hour. Fergus, the Lab who followed him, is content with an infant's plastic wading pool and couldn't care less about the river.

STIRRING UP OLD MEMORIES

One of the things about death and grief is that they often bring back memories of previous losses. Before Troll there was Amos, also a Lab. I remember it was a real tug-of-war to walk him past a bar—and there are plenty of them in midtown New York. Whenever he smelled beer, he would stop in his tracks. Amos loved the taste of beer. If he saw anyone drinking a beer, he would drop his tongue in the glass—if it was a can of beer, he would knock it over and lap up the liquid.

One day, while I was walking Amos and Troll, Amos collapsed from a heart attack. He died within a few moments, just by a tree near the bus stop. It was a long time before I could take the cross-town bus without feeling as if I would fall apart. Finally, about a year after Amos died, I went to that tree and placed a bunch of flowers on the spot.

I was able to say that Amos had had a really great life. When he collapsed, people appeared from everywhere to help. A young man named Joe found a board to make a stretcher and called a friend with a car to take Amos to the animal hospital. Someone else took Troll and cared for him. Now, when I pass that tree or take the crosstown bus, I think of all the good times with Amos. I also think about all the good people who helped me at that terrible moment. I like to think about the positive connections to people who restore our faith in the human race.

DO ANIMALS GRIEVE?

I do not know for sure what constitutes grief for animals, but I know that they do grieve. I've heard stories of dogs that stopped eating after their owner died, then died themselves shortly thereafter. Other tales tell of dogs that went to the train station every day for the rest of their lives after the death of their human friends. There was a story recently on television about a cat that traveled more than a hundred miles to find her owner.

The point is, animal grief is very strong. I wonder how much it depends upon the bond between the animal and another person or animal, or upon their genetic makeup. Elephants have been seen to pick up and hold the bones of other elephants they knew who went off to die. And mother animals of many species hold their dead babies for days, unable to let go and acknowledge their loss.

WHEN IT JUST HURTS TOO MUCH

People in grief usually manage to get past it, but not always. In extreme cases, it might be helpful to consider tranquilizers or other medications to help you through the grieving process. If you are so depressed from your loss that you are barely getting up and out to work on time, or if you are not sleeping at night, then think about medication. Don't be embarrassed or afraid of being criticized for suffering so much "over an animal." Remember, getting medical help is a lot better than trying to "medicate" yourself with extra food or by smoking or drinking too much.

That goes for sex, too. Many people use sex the same way others use food, drink, smoking, and drugs: as an escape from anxiety, tension, hurt, pain, anger, and, of course, grief.

From a psychological standpoint, lots of people fear that agreeing to take medication means that they are out of control. However, if you are experiencing the symptoms of serious depression, you are probably feeling out of control anyway. The same holds true for psychotherapy; many people still think therapy means they are weak or without a best friend or out of control.

One of the big lessons learned in psychotherapy is that grief is not limited to a death. Part of the working through I have talked about in previous chapters includes grieving over what we never had, or what we had and lost in earlier parts of our lives, particularly in childhood. The therapist is concerned with the grief associated with childhood. For the firstborn, that can mean grieving the loss of a parent's attention with the arrival of new siblings. It can mean being the lost girl child in a family where the boys were considered more important. The childhood loss of a pet may also be experienced as grief. And, like the loss of a parent or sibling, it can be a trauma as well.

Grieving is not a solitary event. Every loss seems to recall all the previous losses in our lives. Some of us have to grieve what we missed out on, maybe a love we were not ready for or that we could not handle, or a job or travel opportunity that we believe might have changed the course of our lives. Then there is the child we never had, or the apology we never made or accepted that might be hanging around as part of what we need to explore once again in order to feel better.

One good thing about grief is that each time you experience another round of it, you have an opportunity to reintegrate those past losses on a different level. And it seems to matter little whether that loss involved another person or an animal that was close to you.

EACH IN HIS OWN WAY

What happens when two people grieve the same loss? Each will show feelings differently. Each will be influenced by his or her particular emotional baggage. When Ron's cat, Clueless, had to be put to sleep, he and Tanya made the decision together. When the cat had been gone some months, Ron could not pull himself out of the grief he was feeling. It seemed as though he was pulled back to his father's death five years earlier and to his mother's death, a year to the day after his father's.

There was a curious connection between Ron and the cat. He had found Clueless meowing in an abandoned building in the South Bronx. The cat was not more than a week old and was obviously orphaned. Ron waited about an hour to see if he could find any other feline signs of life in the building, but there were no other kittens and no adult cats. Ron had never dealt with his parents' death or with the idea that he, like Clueless, was an orphan.

Tanya's story was different. She had never lost anyone close to her. Even though Clueless was Ron's cat, Tanya felt this death as the first loss in her life. She liked the cat and talked frequently of missing her. Still, Ron was far more affected by Clueless' demise, not because she was his cat and he had rescued her from death, but because he identified with his pet as an orphan.

Unconsciously, some great part of his feeling for the cat was related to the earlier loss of his parents, particularly his father. Ron was a lot more ambivalent about his father's death because the two did not have a good relationship. He had always felt his mother's love for him and was able to mourn her loss in a more complete way than the loss of his father. This experience was typical; the less ambivalence there is about the deceased, the less difficult it is to let go of them and to get on with one's own life.

Often, people idealize the person or pet that is lost. For example, a person who has lost someone close may avoid forming new relationships, saying it is impossible to find another partner as good as the one lost. The same may be true of a pet. It is important in dealing with any loss to acknowledge the reality of the relationship. Nothing is totally good or totally bad. More important, every relationship is different. While sadness may last a long time, there should be no guilt about moving on to a new relationship. A person might remarry after losing a spouse, or get a new pet after one has died. In no way do those successors take the place of the one that was lost, so there is no reason to feel guilty.

The real work of grieving (for both people and pets) lies in being able to get beyond those special bonds you formed so that you can form new bonds with others. By no means should those special bonds be forgotten—they are warm and dear memories, and they reflect the time and affection that went into building them. They will never be replaced. Grieving people must recognize and accept this and then allow themselves to move on to new relationships, be they two-legged, four-legged, feathered, or finned. When the work of mourning is successfully ended, our capacity to love is available once again.

MOURNING AND MELANCHOLY

Grieving is a normal response to loss. The problem arises when some people become what psychoanalysts call *melancholic*. Perhaps the best work ever written on the difference between healthy mourning and the unhealthy variety was Sigmund Freud's *Mourning and Melancholia*.

Freud said melancholia represents an unhealthy emotional and mental reaction to loss. In some ways, he said, it is difficult to distinguish the healthy and the unhealthy aspects. This is because both can include physical symptoms, as well as a loss of self-esteem, a loss of loving feelings, and a lack of interest in life beyond the front door.

Many people feel a sense of lowered spirits or disheartenment. They seem much less interested in the world and even less interested in love. In fact, a slowing up in activity occurs as a result of mourning a loss. This is normal.

People often report that while in mourning they experience many physical reactions to their loss—including lack of appetite, headaches, stomach aches, and aches in almost any part of the body capable of aching. In fact, physical reactions often mirror the heartache of loss. In the past few years, I have been examining connections between avoiding the emotions connected to loss and the onset or exacerbation of pulmonary disease. It seems that what we keep bottled up is fermenting inside us.

All of this emphasizes the importance of the mourning process. Mourning is the way we redirect the energy we had invested in a lost loved one, be it human or animal, to the living world. According to Freud, the difference between healthy mourning and melancholia is this: "In mourning, the world has become poor and empty. In melancholia, it is the ego itself [that has become poor and empty]."

The *ego* here refers to that part of us that interacts with our real world. In other words, experiencing ourselves rather than the world as having become poor and empty after a loss means that we are not dealing with loss in a productive manner. In melancholia, grieving people beat up on themselves and fight with themselves in a critical and judgmental way about their unworthiness.

MELANCHOLIA AND DREAD

We know that unhealthy mourning can take many forms and can include a whole host of elements, but it generally follows a common scenario. It often includes a catastrophic sense that the survivor will be punished. I once had a client who had lost his dog six years before. The dog had been hit by a car. When Joe came to see me, it was for other reasons, but once when he connected with my Lab, Fergus, in the office, he talked about his departed dog.

Joe said that without question, Dave, the dog, was his best friend. He never thought about getting another dog because he did not think he could replace a best friend. Joe had few human or animal friends— none of them intimate—that he really confided in. He had preserved his relationship with his dog in his mind in such a way that he could not reconnect to life again after his pet and friend died.

There was something terribly dead inside this man. As we worked together, Joe finally recalled the memory that his father had committed suicide when he was in his early teens. He had never dealt with his father's death, and his mother would only talk about the abandonment and betrayal she felt when her husband took "the coward's way out."

In this case, having never grieved his father, Joe had preserved him as an object rather than as a person. He expressed little emotional connection with him, positive or negative. For Joe, his father was not someone to be pitied, to be furious at, to wonder about, to have unanswered questions about, or even to miss as a parent he might have been able to rely upon. In typical melancholic fashion, he blamed himself for not being enough of a son to keep his father alive. He hid the death of his father from his consciousness and used self-criticism and judgmental self-attacks to keep the reality of the loss out of his psychological sight.

Joe reported that he often felt like he was living in a state of dread. I believe it was the loss of his dog, as well as the fact that his father's death was a suicide, that made it so unbearable for Joe to consciously deal with grief in a less pathological manner. Had he been able to do so, he most probably would have been able to get another pet to fill up the place left empty by Dave's death.

Joe's father had committed suicide at the age of 36. As this man was approaching his 35th birthday, I asked him if he, too, was thinking about committing suicide. He assured me that he had no thoughts of it.

Some time later Joe decided to end his therapy. He said it had really helped, but he was feeling good and wanted to try things on his own. Sometimes that's the case; of course, all effective therapy comes to an end at some point. But people often end their therapy rather than deal with the pain involved in revisiting old wounds. While we agreed that Joe had resolved many of the problems we worked on together, I pointed out that he still had not looked at how his father's suicide had affected him.

Some months later, I heard that Joe had committed suicide. I calculated that he had just turned 36 when he took his life. I always wondered if his fate would have been different if Joe had not lost his dog.

I tell you this story to emphasize that when you do not face the need to grieve a loss, it may reappear in many different forms that you do not connect to loss. I hope the result will not be as dramatic as Joe's, but bottled-up emotions always find a way to express themselves. Often, untouched grief appears in the form of physical ailments or the experience of dread.

THE DREAD PARTNER OF GRIEF

Perhaps the most awful of feelings that often accompanies loss is dread. There is nothing great to say about dread—it lives in your stomach in a way that can make your head spin and your ears ring, and cause you to feel dizzy and light-headed while nausea takes over your world. It is a particular kind of fear that is experienced as not being attached to anything concrete, but it is strong enough to leave you feeling emotionally immobilized.

Dread is often a reaction to loss and unfinished grieving that has taken a turn off the normal course. It may also include a fear of the future. On top of grief, you may be concerned about your ability to survive in the future without the lost loved one. "What does the future have in store for me?" can be a very scary question.

Dread signals that there is more work to be done in the grieving process. Frankly, dread is just one of those experiences that either gets better with time or that really needs work with a therapist. Dealing with dread that lasts over a long period is just not something you can work on alone.

THE MEASURE OF GRIEF

For now, the question is, how much of yourself died when your pet died? What part of you was invested in the pet that is no longer? Are you able to find comfort in knowing that you gave the animal a good life? Can you recall the pleasure of having had this pet, or are you so overcome with grief and loss that the past happiness is clouded over? The questions are the same when the loss is a person in your life.

Another thing to remember about grief is that it is always greatest and lasts longest in those relationships in which there was great ambivalence about the deceased. What often makes grieving a dead parent so difficult and so ongoing is the great amount of mixed emotions that most of us have about our parents.

In grieving someone toward whom we have had great ambivalence, it takes time to sort out what we loved about them and what we hated about them—if anything. In doing so, we must decide what memories we want to hold on to. All these issues complicate the grieving process, whether it involves a person or a pet.

For most of us, the pet we have lost was one from which we received unconditional love and toward which we hopefully expressed unconditional love in return. Because there is generally little ambivalence about our relationship with our pets, our grieving for them should be a little easier.

ANNIVERSARY OF GRIEF

Still, predicting the time it takes to grieve the loss of a pet is no easier than predicting the time it takes to grieve over a person. In either case, people mourn their loss in their own style—there is no right way to mourn or go through the grieving process. But while individuals may have their own way of dealing with grief, it *is* necessary to remember the past. Remembering anniversaries, for example, is not being maudlin. The dates when you first got your pet, the pet's birthday, and the anniversary of the pet's death should always be reminders of the relationship that was.

Those dates have a sneaky way of creeping up on you and taking you by surprise. You might find yourself unable to sleep, dreaming about your pet, or having trouble waking up. You may find yourself suddenly teary-eyed or sad for no apparent reason. You may have forgotten those anniversaries, but the unconscious remembers. It is helpful to write the dates in your calendar and spend a few moments thinking about your pet as these dates come up.

When Kevin and Olga's cat died, Olga was devastated. Kevin took care of all the funeral arrangements. He knew that Olga, who was a child of Holocaust survivors, could not tolerate having Sherman cremated. He arranged for the purchase of a coffin and a plot in a suburban pet cemetery. They went together to the cemetery and watched the coffin lowered into the ground. Both wept openly and comforted each other.

Olga continued to grieve the loss of Sherman, while it appeared that Kevin did not. She had difficulty sleeping and frequently came home from work feeling sad. Kevin tried to comfort her, but beyond his initial tears at the cemetery, he seemed just fine. He did not talk about Sherman or show sadness. In fact, in Olga's view he behaved as if nothing happened. She became increasingly upset with what she saw as Kevin's callousness, his attempts to comfort her not withstanding.

In turn, Kevin was hurt by Olga's accusations. He said that he was indeed upset by Sherman's death, but he felt that he had grieved enough while making funeral arrangements. For Kevin, closure came with Sherman's burial. He told Olga that he didn't understand why she expected him to mourn the same way she did. He felt that he was entitled to mourn in his own way.

A couple can do just so much together in working through a shared loss. At some point, each will also have to examine how the loss reflects his or her own lives. This is an important conversation for a couple to have in sharing their grief and in experiencing a deep, intimate process.

Part V

Why Have a Pet?

*Now That We Know That the
Pet Is Not the Problem . . .*

Chapter 24

The Healing Power of Pets

Let's face it: Having a pet can be just as much trouble as having children. Then why do so many of us have pets? I've said it already: Pets offer their owners comfort, unconditional love and companionship. Current studies suggest that people with pets, married or single, live longer. Researchers have cited the human need to be needed, the human need to feel in line with nature, the power of nonverbal contact, and companionship as possible reasons why. Regardless of their focus, the studies show that with age, people tend to withdraw into themselves, and a pet keeps them connected to the external world. Humans also need affection, tenderness, and touching. The touching that goes on between people and pets satisfies this need, although people are often ashamed to admit even to themselves, much less anyone else, that it feels good.

Touch

The fear of reaching out and touching another human being is based on the anticipation of criticism and rejection. In American culture we barely touch our children or our friends. For many people, pets are their primary source of touching and being touched. We Americans find it amusing that in Spanish, French, Italian and Greek cultures people are always kissing and hugging each other—regardless of sex. Greetings in some Eastern European cultures still include men kissing women's hands. Actually, it is sad that we have come to the point of not touching—and even not talking—in our society. I recently heard of a male worker telling a female coworker that she had beautiful hair, a comment which resulted in a sexual harassment accusation.

Studies also suggest that elderly people living in institutional settings live longer when pets are welcomed as part of the community. A great idea for a senior home would be one in which people could bring pets with them—maybe even a home for both senior people and senior pets, retired Seeing-Eye dogs, hearing dogs, police dogs, and Greyhounds. To quote novelist Agnes Sligh Turnbull: "Pets' lives are too short; that is their only fault."

Companionship

In the Edward Albee play *Delicate Balance,* that yearning is stated clearly. The cat in the story will not love the main character, no matter what he does for it. The story ends with the main character killing the cat because he cannot stand being rejected. We *really* need to feel needed!

For some people, pets are their main source of pleasure, playfulness, and joy. Some people never smile except when they're with their pets. For many people, a pet can rescue them because they think no one else cares about them. A pet can rescue a child or an adult from total isolation and aloneness, and having a pet keeps people in contact with something that is alive beyond the TV.

For many single people, the pet is regarded as family. This is especially true for people who inherited a dissatisfying family. A pet may give a person many things that the family did not.

Gail and Arthur tried having a baby. After years of watching thermometers and the calendar, it was finally confirmed that Gail could not conceive. They are currently investigating adoption possibilities, but in the meantime, they have stated openly and directly that they both appreciate having their little Poodle, Boobi, as a member of the household. Both also feel resentment when "knowing" friends and family members feel a compulsion to tell them that the Poodle "must be a child substitute."

Gail has sworn that the next person to make this keen observation will be told that the only reason they have Boobi is for an occasional threesome. "It is so painful to hear someone do that one-upsmanship thing," Arthur said. "And, of course, it is always someone who has kids making the comment." Gail added, "It would be so nice to not have to put up with that business that I often bring the subject up first and cut them off at the pass."

This kind of condescension not only demeans the other person's love of a pet, but it also suggests that something not quite normal is going on. But there is nothing abnormal about filling up our lives with as much love as we can.

VITALITY AND COMMUNITY

Great comfort comes from having a pet and not having to come home to an empty house. Instead, you come home to something vital and alive, something that responds to you. There is a real difference in the feel of a living space when it is inhabited by a pet. People with animals have less of a need to turn on the computer, the TV, or the radio—and a pet is certainly much, much better than an appliance.

Pets also anchor people in the world. Often single people report, "If I did not have my dog, I would never come home." Having something alive to come home to is comforting.

For many single people as well as family groups, a dog community exists where they can meet other people. The dog community in my neighborhood is a vibrant but informal group that networks and helps each other out. Some people have volunteered to walk dogs for the elderly, and a number of people walk the dogs of AIDS patients.

I think often of how some of my patients over the years have become re-energized, happier, and healthier with pets in their lives. Big Ralph was just about the loneliest guy I knew. He was always alone and was always getting into relationships with people who used him and dumped him. He would simply go home, switch on the TV, and ride the remote control until it was time to go to bed.

Ralph did not trust himself to be responsible enough to have a pet. Yet, whenever he was in my office it was clear that he had a real affection and tenderness for my dogs (who are often in the office with me). He always asked about their health and remembered their birthdays.

Finally, someone in one of my therapy groups who had to visit an ailing parent asked Ralph to feed and walk her dog for a few days. After much procrastination, Ralph agreed to care for her dog. Ralph had at last given himself a chance to care for another living thing, and he discovered how little it takes for pets to be happy and pleased. Pets are so not demanding, and given the right choice of pets, as Ralph expressed it, "anyone can feel competent." Ralph had finally learned what other pet people already knew: Pets are great at raising self-esteem and at keeping some other living thing happy. And they ask so little in return. Pets do, indeed, make people's lives richer.

HEALERS IN THERAPY

Over and over again, I have seen the valuable role pets play in people's lives. For starters, pets have an impact upon the early years. One young man who had never talked about his past recalled a dog he had as a child and remembered the warmth and love of that relationship in an otherwise abusive home. The memory of his dog brought back other memories, and the man began to make marked improvement in treatment.

I also have seen the healing effects of an animal in working with people in psychotherapy. Nearly 30 years ago I brought a dog with me to my office. Humphrey was a wonderful therapy dog: He was never intrusive. He would lie by the couch and, if a patient moved into a painful or fearful emotional place, he would lift his head and place it on the patient's arm. Patients experienced this gesture as one of infinite comfort and, as a result, would generally move into even deeper emotions.

These people often told me of dreams in which Humphrey rescued them. Frequently, these dreams had more to do with fears that I could not rescue them. Some patients felt that if they told me everything, I might not like them any longer or want to help them, much less rescue them. But they believed that Humphrey would not judge them. Other patients inquired if I would take care of them the way I took care of Humphrey. Whenever a little child told me a story about Humphrey, I think the child was telling his or her own story.

After Humphrey died, I adopted Amos, a yellow Labrador Retriever who was a retired Seeing Eye dog. Perhaps Amos shone most when he was with children. I had learned a lot from watching kids interact with Humphrey and put that to good use with Amos. Because the dogs were live, warm creatures who couldn't speak, they could be trusted with the children's fears and secrets.

Nothing ever upset Amos—he could handle anything. He was in his glory around kids; they could do anything to him, and he would never object. As a result, severely disturbed children who could not find a way to talk to me would talk to Amos. They would tell Amos about their pain and sadness. They would tell Amos what tortures they had been exposed to and would promise him that they would never do things like that to him. One little boy said, "I would never make you sit on the radiator with no clothes on."

Something about Amos' peacefulness invited childhood expressions of deeply hidden secrets. In an attempt to develop Amos as a therapy tool, I learned to throw my voice like a ventriloquist. This was particularly beneficial in working with very young children who had suffered trauma at the hands of adults. Through Amos, these children could recount, relive, and finally work through their trauma. It was also interesting that older kids quickly figured out I was Amos' voice and learned to confront me and deal with issues of trusting adults.

When Tess, an adopted Bouvier des Flandres, arrived in my life following the loss of Amos, patients weren't sure what she was. Tess walked like a bear, looked like a buffalo, and was as gentle as a lamb. In group therapy, Tess instinctively moved over to whoever was in the hot seat and lay at this person's feet. Her message was one of gentle protection. Tess had her own way of dealing with angry feelings, both in the group setting and in individual treatment. When a patient got too angry, Tess passed wind. Perhaps it was her way of saying, "Lighten up, knock it off." Whatever, she drew a laugh whenever it happened.

With the arrival of Troll, another yellow Lab, I now had a team of canine co-therapists. Tess and Troll did more to raise issues of sibling rivalry in individual sessions than Cain and Abel ever had. One could not be greeted without the other demanding equal attention. Patients had little choice but to examine their own sibling relationships. Their projections onto the dogs offered numerous clues directing us to the root of their problems.

People often ask how I trained the dogs to work with my patients. What is fascinating to me is that I did not train any of these dogs to behave in the office. They all barked when the doorbell rang at home, but not in the office. They did not react in the same way to friends and to patients. All the dogs were much more playful and intrusive at home. Instinctively, they all knew that they needed to behave differently with patients.

This was particularly true for Humphrey and Amos. Troll learned from Amos, as Tess did from Troll. Certainly, I must have sent out my own nonverbal signals as well to indicate my expectations. But their sensitive understanding came from within.

I am continually amazed by the respect dogs and other animals give to human grief and pain. I suspect that this is true of many of the animals we keep as pets. The gentleness of their response is overwhelming to observe. Never once have any of my dogs overreacted or underreacted to a person's grief, mourning, or sadness. Their response always has been exquisitely correct for the person in pain. This may be one of the most astonishing observations of my experience with dogs in therapy.

As the years passed and I continued to develop as a therapist, and as I continued to observe patients interacting with the dogs, I came to an important realization: Not only did the dogs react to the patients' emotional states, but the patients reacted to the dogs by reaching out to touch them.

Gradually, I became aware of patterns in the occasions when patients would reach out for the dogs and touch them. Many patients reached when they were in need of comfort. Others made contact with the dogs when they didn't want to go more deeply into an emotional area we were dealing with, didn't want to know about an issue, or claimed they couldn't remember. I started to note where they touched the dog at these times: on the head, the heart, the ears, the tail, the genitals. I started to play a hunch. If a patient touched the dog's heart, I would say, "I see you are touching Troll's (or Tess') heart. Is anything happening in your heart?" Patients would then attend to what they were experiencing in their body and report feelings they were previously unaware of: "I feel as if my heart is broken, but I don't know why."

Often these interactions following a patient touching a dog would lead to progress in treatment where there had been none before. I came to realize that patients were touching the dogs where their own feelings were housed, if not emotionally experienced.

Making a Real Connection

Today's society with its TV, radio, magazines, the Internet, e-mail, fax, newspapers, beepers, books, cell phones, the movies, home phones, the theatre, car phones, concerts, office phones, sports events, cordless phones, and nameless hobbies is not conducive for keeping us in touch with our emotions. And, in my opinion, these are very often distractions that help us avoid the emotionally unpleasant—call it emotional paper shuffling, if you will. The real issue is that we are not integrating our emotional experiences and relating them to our intellectual experiences. Who has time to feel, especially when feelings are generally regarded as sources of information that aren't as valid as the intellect? Interacting with our pets offers a step back, a way to reconnect with our feelings and ourselves.

Chapter 25

Pets and Singles

∙∙

While most people in our society consider the classical family setup—
two parents and children—to be the norm, a good many people
live alone by choice. Sometimes the choice is a very natural one:
The person just hasn't found someone that he or she wants to couple
with permanently. There are also people who have lived in the
conventional family group and for one reason or another no longer
do so; the spouse has died and the children are out on their own,
for example. There are also those who simply like living alone.
There are so many self-help books and articles assuring us that it is
okay to be single that it may be time to worry. The fact is that it really
is okay.

For some inexplicable reason, people seem obligated to offer
assurances to "those poor unfortunates" who do not have a mate—
and especially to those who do not have 2.4 children—as though
there is something unhealthy about being a single adult.
Unfortunately, all too many people believe that just because they are
with a partner, everyone should be. This is a common, if not somewhat narcissistic, view of how the world should be.

Being single can be a result of choice or circumstance—
depending on how you regard singleness. Being SWORD, (Single,
Widowed, OR Divorced) can be comfortable or heart-wrenching. It

241

is when being single operates as an unconscious response to displacements, projections, and repetitions that it becomes an issue.

NOT EVERYONE IS A COUPLE— IT'S OKAY TO BE SINGLE AND MEAN IT

There are a lot of people in relationships who prefer living alone and getting together when it is mutually agreeable. In some cases, both parties have pets which just could not live under the same roof. In other circumstances, the pet and one of the people are at odds with each other. There are also people who are just plain allergic to a lover's pet and need to retain their own non-pet space.

There is no doubt that a pet is an anti-loneliness device. Taking care of a pet and feeling responsible for it creates feelings of being needed, which seems to be an important aspect of humanity. A new phenomenon is the number of single people gravitating toward cities and urban life. Nearly 50 percent of the population of Manhattan is single, according to a recent article in the New York Times. For many single people, the pet is regarded as "family"—especially for people whose human family experience was less than satisfactory. A pet may give a person many things that their family did not give them.

For example, Serge came from a family in which his older brother was continuously abused by their mother. He was quite sure his mother was very disturbed, but could do nothing to help his brother. Their father also seemed afraid of his wife and looked the other way when she was being abusive. Serge felt helpless that he couldn't come to the aid of his brother. His brother resented him for not receiving the same abuse from their mother. Her pathology was one of splitting the world into all good and all bad people. Serge grew up with a cat, Portia, who for all purposes was his only comfort and contact when he would fall asleep each night with her lying across his throat, softly purring.

Serge could not stay in a relationship with a woman because he did not trust women to not become abusive. He was not interested in a homosexual relationship and had brief encounters with women he met on vacations or during his work-related travels. Serge had a large coon cat, Ferabutta, who recently died of old age. His grief has brought him into therapy and he is beginning to look at the other losses in his life, including a mother he could never trust.

For many people and for many reasons, particularly unconscious reasons, there is a sense of "I am not entitled to have a relationship of my own." Raoul, another patient, reported that when he was growing up, his mother always scoffed at the women he brought home. In his mother's eyes, no woman was good enough for him. They were not pretty enough, smart enough, sensible enough, or rich enough for Raoul. He believed his mother's hype because she had kept him feeling so insecure about himself all of his life. He felt that she could see things better than he could with her "third eye" and she knew things better than he did because she listened with her "third ear." To say that his mother was an insensitive powerhouse of knowledge without knowing anything was an understatement.

STAYING SINGLE BY CHOICE

Many women choose to live alone—especially divorced women who have had it with taking care of someone. Although they may have relationships that are rewarding, they prefer the freedom of not living with another person and being tied down to another human's needs. At the same time, they may not feel that way about having a pet.

Among the single-with-pet group are a great majority of widowed women who stay single because men in their age group tend to marry younger women. Men die younger than women in the United States, leaving many more available women than men.

There is such great comfort in having a pet. There is comfort in not coming home to an empty house. Instead, you come home to something vital and alive. There is a real difference in the feel of a living space when it is inhabited by a pet. There is a grounded feeling; it seems that pets really do anchor people to the world. Often single people report: "If I did not have dogs I would never come home."

IS THERE A GENE FOR FEELING NEEDED?

For many pet owners, owning an animal that depends on your care in order to survive satisfies a sense of feeling needed. It is no different with people. Feeling needed and depended upon is a basic human need—we often rely on human relationships for our sense of feeling needed. Our love and care of another human is often unappreciated or is not what the recipient had in mind. In human relationships, we may be told in so many words that what we have given is wrong. Such is not the case with animals. If what you supplied is not correct, the animal will let you know by its reactions without accusing you.

People often compare having a pet with having a three- or four-year-old child. But feeling needed by a pet is different from feeling needed by a kid. Unlike kids, who eventually become self-sufficient (hopefully), a pet remains a pet—with the same needs from early on in its life until the time to say good-bye. Having a child suggests that there will be someone there in your old age to make sure the home-care workers are at least giving you three square meals a day, a wheelchair ride around the house, and an occasional bath. Having a pet usually implies that you will outlive the pet (excluding some birds and elephants) and often will be responsible for agreeing to some form of euthanasia.

Feeling loved by a pet is different from feeling loved by a child. Kids need to separate, and in doing so they need to occasionally become angry with us, disappointed with us, rebellious against us, fed up with us, and hopefully, when all is said and done, they return to us as fairly well-adjusted adults.

Not so with pets. Pets don't have that many conflicts with the humans in their lives. With the exception of occasional bouts of who is Alpha, pets pretty much accept our caring and love without minding whatever symbiotic fantasies we may bring to the human-pet bond.

Pets offer pleasure, playfulness, and joy. For some people, a pet provides their main source of pleasure. Some people never smile except for their pets. For many people, especially kids and adolescents, a pet can rescue them, as in "no one else cares about me," from total isolation and loneliness. It can keep kids and people in contact with some living thing beyond the people they see on television.

PETS REPLACING PEOPLE?

A pet can also be a substitute for people-relationships. People who have been the victims of a great deal of physical and or psychological damage may go out of their way to avoid human relationships. The pain of previous experiences may have withered the desire for any meaningful contact with people.

Beyond this group of people, there are many others who may try to avoid all but casual or superficial relationships with other people. Some suffer from such a powerful dread of being disappointing or disappointed that they prefer to remain alone. Those who fear they will be abusive as a result of having been abused often remain single. And what of all the people who so fear being found out— whether it be that they are boring, or stupid, or murderous, or not funny? They consciously or unconsciously believe that it is better to be alone than to be uncovered. There are those of us who suffer from addictions that we think of as too humiliating to share with others: eating, alcohol, drugs, pornography, fetishes, or sadism and masochism.

As we learn more about various types of childhood abuse— physical, sexual, and even verbal—we understand more and more about the ways in which children learn to protect themselves. Where there has been childhood damage, the difficulty of surrendering the childhood defenses may preclude the possibility of replacing these defenses with more adequate, workable adult defenses. Sometimes, pets truly do become a replacement for people relationships.

INTIMACY: TO BE OR NOT TO BE?

This chapter on pet owners who live alone (with the exception of the pet) is a good place to say a few words about intimacy. After some 25 years as a therapist, I have come to believe we are all terrified of intimacy. The problem is that the word has been thrown around so much that we may not really know what it means anymore. Somehow it has become another euphemism for sex. We all like to think of ourselves as capable of great depths of intimacy. Usually if we are not experiencing what we consider to be intimacy, we blame it on the other person in the relationship, or on some set of external circumstances.

The word *intimacy* comes from the Latin *intimus*, referring to the essential, the most inward, the most private. To be intimate is to be able to give voice to the innermost private parts of ourselves. It means surrendering the mystery of the essential core of our being and offering expression to our fears, hopes, fantasies, joy, spirituality, and bewilderment. Being truly intimate with another usually *culminates* in physical expressions of love. Intimacy suggests risking criticism, judgment, ridicule, and rejection, and collapsing in total devastation and humiliation if the intimate gesture is not fully accepted and reciprocated.

SAVING THE WORST FOR LAST

We know that there are parts of ourselves that keep us from feeling whole and complete, which keep us from being intimate. In the most extreme scenario, these parts keep us from getting into, staying in, or even thinking about relationships. Generally, when we meet new people, we keep these parts of ourselves out of the new relationship. It should take time and trust to get to the point of feeling secure about sharing these things. Psychologists know that when couples talk about the honeymoon being over, it usually indicates they are becoming more self-revealing.

Some of us are so afraid of those unconscious internal impulses that involve sexuality and anger that we unconsciously avoid being around anyone for too long a period of time. Some people unconsciously believe they need to be punished for their thoughts and feelings. Just having the thoughts and feelings without acting on them, they believe, will bring on retaliation, more destruction, and greater punishment. Remember all those stories and films in which the characters reveal their most intimate selves to strangers on a train or ship? It is difficult to help people talk about themselves intimately within relationships that are important to them.

Part VI

Putting It All Together

Looking Back on What We've Learned and
Looking Forward to a Better Relationship

Chapter 26

A Final *Ah-hah*

In summing it all up, the animals we keep as pets, and how we interact with them, are often windows into our own emotional souls. I have tried to show, through case histories, how the way we behave with these animals and respond to them is so often colored by what is going on within our unconscious selves.

In the course of these explorations we have learned about the basics of human—and perhaps pet—behavior. We've seen how displacements, imbuing our pets with qualities of people from our past, can distort how we perceive the pets in our lives.

One of the most basic lessons we have learned—a lesson that is applicable to all psychology—is that nothing experienced or learned is ever lost. From birth we experience, and learn to discriminate, what is pleasant from what is painful and unpleasant, and learn to accept or reject it. If something cannot be rejected, the experience lies in waiting in that area of the mind we call the *unconscious*. One way or another, what lies in that unconscious will make its presence known.

We have also discussed projection, which is refusing to acknowledge those characteristics within yourself that you dislike, and instead seeing them in others whether they are really there or not. The adventure of Fred, the dog, and his "parents," Barry and Estelle, gave us a clear picture of how projection works as a defense against our own unpleasant parts.

As we continued to explore the interaction of our various defenses we saw how they were compounded by drawing a pet into people relationships in such a way that the animal is no longer just a pet. We also looked at jealousy, revenge, control, grief, dread, melancholia, custody battles, and a whole host of elements that combine to interact with an already complex mixture of psychological defenses.

To put it simply, we are our own creations, but we all had help from the outside.

HEALING ISN'T EASY

Most people today want here-and-now solutions to their problems. In this computer age, there is a real sense that we can feed all the information into a single file, and when all the information has been submitted, there should be some kind of quick response. As a therapist, I've heard many times, "I've told you everything about this, I am not holding anything back. Now tell me the solution." That's a great idea for math problems, but not for life therapy. In most life situations, there is no magic formula that makes everything turn out as one would like.

One of the questions I am most often asked is "Why do I have to go back and look at the past?" As I mentioned earlier, the great philosopher Santayana challenged, "Those who cannot not remember the past are condemned to repeat it." Søren Kierkegaard, a 19th century Danish theologian and early existential philosopher, put it a bit differently: "Life can only be understood backwards, but it must be lived forwards." Therapy helps us to remember the past with the mature perspective of an adult, and allows us to put it together in a new, real way.

IF THE PROBLEM STEMS FROM ME, WHAT DO I DO ABOUT IT?

Like any good student of psychology, you may have found yourself at different times while reading this book thinking, "Oh! This is *me*, what do I do about it?" Before you e-mail all of your friends in a panic, you need time to digest the information in this book. Maybe it is you and maybe it isn't. At any rate, some more reading, and of course talking with your friends and significant others, will help confirm or dispel your panic. If it is you, there are some real choices. Keep reading, keep talking, check in with the vet, and maybe even consider therapy.

If your conclusions involve some questions about the pet, yours or another's, there is a lot of literature on just about every species—to say nothing of all the television documentaries, and, of course, there is always information to be found at your local veterinarian or SPCA.

WHY A THERAPIST?

I have mentioned the value of professional help throughout the book and want to add a few more reasons why someone might want some professional help. In a sense, our defenses take on lives of their own; they want to survive, just like we do. Even ineffective, inadequate defenses seem to have lives of their own. Once they have been uprooted from their home in the unconscious, these defenses may lose some of their potency but not enough to relinquish their grip on you. When they are dragged into your consciousness, these defenses engage in a final tenacious attempt to hold you in your past, before surrendering to more viable, effective defenses.

Uncovering the old defenses almost always requires some professional help to get beyond just identifying them. It is necessary to understand why they exist (what they are protecting you from) before they can be overthrown. Undoing a defense means somehow luring it into the preconscious, taking it unaware so to speak, before it has time to return to the unconscious at the speed of sound.

It takes someone with a special kind of training to make this happen. It is not enough to know all about what displacements, projections, and repetition compulsion are. It takes a person who knows how to listen to what the patient is saying or not saying. It takes a person who can offer a psychologically safe environment in which the patient can allow him- or herself to view those often painful, humiliating, and sometimes-frightening memories behind their emotional pain. We are each individuals, products of all of our experiences, feelings, and responses to life.

Theodore Reik, a student of Freud and founder of his own institute, The National Psychological Association for Psychoanalysis, wrote a wonderful book worth reading (even in today's new millennium) entitled, *Listening With The Third Ear*. That is exactly what the therapist does. A therapist is listening for the intent of your message rather than the content, waiting for the little glimmers emanating not too frequently from your unconscious and turning them into meaningful communications to be shared with you.

No self-help or "how-to" book will give you the whole answer. For some people, such books are of little help—they have been reading or have been in therapy and already know much of what is in the book. For others, their own anxieties, defenses, displacements, projections, and repetition compulsions may be clouding over, and even distorting, the information being gleaned from the text.

In one way or another, we are always revealing our innermost unconscious secrets. Our pets often become the door to such revelations. When we find ourselves using pets to deliver unconscious messages about ourselves, it is time to decipher the message, resolve our feelings, and move on.

Remember that therapy is never a demand to change, only a request to have the opportunity to see the whole picture.

Glossary

··

ABANDONMENT: A state of being in which a person or animal is either left behind or rejected physically, emotionally, or both. Abandonment strikes at the very heart of the individual's sense of security. For the young of all species, abandonment by a caretaker is tantamount to being left to starve and die. Being left alone by a person or animal because they have died may be experienced emotionally as an abandonment, however since death is rarely an act of will, it is more accurate to describe death in terms of fear, loss, and aloneness.

AGGRESSION: Instigating a hostile act occurring as a result of having angry thoughts and feelings which have their foundation in real or imagined circumstances. The end result is provocative behavior. In animals, aggression is usually a fear response to being cornered and unable to flee. Humans too, may exhibit aggression as a fear response; however, they may also use it to create fear in order to gain an advantage of some sort. In humans it is more about initiating hostilities either physically or verbally. In wealthier, more sophisticated circles, aggression takes the form of lawsuits.

AH-HAH EXPERIENCE: Becoming aware of an insight that is usually a result of connecting a thought with an emotion to produce a deeper understanding of some cause and effect in a person's life. Very often the connection had been there all the time at an unconscious level of awareness and was brought to consciousness in the course of psychotherapy or by an associative event in the person's life. Ah-hah experiences originate from Harry Harlow's work with chimpanzees, particularly a chimp known as Sultan who linked together a broom and the handle, as well as assembling other items, and was able to repeat the learning over and over again with some outward appearances of pleasure and satisfaction with his accomplishment.

ANGER: Well, that's another whole book isn't it? Anger as an emotion is not the same as having angry thoughts. Often the experience of angry thoughts is masked by physical experiences of tension, anxiety and fatigue. Anger may be released in the form of an outburst or may be turned against one's self. The person may chastise himself: "I should have . . . I could have . . . Why didn't I say . . . ?" The emotional experience of anger, when contained within, is a warm tingling kind of feeling that is experienced as energizing as it expands within the body of the angry person. Anger is an emotion, which differs from aggression, which is an act.

CONSCIOUS: A state of being in which there is an awareness of sensory perceptions, thinking and feeling in a fully awakened state. In a conscious state we operate with intentionality and with an awareness of interactions between our internal states and our external environment. As part of Freudian theory, consciousness is one of three levels of human awareness the other two being the preconscious (just below the level of conscious awareness) and the unconscious (not experienced consciously).

DEFENSE: Psychological mechanisms that protect us from the experience of pain. We defend against threatening thoughts, feelings, and impulses by the use of psychological mechanisms operating unconsciously within us. Defenses appear at each level of human development from early infancy and evolve throughout our lives. As we mature, our psyche discards those defenses that no longer serve us and replaces them with more effective defenses. Unfortunately, everyone is stuck with a few defenses that are no longer useful but have to be identified and examined in psychotherapy before they are replaced with more effectual, utilitarian defenses. When defenses appear in psychotherapy treatment, they are referred to as resistances.

DENIAL: One of the early developmental defenses used in which we deny our role in past or present events. Denial can be seen in little kids. For example if you ask who broke the cookie jar, you may be surprised to learn that cousin Judy broke it. While this may appear to be simple lying, it is not, in so far as there is a real belief that Judy in fact did the deed.

DEPRESSION: Depression can take many forms; it is important not to toss this term around with too much abandon. With the advent of advanced knowledge in psychotropic drugs many people and physicians are treating various psychological states as depression, sometimes inaccurately. Depression, as a state, is often regarded as shameful leading people to self-medicate themselves with sex, drugs, nicotine, food, and alcohol. People often confuse sadness, pain, and grief with depression. There are many forms depression can take from chronic depression to an agitated depression, which should not be confused with manic-depression. If you think your pet is depressed check back to the chapter on projection as a defense or with your veterinarian.

DISSOCIATION: Psychic removal of one's self emotionally and intellectually from situations and issues which can not be tolerated and integrated by the ego. Dissociation often follows a trauma in which the person does not let the experience end. The person's ability to percieve and integrate experience is lost.

DISPLACEMENT: Used in a very specific sense in this book rather than in the classical Freudian sense. Traditionally displacement is one of the defenses we use primarily in our dreams in which a feeling is shifted from one image to another. For example, a young woman dreaming of passionately kissing her grandfather or her therapist might be displacing passionate feelings toward her father which are too threatening to be consciously acknowledged. In this book, displacement is used more in the sense of transference but is expanded to include the interactions that occur in the use of projection and the repetition compulsion in conjunction with transference reactions. The word transference is primarily intended for use within the realm of actual psychotherapy sessions in which the client transfers feelings and experiences from the past onto the person of the psychotherapist.

FAMILY: For purposes of this book, family may refer to a person's or pet's family of origin or to any combination of people and animals bound together by an emotional tie and referred to as family by members of a grouping.

FEELING(S):   Feeling is not the same as doing. While all feelings are acceptable, that is, there is no such thing as a wrong feeling, there are wrong actions. If you convert a feeling into an action destructive to you or others, be prepared for the consequences. Otherwise enjoy your feelings and see where they take you.

GRIEF: A lifetime process of experiencing and recovering from a loss. It has many stages ranging from denial to anger and acceptance. Each new loss that we experience awakens our feelings about all our previous losses and invites us to rework our experience of mourning. See chapter on grief and how it is different from its more neurotic sidekick, melancholia.

IDENTIFICATION WITH THE AGGRESSOR: Unconsciously becoming just like the persecutor in order to avoid further psychic, emotional, or physical pain.

IMPRINTING: A stage found in most species indicating a specific time frame or stage of development in which the animal acquires traits or species-specific behaviors. For example a duck will imprint with its mother or any other living creature it is near when it is 8 to 12 hours old. A lost duck imprinted to Tess, my Bouvier des Flandres, as its mother for the rest of its life. Puppies learn to socialize and desire human company between 8 and 10 weeks of age. For more information about imprinting read the work of ethnologist, Conrad Lorenz.

IMPULSES: Popularly regarded as a seemingly inexplicable urge to want or do something. From a biological standpoint, it is the result of the electrical energy that travels from nerve to nerve within our bodies. Psychologically, impulses usually refer to psychic energy in the form of thoughts, affects, and fantasies that either get discharged into action, repressed (see Repressed), suppressed (see Suppressing) or become something else that hopefully won't get us into trouble. We have all kinds of impulses ranging from sexual impulses, to childlike impulses, to murderous impulses.

INTEGRATE: In psychology, it means to coordinate and blend our sources of sensory information with what we think and what we feel. Psychologists speak of integrating experiences into the ego. The ego is regarded as the conscious source of functioning; it maintains contact with reality and the real world. The ego integrates information from these sources with our individual and experiences, and personal history. For Piagetian psychology, a Swiss school of psychology studying the way children learn to learn, integrating takes on the roles of "accommodation" and "assimilation" of new information.

INTERMITTENT CONDITIONING: This is one of the many forms of behavioral conditioning developed by Behavior Psychologist, B. F. Skinner and from the work of Pavlov. There are many forms of conditioning behavior in animals and humans. In this particular form of conditioning, each time the subject completes a desired behavior s/he may or may not be rewarded, regardless of how well the subject performed. Because the individual never knows if a reward is forthcoming, he keeps trying. People with inconsistent parenting learn that they can be rewarded by a parent on Tuesday and punished for the same behavior on Saturday; they are subjects of intermittent conditioning. Of all the forms of conditioning, the intermittent form is the most difficult to extinguish and some behavioral psychologists believe that it cannot be completely extinguished.

INTIMACY: A process in which individuals attempt to get to know and trust each other with continuing depth of feelings and verbal expressions of their innermost experiences, fantasies, fears, wishes, and thoughts. Many of our psychological defenses defend us against intimacy for fear of being emotionally injured or humiliated. Often, couples in therapy will find an excuse for an argument after an intimate encounter as a defense against having gotten too intimate.

JEALOUSY: Jealousy may be regarded as a feeling or as a state of being. A number of emotions may combine to form the feeling of jealousy. These may include love, embarrassment, humiliation, fear, rage, and revenge. Jealousy may be a normal response to a situation, or it may become pathological; it may be momentary or ongoing. Jealousy involves a triangle in which the jealous person believes the object of desire loves the third party more than the jealous individual. Jealousy often reflects a possessive quality wherein the jealous person regards the object of affection as personal property rather than as another separate being.

LOSS: Any experience or relationship that existed (real or imagined) then ended. Not only do we suffer psychological loss when a relationship ends, there may be a resurgence of earlier experiences of the loss of emotional support we needed as infants and children, but did not receive. If you had an absent parent or a substance-abusing parent, then you have suffered the losses that come with an unavailable parent.

MELANCHOLIA: An excessive grief reaction, well beyond the range of "normal," in terms of types of reactions and time-duration to loss and grief.

MOTIVATION: A process that assumes that priorities and choices are being made by an individual to determine what actions shall be engaged in based on a goal. Goals can be short-term or long-term and may be basic life survival activities or more esoteric activities such as academic motivation, professional motivation, or personal relationship motivation.

NURTURANCE: Supplying life supporting needs to another human or animal. Feeding, educating, sheltering, clothing, and training another are all nurturing activities. Helping a human to learn to distinguish emotions and give names to various feelings is part of psychological nurturance.

PRECONSCIOUS: That part of memory that is close to conscious recall and can be brought to consciousness through dreams, free associations, or incidents that sparks a memory connection. Remembering and recalling dreams is drawing information from a preconscious state to a conscious state.

PROJECTION: One of the major defenses we have in dealing with the world. Anything that is uncomfortable, threatening either physically or emotionally can be projected onto other people, pets, objects. See Part II on projection.

PSYCHOANALYSIS: The study of human behavior as developed by Sigmund Freud in the late nineteenth and early twentieth centuries. Freud identified the unconscious and most of the defense mechanisms we use to protect ourselves in the world. In working with patients, Freud discovered the role of dreams and the unconscious. Her also constructed a theory of human development, which included concepts of infantile sexuality and aggression as normal parts of childhood. Despite much criticism from contemporaries, Freud contributed more to our understanding of clinical psychology than any other individual. Though his theories have been attacked over the years, all other theories of psychotherapy still rest heavily upon Freudian theory as it has evolved over the past century.

PSYCHOLOGIST: There are many kinds: PhD's usually specialize in the fields of behavioral, clinical, cognitive, developmental, educational, experimental, forensic, industrial, learning, neuro, and social psychology—you get the idea. There are also psychiatrists who are MDs engaging in diagnosis and prescribing medication; they may or may not be in psychotherapy practice. Psychoanalysts who engage in clinical treatment using a specific mode of treatment that includes free association, dream analysis, and the exploration of transference; they may have MD, MSW or PhD degrees; there are also trained lay analysts.

RAGE: OUTRAGE and ENRAGE. Most people associate rage with anger, but that may not be so. Sometimes rage can occur from an external experience and sometimes it occurs as an internal experience. As with all other experiences, degree determines what is neurotic and what is out of control. Rage may be a form of discharging anger without having to feel it as an internal experience. When this happens, one may go into outrage, in which the experience is externally discharged in the world; when one becomes enraged, the experience is turned in against the self. Either way it is a way of not having the actual emotional experience of anger. Rage can come from constructing a scenario in your head, without any data, in which you imagine things being said about you that lead to a rage reaction. It's much like the old story of a farmer who goes to borrow his neighbor's shovel and is so sure that he will say no, that when the neighbor opens the door, the farmer says, "keep your damn shovel."

REPRESSED: The unconscious (always unconscious) and automatic act of forgetting or removing from consciousness the thoughts, feelings, wishes, desires and fantasies that are too painful or believed to be too dangerous to continue to hold in consciousness.

REPETITION COMPULSION: An unconscious re-enacting of unfinished business from the past with an unsuspecting person(s) or pet(s). Most couples engage in a repetition compulsion, which keeps the high drama of their relationship in high gear.

RESISTANCE: The use of various defense mechanisms to protect us from real or perceived dangers within the real world and within our internal world of wishes, fears, fantasies and dreams. According to Anna Freud, Sigmund's daughter and a psychoanalyst in her own right, there are ten basic mechanisms of defense or resistance. These are repression, denial, reversal, reaction-formation, rationalization, intellectualization, regression, altruism, projection, and introjection.

SELF-DESTRUCTIVE: Any action or thought that is not in a person's best interest in fostering a nurturing environment for one's self and those the person cares about, animal or human.

SELF-FULFILLING PROPHESY: Comes in many forms. A self-fulfilling prophesy can be in the form of believing you know how an event or some other thing will turn out before it actually occurs—without having sufficient data to substantiate the prophesy. Nevertheless the prophesy comes true because of the unconscious modifications in thoughts, feelings, and behavior that lend themselves toward the actualization of the prophesy. A simple example might be the person going for a job interview who is certain s/he will not get the job and of course does not get the job.

SELF-LOATHING: Not liking oneself to the extreme. Self-hatred and self-contempt (both part of self-loathing) are often a result of destructive fantasies that are turned against the self because they are too dangerous to maintain in the form of being directed toward others. Self-loathing can be a way of protecting a parent or other significant person from one's own anger, jealousy, envy, and fury.

SEPARATION ANXIETY: Different, age-specific, developmental issues of the young (and not so young) of any species separating from their parents and becoming aware of their existence as separate from all other living creatures. In humans, separation anxiety or the realization that mother and infant are separate beings begins around 8 months of age for the infant. For most mammalian species, separation is acknowledged with the onset of whelping. Separation and individuation for people means separation from parents and family to become an emotionally separate individual. Generally, individuation implies the ability to hold onto and value the things parents gave to you that are worth holding on to, and being able to let go of the stuff that is of no further value. To be emotionally separate from our parents and our children is a lifelong work that has different expressions with each stage of development from early infancy through each decade of our lives.

SUBCONSCIOUS: A 1940's Hollywood term meaning preconscious (see Preconscious).

SUPPRESSING: The postponement of a thought or a feeling. For example, if you are feeling sad and cannot bring your sadness to work with you because it will severely affect your productivity, you may choose to postpone or suppress your sadness until the end of the work day.

TRANSFERENCE: In psychoanalytic treatment, any feelings, thoughts, ideas, and fantasies that belong to people in the patient's past that are presently being attributed to the analyst or therapist as if they belonged in the present. Because the analyst maintains a neutral position with regard to the client's presenting material, it is possible to determine what the past unfinished business is about. It is interesting to note that transference, and displacement as well, are forms of acting out to the extent that something is getting replayed instead of being talked about.

TRAUMA: An external event that is so overwhelming to the human psyche that it cannot be digested factually or emotionally; it sticks out from the rest of the person's personality.

TRIANGULATION: We often create scenarios in which we form triangles with people, pets, organizations, and institutions. In an unconscious sense we are attempting to re-create our relationship with our parents, or repair or undo a parental relationship, and sometimes even attempt to master our own role in a parental relationship. Often triangulation is an alternate reality to unconsciously acting out Oedipal strivings.

UNCONSCIOUS: All the activities of the psyche that are not consciously available to the person. They may include unconscious fears, thoughts, impulses, fantasies, memories and feelings. Any of the unconscious processes may be moved toward consciousness through the preconscious with the aid of psychotherapy.

UNCONSCIOUS WISHES: Psychologically, a desire or longing that might be too dangerous to acknowledge consciously and therefore remains in the unconscious or else becomes reversed in reality. For example a wish to be an exhibitionist may be covered over by shyness as a way of not embarrassing oneself with the wish.

WORKING THROUGH: As we learn about ourselves though psychological awareness we need to continually work through this new knowledge and integrate it into the whole of our personality. Working through means dealing with all the defenses that have kept us from the psychological awareness in the past. Sometimes working through follows an *ah-hah* experience.

About the Author

....

Dr. Joel Gavriele-Gold has been a psychologist and psychoanalyst in private practice in New York City for the past 25 years. He is currently the Executive Director of the Institute for Expressive Analysis in New York City. Dr. Gavriele-Gold has also served on the Board of Directors of the National Psychological Association for Psychoanalysis, as well as the New York Society for Clinical Psychologists and the New York State Psychological Association. He is a past recipient of the prestigious Gradiva Award for the best article on psychoanalysis in 1997. He has presented various papers at Oxford University in England and has been a guest lecturer at Charles University in Prague, Czech Republic.

Dr. Gavriele-Gold has published articles on dogs used in psychotherapy with children and adults. He has served as the Northeastern Director of the American Bouviers des Flandres Club rescue efforts and is a member of the Dog Fanciers Club, the Sussex Hills Kennel Club of New Jersey, and a member of the Dog Writers Association of America. In addition, he is the cofounder of Pet Talk, a pet problems support group in New York City.

Dr. Gavriele-Gold also serves on the Board of Directors of Pets Alive, a no-kill animal shelter in Middletown, New York. In his free time, Dr. Gavriele-Gold is preoccupied with Gavriele's Gijsbrecht von Elodie (more often referred to as Broodje) and Gavriele's Charlotte Rouge—both Bouviers des Flandres—and Fergus Coe, an extraordinary yellow Lab.

Index

Index

Notes